Collaborative Working in Higher Education

Collaborative working is an increasingly vital part of Higher Education academic life. Traditionally, university culture supported individual research and scholarship. Today, the focus has shifted from the individual to the group or team. *Collaborative Working in Higher Education* takes the reader on a journey of examination, discussion and reflection of emerging collaborative practices. The book offers suggestions for developing practice via an overview of the key aspects of collaboration and collaborative working, informed by focused case studies and the contributors' international perspectives.

The book has three main parts:

Part I: Examines the social nature of collaboration from a practical and critical perspective, focusing on four dimensions: academic practice, professional dialogues, personal and organizational engagement, and social structures. It considers organizational models, varied approaches, potential challenges and the management of collaboration at different stages.

Part II: Focuses on the different aspects of collaborative working, addressing the crossing of boundaries. It looks at different contexts for collaboration (e.g. discipline-based, departmental, institutional and international) using case studies as examples of collaborative strategies in action, and providing learning points and recommendations for practical applications.

Part III: In addition to considering forms of collaboration for the future, this part of the book engages the reader with a thought-provoking round-table discussion that itself embodies an act of collaboration.

Collaborative Working in Higher Education is a comprehensive analysis of how collaboration is reforming academic life. Higher Education faculty, administrators, researchers, managers and anyone involved in collaborative working across their institution will find this book a highly useful guide as they embark on their own collaborations.

Lorraine Walsh is Assistant Director (Educational Development), Library & Learning Centre, at the University of Dundee. Her main areas of research include academic identities and inter-disciplinary working. Lorraine is co-author with Peter Kahn of *Developing your Teaching* (Routledge, 2006). She is a Fellow of the RSA.

Peter Kahn is Educational Developer at the University of Liverpool, where he co-directs the MA in Learning and Teaching in Higher Education. His research interests now focus on applications of social theory in the study of Higher Education. He is a Fellowship holder of the Staff and Educational Development Association.

Collaborative Working in Higher Education
The Social Academy

Lorraine Walsh and Peter Kahn

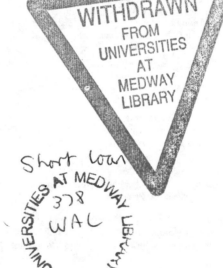

Routledge
Taylor & Francis Group

NEW YORK AND LONDON

First published 2010
by Routledge
270 Madison Ave, New York, NY 10016

Simultaneously published in the UK
by Routledge
2 Park Square, Milton Park, Abingdon, Oxon OX14 4RN

Routledge is an imprint of the Taylor & Francis Group, an informa business

© 2010 Taylor & Francis

Typeset in Minion by
Keystroke, Tettenhall, Wolverhampton
Printed and bound in the United States of America on acid-free paper by
Walsworth Publishing Company, Marceline, MO

Library of Congress Cataloging-in-Publication Data
Walsh, Lorraine, 1964–
Collaborative working in higher education : the social academy /
Lorraine Walsh and Peter Kahn.
p. cm.
Includes bibliographical references and index.
1. University cooperation. 2. College teachers--Professional relationships.
3. Group work in education. 4. Group work in research. I. Kahn, Peter.
II. Title.
LB2331.5.W35 2009
378–dc22
2009005678

ISBN 10: 0–415–99166–8 (hbk)
ISBN 10: 0–415–99167–6 (pbk)
ISBN 10: 0–203–87292–4 (ebk)

ISBN 13: 978–0–415–99166–7 (hbk)
ISBN 13: 978–0–415–99167–4 (pbk)
ISBN 13: 978–0–203–87292–5 (ebk)

Dedication

To all our family, friends and colleagues.

Contents

Case Studies

Figures

Tables

Foreword

Collaboration is surely an idea whose time has come. After all, if we now live – as we assuredly do – in a 'network society' (Castells, 2000), then collaboration is but a formalization of ties that are already present. We are already linked to each other whether we like it or not. No man is an island, so the saying goes. We might as well, therefore, make the best of things and work purposively together.

But collaboration, as this volume gracefully shows, comes in all manner of different shapes and sizes. In higher education, collaboration may be found in research and teaching and consultancy (and other, so-called third-stream activities); it may be exhibited at institutional, regional, national or global levels; it may be found within disciplines or across them; it may be found among paid-up academics or those who work in academically related activities; and it may be seen in teams that are a composite of academics and other colleagues in the university, whether in the library, in computing, in technical services, or among those who have managerial or administrative roles.

Collaboration in higher education is not new. In particular, research in the physical sciences has required teamwork for over a hundred years. The characteristic mode of securing advances in knowledge in those areas is precisely through individuals working together. But collaboration has recently come to be ubiquitous. Most programmes of study are designed nowadays by groups of staff, and even individual units or modules are the responsibility of more than one individual. And in research, collaboration has found its way into the humanities as well as the social sciences. Partly, this latter development is a reflection of disciplines in general adopting methods associated with the natural sciences, including the digitization of material such that large data-sets are produced.

Together, these developments are bringing fundamental shifts in the character of academic work. The lone scholar, whether as scholar-teacher or as scholar-researcher, is not yet extinct, but is a diminishing species of academic life. We are witnessing here, as the subtitle of this volume suggests, the arrival of the social academy.

It is, as I have already intimated, a somewhat strange depiction. Isn't it a category mistake? For the academy was always 'social'. It was formed precisely out of individuals coming together to sustain mutual interests in scholarship, inquiry and learning. But the designation of 'social' in 'the social academy' draws attention to the way in which the academy is being enjoined in this direction. There is abroad an impulse towards the social.

How might we account for this new impulse? There is surely a combination of forces at work. Some are doubtless connected with the incorporation of the academy into the institutional web of society. Universities are large and complex institutions, increasingly playing major roles in society through large-scale research and teaching missions. Many of their activities span complex fields. A course that is entitled 'Music Design Technology' simply has to be put together and offered by staff from several fields working together. Other forces are more organizational and spring from the drive to manage institutions effectively and efficiently – and teamwork seems to offer both happy outcomes.

But 'collaboration' surely has more positive ideals in its backing. If the medieval university was established largely through the efforts of individuals coming together (on some marshy ground somewhere) collectively to meet common challenges and impulsions, that collective impulse can only be heightened today. For the challenges of a global village, of proliferating and intersecting knowledge fields, of an expansion in the scope and scale of activities, of the press of time, and of a heterogeneity of 'stakeholders' must reinforce the urge towards the collective. Society has come into the academy; in turn, it makes sense for the academy to take seriously its own sociality if it is to meet adequately the challenges that it now faces.

The collaborative university – as we might term it – is a new kind of university. It takes its networking seriously. Frameworks of understanding are already networked, criss-crossing and overlapping in ever more complex forms. The metaphors themselves proliferate in a vain attempt to capture this complexity. Some conjure images of spaghetti or seaweed tangled in a mess; some point to the fuzziness and interpenetration of boundaries; some call up metaphors of the liquid, referring to intermingling pools, streams and currents; and others refer to the randomness that creativity has now become, with perhaps billions of streams of data, images, representations and texts intermingling in crazy ways. In this milieu, the individual as a moment of academic activity has lost his or her sell-by date: the collective offers the only hope of forming responses that are halfway adequate to the networked world in which we all now find ourselves.

As a result, some large questions arise. Is academic work now the work of collective minds? In the West, the idea of individuals having profound or revolutionary thoughts has exerted a large influence: Nobel prizes are awarded to individuals, despite the team effort often involved. In the United Kingdom, too, its periodic research assessment exercise has focused its attentions very much on the output of individuals. And degrees are awarded to students as individuals. But should we now accommodate to the idea of the collective mind: the idea that thoughts are both generated by and held collectively; the realization that cognitions themselves are held in networks, in a virtual space? Should the idea of 'the great mind' – or even, simply, 'the mind' – be abandoned as a fiction, for minds are always working in the company of other minds, albeit connected via the internet? Even the ideas of creativity and innovation should perhaps be attached much less to an individual's efforts and much more to those of a team.

This would be taking networking really seriously, effecting a fundamental shift in our conceptions of academic work and academic identity. The business card, on this depiction, would say much less about the individual as such (her or his various designations and qualifications) and much more about the team or collective endeavour of which the individual is part. Here, to draw on a phrase from this book (pp. 40–41), would be a subjugation of self, a subjugation of self that is already well in train.

To ask whether this subjugation of self is desirable or not is to miss the point. For, as this volume implies in its extensive examination of collaboration in so many different arenas of academic life, the collective has now become a more or less necessary mode in which the academy engages seriously with the challenges before it. This collectivity brings mutual learning, and new kinds of creative possibility. This volume is testimony, over and over again, to the spontaneous desire of academics to work together on common challenges. Voluntariness, indeed, emerges as a *sine qua non* of successful collaboration. In its case studies, this volume implies that where activities are unsuccessful or fail to reach their putative potential, the failure is often the result of collaboration being coerced and oriented towards pre-set ends to which the parties concerned were not signed up. 'Collaboration', accordingly, may be read as a realization of the old-fashioned idea of 'academic community'.

If collaboration is in part a response to complexity and uncertainty, it should not be seen as an end to complexity and uncertainty. Collaboration is no way to the easy life. As this volume makes clear, collaboration opens up yet more complexity and more uncertainty. In this collaborative venture, is there to be an integrative idea? Will the group have its own *ideology*? If so, how might it, how could it, emerge? What is the range of perspectives to come into view? Are some perspectives – and even some individuals thought to be representative of those perspectives – to be excommunicated a priori? How are individuals' egos to be managed? Whose name is to go first in any listing of the collaborators? Is freelance work to be permitted? To what degree will the group take its bearings from real-life and pressing societal problems and to what degree from more theoretical considerations? Where, in short, is the group to place itself on Mary Douglas's (pp. 33–34) grid?

Academic collaboration, as this volume makes clear, is necessarily epistemo-logical in its implications. For in collaboration lie not merely questions as to the cognitive scope and the boundaries of the work in hand, but also questions as to the language in which the endeavour is to go forward. Will a new overarching or transdisciplinary language emerge? Or perhaps even 'transdisciplinarity' does not do justice to what is on the cards. But, as this volume at least implies too, collaborative work is – in the most generous sense – *pedagogical* in character. For those involved in a collaborative venture will, *ipso facto*, learn from each other; and so, tacitly, will teach each other. And so further issues arise as to the relationships within the group and the principles they might observe for intercommunication.

This volume is no mere assembly of texts on the idea of collaboration in the academy. It is held together by a core set of concepts, themselves seen as held in a dynamic set of relationships. Those interlinked concepts – of 'social vehicles', 'practice', 'context', 'professional dialogues' and 'engagement' – play out in different ways through the volume as different aspects of collaborative working are taken up; and each issue is richly illuminated by a set of case studies that are widely drawn across higher education institutions and disparate activities. This is a powerful book and one that is much needed. I believe that it could come to stimulate much further thought and action, even critical thought and critical action, in relation to collaboration.

Ronald Barnett
Institute of Education, London
January 2009

Reference

Castells, M. (2000). *The Rise of the Network Society*, 2nd edn. Oxford: Blackwell.

Acknowledgements

We would like to thank the many friends and colleagues who have contributed in some way to the development of this book. To Ron Barnett and Matthew Taylor for their willingness to participate in the round-table, and for the many ideas which they helped to spark through our discussion. To Gordon Roberts for his wit and wisdom, as always. To Philip Morrison for his suggestions for further reading, and to all the colleagues who contributed a case study and who have helped to shape this book, not least James Wisdom, who helped stimulate our original ideas. To Kathy Kahn for comments on one of our illustrations. And to Sarah and Alex at Routledge for their roles in bringing this book to publication. We are grateful also to those who work alongside each of us in Dundee and Liverpool for their encouragement and ideas. Peter would further like to thank his family for their support; and Lorraine would like to send special thanks to her husband for his support, and to Peter for making this such an enjoyable collaborative venture.

Contributors

Imelda Bates is a clinician, researcher, consultant and teacher with a particular interest in strengthening educational and research capacity in developing countries. Her work includes establishing collaborative partnerships with individuals and institutions in, for example, Ghana and Malawi, to design, deliver and sustain courses in education and research.

David Baume is an international higher education researcher, evaluator, consultant, academic developer and writer. He was founding chair of the UK Staff and Educational Development Association (SEDA), founding editor of the *International Journal for Academic Development* (IJAD) and a Director of the Centre for Higher Education Practice at the United Kingdom's Open University. He is External Examiner to the Diploma in Project Design and Management described in the case study.

Michael Connolly is Emeritus Professor at the University of Glamorgan, as well as a Visiting Professor at Nottingham and Bath Universities. He has published widely in the field of public policy and management, including education management.

Jason Davies is a Senior Teaching Fellow in University College London's Centre for the Advancement of Learning and Teaching. His chief research interest is the social negotiation of knowledge systems, encompassing ancient historiography, religion, medicine and oneirology, interdisciplinarity, and the praxis and transmission of knowledge (education). His chief publication to date is *Rome's Religious History* (Cambridge, 2004).

Peter Goodhew is Professor of Materials Engineering at the University of Liverpool and Director of the UK Centre for Materials Education. He leads the United Kingdom–Ireland region of the Conceive, Design, Implement and Operate (CDIO) collaboration and is the academic responsible for major curriculum reforms and the simultaneous building of new teaching spaces for active learning at Liverpool, in both cases for a 250-strong annual cohort of engineering students enrolled on a range of programmes from civil engineering to aerospace engineering.

Neil Haigh is Associate Professor at AUT University, Auckland, and a long-standing member of the academic developer community. The primary agenda for his teaching is helping colleagues, and their students, develop the capabilities required for thoughtful and scholarly professional practice. His related research focuses on the relationship between academic development and student learning, and initiatives to support the scholarship of teaching and learning.

Paul Liam Harrison is an artist and researcher based at the Visual Research Centre, Duncan of Jordanstone College of Art and Design, University of Dundee. He is Principal Investigator on the Designs for Life Project, and through his practice, which is based in print and collaboration, he has worked on several other projects in recent years that concentrate on his interests in developments in the biosciences.

Alison Holmes is in her fifth year as the Director of the University Centre for Teaching and Learning at the University of Canterbury, Christchurch, New Zealand. She has worked as an academic developer for over ten years with the TQEF National Coordination Team, and as Quality Enhancement Adviser at the Universities of Northumbria and Derby in the UK.

Norah Jones is Professor of Education at the University of Glamorgan and Head of Campus Blended Learning in the Centre for Excellence in Learning and Teaching. She has published a number of papers on education management. Norah is a chartered psychologist and Fellow of the Chartered Institute of Personnel and Development.

Helen King has been working in discipline-based educational development since receiving her geoscience PhD in 1996. In 2006 she was awarded a National Teaching Fellowship and achieved the SEDA Fellowship in recognition of her national and international work in this area. In 2007, Helen left her role as Assistant Director of the Higher Education Academy GEES Subject Centre to live in the United States. She is currently working as an independent consultant with clients in the United Kingdom and United States.

Virginia S. Lee is a Senior Consultant and managing member of Virginia S. Lee & Associates, a consulting firm with a focus on teaching, learning and assessment in higher education. She is currently President of the Professional and Organizational Development Network in Higher Education.

Julie Lydon is Pro-Vice-Chancellor at the University of Glamorgan; previously she was Assistant Vice-Chancellor at the University of the West of England and Associate Dean at the University of Wolverhampton Business School. Her management experience includes the strategic development of curriculum, learning and teaching, partnerships and academic quality. She has been involved in the development of international partnerships and exchange arrangements since 1989. Her research interests are in the fields of organizational change and collaboration within higher education.

Jane MacKenzie, originally a research biologist, is an Educational Developer at the University of Glasgow. She coordinates a postgraduate certificate in Academic Practice for new academic staff. Her research interests include community in educational and professional development, identity formation in science education, and how the scholarship of teaching and learning is promoted, supported and understood in different contexts.

Philip S. Morrison is Professor of Human Geography in the School of Geography, Environment and Earth Sciences at Victoria University of Wellington, New Zealand. His primary specialisms are local labour markets, housing, migration and population geography.

Kogi Naidoo, Deputy Director and Associate Professor in the Centre for Learning and Professional Development, University of Adelaide, is national project leader in New Zealand, investigating the impact of academic development on first-year students. She has extensive work experience in this area and has published widely, receiving several awards and fellowships.

Mathew L. Ouellett is Director of the Center for Teaching, University of Massachusetts Amherst. He has consulted with hundreds of graduate students, faculty members, departments and colleges on multicultural course design and organizational development issues. He was President of the Professional and Organizational Development Network in Higher Education from 2006 to 2009.

Jan Parker is Senior Research Fellow in the Institute of Educational Technology at the Open University. She is Editor-in-Chief of *Arts and Humanities in Higher Education* and Executive Editor of *Teaching in Higher Education*.

Lorraine Stefani is a senior academic with over twenty years' experience working in higher education, currently in the post of Professor/Director of Academic Development at the University of Auckland. She has extensive experience of educational change management; a high-level research output on a range of topics, including e-learning, assessment of student learning and student engagement; and an enthusiasm for developing models for sustainable, distributive leadership.

Mhairi Towler gained her undergraduate degree in biochemistry from the University of Dundee in 1996 followed by a PhD in Molecular and Cell Biology in 2000. She was then awarded a Wellcome Trust prize fellowship to undertake postdoctoral work at the University of California, San Francisco, on the subject of membrane traffic in muscle cells. The final year of the fellowship was carried out in Dundee, where she studied signalling events in muscle tissue in response to exercise. Mhairi is currently focusing on metabolic regulation by the enzyme AMPK. She has a keen interest in art and has been involved in two 'Sci-Art' collaborations to date.

Hannah Whaley is Assistant Director (Research and Systems), Library & Learning Centre, at the University of Dundee. She specializes in designing and programming innovative software solutions to enhance learning in higher education, including work in self- and peer-assessment and groupwork assessment. Hannah was named UK Learning Technologist of the Year by the Association of Learning Technology in 2007.

Alastair Wilson is a Senior Research Fellow in the Applied Educational Research Centre, University of Strathclyde. His research interests include education and social justice, the experience of disability, and the role of new technologies in learning and teaching. Alastair has a particular interest in the use of new technologies in collaborative inquiry.

Part I
Collaborative Working
in Higher Education

1
Opening Up Collaborative Working

> Biologists would rather share their toothbrush than share
> a gene name.
> **Mike Ashburner, geneticist (Pearson, 2001)**

Collaboration is rich with potential, and is often seen to offer greater possibilities than solitary working. A set of stock phrases have grown up to give expression to this sense of promise that we associate with collaborative working. Huxham (1996) talks of the 'collaborative advantage' that arises when we work together. Kanter (1994) also speaks of 'creating new value together' and collaboration leading to a 'stream of opportunities'. And we could go on to quote numerous other authors. But why is collaborative activity viewed in this way? What does collaboration allow, what does it look like and what are we *doing* when we collaborate?

At its most basic level, collaborative activity can be considered to take place where two or more parties work together to achieve a common goal, whether those parties involve individuals, groups or institutions. Increasingly, university staff and their institutions are engaging in collaborative working and partnerships in a variety of arenas. The complexity and networked nature of our twenty-first-century world seems increasingly to demand new patterns of working from all of us, while the changing nature of knowledge also affects the ways in which we work, opening up scope for yet further innovation.

So how can this potential of collaborative working be most effectively realized? The fact that several individuals or organizations in themselves agree to 'collaborate' is not sufficient to bring forward a useful and creative collaborative venture. Working collaboratively can be very time-consuming. It is challenging, is fraught with potential pitfalls and can result in tensions and disagreements. Opportunities need to be developed to afford and realize possibilities for constructive participation across a collaboration. Language needs to be shared – or created – and understood by all those involved. Effective collaborations require energy, commitment, resource (human and capital), enthusiasm, determination and possibly a good dollop of sheer doggedness to see them through to a successful conclusion. So why do it?

The primary purpose of this book is to assist readers in both understanding and shaping their collaborative practice within the academy. It is designed as an accessible examination and discussion of the world of collaboration and partnership working in higher education and is presented in three sections. In its approach the book bears many similarities to a set of matryoshka – Russian dolls. The largest doll, the book itself, is about collaborative working in higher education. Layer upon layer of this text reveals further facets of what a collaboration involves. We begin in this first part of the book, Part I, with a discussion that opens up to examination the nature of collaborative working. In Part II the issues within the book are illuminated and contextualized by case studies drawn from many countries, which detail a range of experiences of collaboration. And in Part III we include the commentary from a round-table discussion on collaborative working with Matthew Taylor, Chief Executive of the Royal Society for the Encouragement of Arts, Manufactures and Commerce (RSA), and Professor Ron Barnett from the Institute of Education, London, and then turn to consider future possibilities and directions for collaborative practice within the academy. Essentially, this book appears to us to reflect the nature of academic experience in the twenty-first century, where collaborative working is fast becoming the norm.

Our examination of collaborative working in higher education begins in this chapter with a discussion of the 'why' and the 'what' behind collaborative working, addressing both drivers and barriers to such activity. Drawing on the first of the case studies that inform this book, we then explore from both a practical and a critical perspective how collaboration is essentially social in nature. This discussion allows us to introduce a model for collaborative working in higher education, a model that we then use to underpin the book as a whole, informing our discussion of collaboration in relation to teaching, research and administration at individual, institutional, national and international levels. This context of the academy provides an important backdrop for our analysis, taking us beyond much of the existing literature in the area, which focuses either on collaboration in generic organizational contexts or on working together in narrow areas such as partnerships with industry or other educational sectors.

The Promise of Collaborative Working

On one level, then, the advantages of collaborating seem clear: more effective working; improved outputs, produced more quickly and more efficiently; and shared ideas and shared effort. In other words, collaboration represents a philosophy based on the idea that 'two heads are better than one'. Collaboration offers huge scope for delivering cost savings and efficiencies. One approach has been to create larger, combined contracts to improve service and achieve savings. Similarly, purchasing consortia within higher education represent an area where collaboration is already extensive, and for clear financial reasons.

Nonetheless, it is important to recognize that collaboration, particularly in an educational context, is not primarily about economies of scale, but concerns extending the possibilities for research, opening up new avenues for learning and furthering a multiplicity of aims within the academy. We can thus see such advantages arising from collaborative working as the following:

- a greater resource than just the individual upon which to draw;
- several, rather than only one, potential 'leads' to maintain the momentum of your project and to refresh the initiative with new ideas and energies;
- cross-fertilization of ideas and enthusiasm;
- the satisfaction of realizing a significant project that would have been unthinkable, and less enjoyable, without the support of others.

In some cases, also, we can see that collaborative working serves first of all to benefit others rather than one's own interests. An example of this is provided in an issue of the *International Journal for Educational Integrity* (2008), where the editorial, in reference to two articles submitted by African scholars, comments, '[A]cademics in more privileged institutions have a *responsibility* to collaborate with our colleagues to ensure that these stories reach a wide audience' (our emphasis). The idea of a responsibility to collaborate is an interesting one, and resonates strongly with the notion of the academy; and indeed we explore these issues further through a case study in Chapter 4 by Imelda Bates and David Baume, looking at a collaboration bridging the United Kingdom and Ghana that has already spanned more than twenty years.

Another facet of this 'piggy-back' approach to collaboration, where one half of the partnership is seen to be less advantaged in some way than the other, can be seen in the idea of 'cognitive authority'. Pilerot (2006, in Rich & Smart, n.d.: 223) contends that 'information professionals can gain cognitive authority through working alongside academics [as they are] more influential when seen to be collaborating with academics, and when their contribution is visibly endorsed by academics, than when they appear to work in isolation'. The extent to which this may be smoke and mirrors is immaterial if genuine benefit is derived. It provides a further example of an 'added extra' in terms of the collaborative process, where the outcomes of the actual collaboration itself, in this case between academic and information professional, are further enhanced by the added benefit of cognitive authority through association. Furthermore, this mutuality can work both ways. Even though it may be that authority stems first of all from one partner, that partner may themselves gain as much from the collaboration as the others involved – and this indeed may well be the case in relation to the two articles just cited. We see this with the musicians within a jazz band, who improvise together, picking up threads of the riff one from the other as the music develops and builds or meanders and settles; or with dance partners, who in practising new steps must learn to accommodate one another, to alternately lead or follow and to respond to individual strengths and weaknesses. Within both of these examples, mutuality, trust and values are developed, shared and realized.

A key reason to engage in a collaboration is thus to learn. Goals that relate to teaching and research intrinsically involve a social dimension. Thus, for example:

- Teaching primarily involves a social process, where the aim is to catalyse the interest and engagement of the student, rather than to download information into their minds.
- Research is not just designed to lead to outputs that collect dust in a library or languish 'un-clicked-upon' in cyberspace; the aim is that others build on this work and learn from it. And such wider learning is more likely to occur if one's research involved a collaborative process.

Collaboration provides a way to realize these goals for learning, forming as it does a key aspect of academic work for teachers and researchers. We can see that a further benefit arises when staff engage in collaborative working, in that they then model effective practices to their students (Rich & Smart, n.d.: 220). This is useful for a number of purposes – not least the very practical one that collaborative working can support learning among students of differing abilities (see Pilerot, 2006, in Rich & Smart, n.d.: 223) – and also reflects skills expected by the twenty-first-century workplace. One can see why Sachs (2003) identifies a collaborative approach as one of six components of a new activist teacher professional identity.

This may be all very well, but to what extent do research or teaching *improve* as a result of, as opposed to being facilitated by, collaborative working? Is there any evidence for improvement? After all, we may be asked to participate in collaborative activity by our managers, or may need to justify our collaborative activities to them. In fact, advantages of collaborative working, in terms of improving the 'mechanics' of going about research, have been acknowledged for many years. For example, Pelz & Andrews, writing in the 1960s, identified providing new ideas, catching potential errors and keeping colleagues 'on their toes' as useful outcomes of a collaborative partnership (Presser, 1980), all of which can help to provide improvements in practice over the lone individual working in isolation. Whether this produces directly, or helps lead to the production of, better research is more difficult to establish, owing to the number of issues in play, not least of which is how research value is quantified. Beaver (2004) suggests at least that collaborative research in the sciences has greater epistemic authority than solitary working, in that papers produced through collaboration are cited more extensively than papers produced by an individual; but this analysis depends primarily on an analysis of citations rather than taking in wider aspects of collaborative activity – the gain is primarily seen on the level of epistemic authority. It still remains difficult to determine whether or not a single driven individual might be able to achieve this on their own, given a suitable task. Relying entirely on bibliometric approaches to ascertaining the value of collaborative working, such as counting the number of co-authored papers, is problematic given that this addresses only one part of the collaborative activity, as Katz & Martin (1997) observe.

What Is a Collaboration?

This discussion of the potential benefits of collaborative working also helps us to appreciate its nature as well, rooted as it is in people coming together from different places and situations. Collaborations between individuals or groups are easy to relate to, and you can probably recall examples from your previous or current experience: collaborating with another colleague to write a journal article, or working as part of a group developing a new course of study. Such collaborative working is increasingly conducted at a distance, whether as a result of restraints on conference budgets, concerns over individual carbon footprints or the way in which technological media shrink the world, easing the restrictions of different time zones and the constraints of travel.

But collaborative activity can also be identified at wider levels, whether institutional, sectoral, national or international. Some of these levels are strategic, some operational, and some will involve aspects of both as an integral part of their working relationship, as we can see in a range of examples of such higher-level collaborations:

- *institutional* – a partnership of individuals and institutions working together in support of a particular cause, as with the Best Evidence Medical Education Collaboration (see www.bemecollaboration.org);
- *sectoral* – a number of individuals, groups and institutions working together collaboratively in support of a sector-wide initiative, such as the Quality Enhancement Themes in Scotland (Quality Assurance Agency Scotland; see www.enhancementthemes.ac.uk);
- *national* – sponsorship or funding of collaborative initiatives, for example, the Australian Learning and Teaching Council Exchange, which provides an online facility to support communication and collaboration across the higher education sector (see www.altc exchange.edu.au/);
- *international* – pan-European projects such as MINERVA and SOCRATES, which includes the open and distance learning project 'Collaboration across Borders' (see www.isoc.siu.no/isocii.nsf/project list/110681).

We see in all of these varied forms of collaborative activity that identification of what counts as a collaboration depends on one's initial perception of what the activity *is for*, and to what extent the emphasis is on the *product* as opposed to the *process* of the joint working. Some collaborations have predetermined outcomes – for example, this book was the planned end product of our collaboration – but other activities may be much more open-ended or perhaps speculative, in which case their outcomes may be more emergent than planned. In these examples it is the power of the joint working behind the collaboration, rather than an initial focus on the product, that helps such ventures ever get off the ground. One of our colleagues – a great global networker – has plans to develop a venture in Southern Africa based around community, sharing and contribution. His own personal enthusiasm and willingness to give of himself draw others into collaboration with him. And although the end product is by no means certain, and both the vision and the reality will no doubt change as the project goes along, others are willing to commit to it, demonstrating the centrality of both the personal and the social dimensions for successful collaborative activity. We can see ways here in which the process of working together in support of effective collaborations – the social – is as important as that of the end product itself.

Indeed, we can at times also see that the process of collaborative working is identified at the outset as being as important as, or more important than, the end product, as exemplified by activities such as collaborative action research and the observation of teaching. In such action research the forum that is created for discussion between the parties helps to shape an environment for practice that is as important as the research outcomes. In teaching observations the joint working of observer and observed collaborating together to examine the process of effective teaching and learning generates a conversation around the act of teaching from which real learning occurs. The discussion integral to this collaboration, the process, is more important than the completed observation form, the product, which may be the perceived end result. Colleagues act together to create something that could not be achieved by individuals working alone.

Drivers and Barriers in Collaborative Working

Even aside from looking for such benefits and outcomes, there are a range of further factors that are driving a seemingly ever greater reliance on collaborative working in higher education, as Table 1.1 illustrates. The push to become involved in collaborative activity can come from a number of directions. These might be from your immediate working practice, as the result of a sector-wide initiative, from a colleague (close by or at a distance), from your line manager, or from your own ideas and plans. You might interpret some of these drivers as opportunities but others could be seen as demands. But if a funder is willing to offer you a substantial grant on the condition that you work together with others, then there is a clear inducement to build this into your bid. Perceptions matter as much as the reality in such a case.

Table 1.1 Drivers for collaboration in higher education

External	Institutional	Personal
Complexity of academic working in the twenty-first century	Institutional structures and frameworks	Attitudinal/personal orientation
Sector structures and frameworks	Strategies and policies	Disciplinary emphasis
Legislative requirements	Enhancement agendas	Career advancement opportunities
Funding body initiatives	Educational development funding	'Pressure' from colleagues

We also see a range of drivers identified in the round-table discussion in Chapter 8. The ever-increasing complexity of research is one such factor, as is the networked nature of the world. And the growth of new forms of knowledge and new disciplines constitutes a further factor in the uptake of collaborative working. The inclusion of new subject areas within the academy in effect acts as a driver for a wider uptake of collaborative working. Health-related subjects and new social sciences, such as nursing, midwifery, social work and community learning, in addition to art-, media- and design-based subjects, have all introduced new approaches to academic practice, most notably interprofessional working and new concepts of what can be regarded as academic output and knowledge creation within the academy. Collaborative working forms an integral part of these new disciplines, resulting in wider shifts and new patterns of professional dialogue across the academy at large.

But the drivers are of course not all towards collaboration. Matthew Taylor picks out in the round-table discussion an increasing sense of competition between universities, as institutions vie to recruit research stars from each other. And, indeed, some traditional working practices in higher education are inclined more to solitary than to collaborative working, as the quotation at the head of this chapter might suggest! Historically, academic and scholarly work has been an independent and solitary activity in which joint working practices have featured very little, if at all. And while scientific researchers, and especially those working in laboratories, have adopted a collaborative approach to their practice for some time, researchers from the arts and humanities still tend to follow a more solitary path that Becher & Trowler (2001: 125) identify as being the result of their having 'a different set of social and cognitive norms'. In these fields, interpretive approaches and theoretical standpoints are developed and promulgated by researchers as *individual* viewpoints, viewpoints upon which their reputations and careers either blossom or wither on the vine.

However, in the same way that the student body of the twenty-first century has changed in terms of diversity and sheer size, academics' professional context has also changed. Your level of awareness may well depend on the nature of your institution or your discipline area, but the changes are there to see. Academics from the arts and humanities no longer exercise the same degree of influence over their institutions as once was their wont. This stems partly from the increased flow in funding associated with scientific and medical research. But even in the arts and humanities the tendency towards lone working is also reducing, as research assessment exercises look for coherence across a team of researchers, or funders stipulate wider engagement – although there still continues to be an inhibitory factor to collaboration in the arts and humanities, where the monograph is viewed as pre-eminent and where the tendency may well still be for research assessment exercises to accord most value to work by individuals.

Differences in aims, professional language and cultures; unwarranted assumptions; and genuine or perceived power relations can still, though, constitute real barriers to collaborative activity. Furthermore, tensions between autonomy and accountability, lack of agreed structures or clarity over responsibility for moving a project forward, and a lack of time needed to manage the logistics can all lead to a situation of 'collaborative inertia' (Huxham, 1996: 4). Huxham argues that while 'differences ... provide the leverage that is to be gained from collaborating', too many unacknowledged or unresolved difficulties can lead to stalemate at best and collapse of the collaboration at worst, with all the attendant fallout. In addition to being destructive with regard to the current collaboration, such difficulties or challenges can be demotivating with regard to future collaborative activity. And to what extent is it necessary to subjugate the self within a collaboration? Or alternatively, what opportunities exist or can be created for personal growth and development, and to accommodate the gift of agency? These questions provide themes for further exploration throughout the book, but that some aspects of academia have the potential to actively militate against collaborative working can easily be imagined, not least as a result of the competitive side of academic life.

The Social Nature of Collaborative Working

Much of our life as social beings revolves around joint working practices to a greater or lesser extent, ranging from simple cooperation with complete strangers in order to smooth the path of day-to-day living, to highly complex collaborative ventures built on trust and personal investment, such as marriage. Indeed, some authors look to distinguish different categories of working together. Elliott (2007: 28) suggests that such activity can involve coordination, cooperation or collaboration:

Coordination (which is not dependent upon either convergent or divergent problem solving) provides synergistic potential through the harmonisation of proximal relationships, thereby forming the sufficient conditions for cooperation and all other forms of collective activity. Cooperation on the other hand relies upon procedural compliance in a shared pursuit (enabled by the synergy of coordination), which in turn provides the collective convergent production mechanisms necessary for 'well formed' contributions to a collaborative venture. Collaboration transcends and includes cooperation in its reliance upon procedural compliance and is distinguished from the 'shared pursuit' of cooperation by the inclusion of collective creation (and thus divergent production).

Other authors also look to distinguish different forms of work in common. Sachs (2003: 32) distinguishes collaboration quite clearly from cooperation, where

> role boundaries and power are left unquestioned and reinforced through formal and informal structures . . . [with] little mutual learning in what is in essence an expert–client type of relationship, where the benefits are more one way, that is, in the interests of those who have most to gain.

Even activities that are viewed as solitary occupations, such as reading or writing, essentially involve joining with others in a way that is virtual or ideological in nature, as opposed to physical and literal. As Bruffee (1999: 8) notes, '[R]eading is one way to join new communities, the ones represented by the authors of the texts we read. . . . Library stacks from this perspective are not a repository; they are a crowd.' As all academic work builds on and develops from the work of others in order to create new ideas and new understandings, the process of academic writing can be seen as a particularly distinct form of collaborative working which in effect forms a process of joint authorship that is itself 'mediated by the emerging document' (Parunak, 2005, in Elliott, 2007). Mass collaboration around literary projects such as One Million Monkeys Typing, and the way in which the novelist Sebastian Faulks has 'collaborated' with the ideas and concepts developed by the original author, Ian Fleming, in order to create a new James Bond story, demonstrate the potential and the exciting avenues that collaborative activity may follow. The facets of effective collaborative working that are woven into the fabric of academia are in effect therefore very familiar to all of us.

But partly because of this apparent familiarity, it is helpful to look at more explicit models of collaborative working. One such model is that offered by Kezar (2005). Her three-stage model, which was developed specifically for the context of higher education, is given in Table 1.2. We see several drivers for collaboration at work within this model, but she also picks out the powerful role that personal relations and underlying social structures have to play in collaborative development; and thus ultimately in its success or failure:

> In recent years, there has been growing debate about what plays a greater role in the development of a context for collaboration/collaborative

Table 1.2 Stages of collaboration

Stage 1: Building commitment	Stage 2: commitment	Stage 3: sustaining
• External pressure	• Sense of priority	• Integrating structures
• Values	• Mission	• Rewards
• Learning	• Networks	• Networks
• Networks		

Source: Adapted from Kezar (2005).

initiatives – learning, assessment/evaluation, or relationships. In this study, relationships or a campus network emerged as the most important conditions across the three stages . . . [which] may be a distinctive feature of higher education collaborations. Because higher education institutions are professional organizations where individuals are greatly influenced and persuaded by peers and rewards are less important than prestige.

(ibid.: 857)

Networks feature also in many of the case studies from practice that we include within this book. This chapter concludes with a case study by Jane MacKenzie on the introduction of a learning community at the University of Glasgow, in Scotland. Her account demonstrates the centrality of building good social relationships in supporting the collaborative endeavours of a learning community. We quote now from this case study in order to illustrate ways in which collaborative working is inherently social in nature:

In 2001–2002 a new category of academic staff – University Teacher – was introduced at the University of Glasgow, with an expectation that they would engage in scholarship rather than research. Scholarship, for the purposes of their contract, was then defined as: 'maintaining and developing knowledge within an individual's specialism, and academic professional discipline, as necessary to fulfil an effective research-informed teaching role'.

MacKenzie observes that in 2006, Scholarship of Teaching and Learning (SoTL) was still an unfamiliar term within the institution, and that the requirement to engage in and provide evidence of it was causing anxiety among the University Teachers. She goes on as follows:

I'm a University Teacher, and I shared this anxiety. My first career was as a research biologist and I was therefore used to working in collaboration; most biological research takes place in the research group. By the time of this project I had already engaged in educational research, but I had made a conscious effort to do this in collaboration with colleagues in other departments across the university, mainly in the biology faculty. This is where I felt and continue to feel comfortable: working in partnership with others. Therefore, being aware of and sharing the anxiety of University Teachers in the institution, I wished to support my colleagues in their SoTL efforts. To this end in 2006 I set up and facilitated a Learning Community of University Teachers.

This particular learning community was based on a specific model drawn from the work of Milton Cox of Miami University, Ohio, and his idea of Faculty Learning Communities whose purpose is to 'establish networks for those pursuing pedagogical issues, meet early-career faculty expectations for community, foster multidisciplinary curricula and begin to bring community to higher education' (Cox, 2004).

In looking to understand the social basis for this particular collaboration, it helps to employ Kezar's model. We can see that the elements of Stage 1 are all clearly involved in the development of this learning community:

- the professional restructuring at the university provided the 'external pressure';
- the values espoused by SoTL provided the focus;
- learning was central to the activity of the community;
- a network of colleagues from across the institution was established.

The learning community began with a two-day retreat, and the group continued to meet once a month throughout the year. All of these events involved a significant social element, as also advocated by Cox (2004). Those involved in the community further agreed to write a short paper and to carry out an individual Teaching Development Project during the period of the year. Kezar goes on to identify 'sense of priority', 'mission' and 'networks' as key attributes for collaboration at Stage 2. These can be clearly seen in the development of the University Teachers' activities as their learning community developed:

- the decision to produce regular short papers and to support teaching development projects that provided the 'sense of priority' and 'mission';
- sub-groups and additional meetings consolidated both the 'mission' and the networks;
- the social elements of the learning community reinforced the newly established networks.

MacKenzie's reflections as facilitator of the learning community stress the importance of the social dimension in fostering the enthusiasm and engagement of the individuals involved, so that they would be willing to prioritize the activities involved:

[T]he social aspect of the learning community was seen as crucial. Certainly, the initial retreat exceeded my expectations in terms of participants' enthusiasm and levels of energy. The group would not have formed so rapidly and successfully without the retreat. I believe that simply being removed from their normal working environment and spending time with people with common interests allowed individuals to get to know each other and feel confident to talk about their SoTL endeavours with enthusiasm. . . . The social links that were made during the year of the learning community continue. Members continue to meet informally and have told me how pleasant it is to 'bump into another member and go for coffee'.

It is important to note also that while the case study author herself played an important role as a broker to catalyse the collaboration, the participants then went on to develop their own spaces for collaborative working.

The most collaborative aspect of the community was most certainly the sharing of and discussions around the Teaching Development Projects. The mini-groups met outside the monthly meetings (i.e. I had nothing to do with the meetings). It was within the mini-groups that members described making the best contacts and friends. It is the mini-groups that continue to meet informally on campus; it was here that the most important links were made.

We see that these mini-groups provided opportunities for professional dialogues between all those involved, as also did the space for exchanges of ideas provided within the initial residential. These two structures further helped to sustain the community, fitting again with Stage 3 of Kezar's model. Such structures, for instance, can help to ensure space for all those involved to make a contribution.

It is evident from the ways in which collaborations grow and develop through formal, informal, chance and often opportunistic meetings and interventions within and across higher education that 'trust' as a meaningful, concrete concept is vital to the success of any collaborative venture. Chance meetings of colleagues at a conference or via an introduction through an extended network or as a result of reading an interesting paper or article all have the potential to develop into fruitful and productive collaborations; in some cases the individuals may never meet but have purely virtual relationships. We can see why one of the five principles of collaboration theory outlined by Gajda (2004: 67–70) is 'with collaboration, the personal is as important as the procedural', where she emphasizes the importance of trust and 'healthy inter-personal connections' to the development of sound footings for collaborative working.

Clearly, we may regard a learning community as a specific form of collaboration; and a community itself can take many forms: disciplinary, geographical, spiritual, virtual, etc. A learning community is a community without place, but many of the key aspects of effective communities – trust, integrity, authenticity and reciprocity – are more closely related to the ideological than to the literal. Indeed, the idea and concept of 'community' can also be seen as being as much a 'value' (Frazer, 2000, in Smith, 2001) as a physical or metaphysical entity.

Hoggett (1997, in Smith, 2001) states that '[d]evelopments in what might be called the sociology of identity and selfhood have played an important role in "opening out the conceptual space within which non-place forms of community can be understood" '. Hoggett's ideas sit well with the example of the University Teachers and their need to establish, explore and validate the nature of their identity as University Teachers within a culture that highly prizes research, sometimes to the detriment of teaching.

A Model for Collaborative Working in Higher Education

One of the challenges in this book is to make sense of such experiences of collaboration. We always experience collaborative working in concrete situations, involving indeed specific named individuals and organizations. In looking to analyse both this story of the creation of learning community and the substantive body of case studies that comprises Part II of the book, it is important to develop analytical perspectives. While Kezar's model is helpful in relation to the process of establishing and sustaining a collaboration, in this book we are also looking for an understanding of collaborative working that is rooted more fully in theoretical perspectives. Thus, in Chapter 2 we develop our own model for collaborative working in higher education, while in Chapter 3 we provide an overview of ways to establish and sustain collaborative working. We will then be in a position to use the analytical perspectives from Part I to inform our understanding of both the case study material in Part II of the book and the wider perspectives and future possibilities that we offer in Part III.

But even at this stage it will help to draw out from this case study at Glasgow the key ideas that we incorporate into our own model for collaborative working in higher education. Thus, the *practice* of carrying out an individual teaching development project provided an important focus for working together, linking to the original motivation for drawing the community together in the first place, so that University Teachers could carry out their professional responsibilities in a constructive fashion. This individual focus for the practice involved also draws our attention to the need for each individual concerned to commit themselves to the programme of work and the dialogues involved; their *engagement* was clearly an essential feature of this activity. Both this engagement and the practice entailed were linked to a series of *dialogues* between the professionals working together, involving interactions and exchanges of ideas around this practice. And in turn we can see that such dialogue was underpinned by a set of *social structures*: someone taking on the social role of facilitator, an initial event, ongoing meetings, and so on. And indeed, the community as an entirety of interactions may be regarded as a social structure. We may be inclined to think that such social structures exist only as intellectual categories, but nonetheless a residential event remains entirely real and far from notional. It is these ideas, which find expression within specific forms of collaborative working in the given *context*, that we draw out in Figure 1.1.

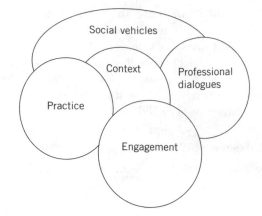

Figure 1.1 Model for collaborative working in higher education.

Social Vehicles

We can see that these underlying social structures form an integral dimension to the way in which the learning community unfolded at Glasgow. We thus use the term 'social vehicle' to describe the fundamental social structures that underpin any collaboration. These structures concern both relationships between individuals or groups, and the stable patterns in which these relationships are ordered. They thus involve also the practices of the members involved, as Manicas (1998: 318) argues, or the pattern of events that brings them together. In this case it is the social structures that enable professional dialogue, engagement from individuals or organizations, and practice itself. The word 'vehicle' further suggests that we are referring to a medium for communicating, expressing or accomplishing something.

Practice

Collaborative activity is furthermore intrinsically bound up with practice, whether of individuals, groups or organizations. In our discussion of practice as an element of our model we will want to consider how our approaches to practice impact on collaborative working; what changes take place in our practice as a result; what pressures might be placed on practice; and, ultimately, what new interpretations of what 'counts' as practice may emerge from these close working relationships with colleagues, students and others.

Engagement

The importance of freedom to collaborate and restrictions on same – whether real or imagined – cannot be overestimated in understanding what drives collaboration, as MacDuff & Netting (2000) argue. Engagement at a personal level is dependent not just on one's interest in a potential collaborative project but also on one's ability to participate. More experienced colleagues will have greater leeway over their working practices and timetables than more junior colleagues – and not just in being able to say yes, but also in being able to say no to involvement in prospective projects. The element of freedom to engage can have repercussions on individuals' levels of commitment to any collaboration and to the levels of effort and energy they will expend on the process. In such cases the need to create and maintain the affective building blocks of effective community becomes all the more important. But commitment is also relevant when considering collaboration between groups or institutions, as our round-table discussants remind us.

Professional Dialogues

Embodied within professional dialogues are the ideas of criticality, professionalism and discourse. Sachs (2003: 32) talks about collaboration as a process of joint decision-making that requires 'time, careful negotiation, trust and effective communication [where] – all parties are learners [and] in which the outcome is improved professional dialogue'.

Knowledge development and knowledge transfer – professional learning – comprise both the process and the product of collaborative working. The development of new understandings and new knowledge is reliant on individual interpretations of reality; yet to be realized, both within a collaboration and across the wider stakeholder group, the appropriate discourse(s) must be created. Effective professional dialogue underpins all successful collaborative effort.

Context

To what extent can we say that societal and sectoral drivers have ensured that collaborative working is now an integral part of a twenty-first-century academic's professional toolkit for practice? Such trends clearly play out in different ways depending on our own unique contexts. And thus while collaborative working may be more dominant in some sections of the academy than others, it is the unique context within which any collaboration unfolds that determines a great deal. Furthermore, the context of higher education itself is also highly relevant, as we shall explore further in Chapter 2.

Conclusion

Collaborative working in higher education undoubtedly constitutes a multi-faceted phenomenon, and one that is shifting. The very nature of collaborative working, in that it is internal- and external-facing, inquiry based, relationship-dependent, and both social and process-reliant, means that frameworks of understanding that emphasize the wider socio-cultural context have a central role to play in the formation of cognition, meaning, relevance and knowledge creation. Elliott (2007) indeed argues that the context specificity of collaborative practice creates difficulties for developing more generalized understandings across and within different disciplinary contexts.

Our challenge in this book is to find a way through this thicket that is both conceptually coherent and relevant to making sense of the practice that we find in specific contexts. In our theoretical examination of collaboration we thus return consistently to the social nature of the activity, but in doing so we give due prominence also to the application of our ideas to specific collaborations. It is indeed through such real-life experiences that we expect you, the reader, to engage with this text, applying and extending our ideas in relation to your own context and perspectives.

References

Australian Learning and Teaching Council Exchange. Online, available at: www.altcexchange.edu.au/ (accessed 21 December 2008).

Beaver, D. (2004). Does collaborative research have greater epistemic authority? *Scientometrics*, *60*, 399–408.

Becher, T. & Trowler, P. (2001). *Academic Tribes and Territories*, 2nd edn. Buckingham, UK: Society for Research into Higher Education/Open University Press.

Best Evidence Medical Education Collaboration. Online, available at: www.bemecollaboration.org (accessed 21 December 2008).

Bruffee, K. A. (1999). *Collaborative Learning: Higher Education, Interdependence, and the Authority of Knowledge*, 2nd edn. London: Johns Hopkins University Press.

Collaboration across Borders. Online, available at: www.isoc.siu.no/isocii.nsf/projectlist/110681 (accessed 21 December 2008).

Cox, M. (2004). Introductions to faculty learning communities. *New Directions for Teaching and Learning*, *97*, 5–23.

Elliott, M. A. (2007). Stigmergic collaboration: A theoretical framework for mass collaboration. PhD thesis. Online, available at the University of Melbourne Digital Repository: http://dtl.unimelb.edu.au/R/UUI5K53SRYSXBBP9YDR2SMCI3LUAE6X77N4L6ULXUMXPBJXLKR-01502?func=dbin-jump-full&object_id=67608&pds_handle=GUEST (accessed 21 December 2008).

Gajda, R. (2004). Utilizing collaboration theory to evaluate strategic alliances. *American Journal of Evaluation*, *25* (1), 65–77.

Huxham, C. (ed.) (1996). *Creating Collaborative Advantage*. London: Sage.

International Journal for Educational Integrity (2008) *4* (1), Editorial. Online, available at: www.ojs.unisa.edu.au/index.php/IJEI/article/view/195 (accessed 21 December 2008).

Kanter, R. M. (1994). Collaborative advantage: The art of alliances. *Harvard Business Review*, *4*, 96–108.

Katz, J. S. & Martin, B. R. (1997). What is research collaboration? *Research Policy*, *26* (1), 18.

Kezar, A. (2005). Redesigning for collaborations within higher education institutions: An exploration into the developmental process. *Research in Higher Education*, *46* (7), 831–860.

MacDuff, N. & Netting, F. E. (2000). Lessons learned from a practitioner–academician collaboration. *Nonprofit and Voluntary Sector Quarterly*, *29* (1), 46–60.

Manicas, P. (1998). A realist social science. In M. Archer, R. Bhaskar, A. Collier, T. Lawson & A. Norrie (eds) *Critical Realism: Essential Readings*. London: Routledge.

One Million Monkeys Typing: A collaborative writing project. Online, available at: www.1000000monkeys.com/ (accessed 21 December 2008).

Pearson, H. (2001). Biology's name game. *Nature, 411*, 631–632.

Presser, S. (1980). Collaboration and the quality of research. *Social Studies of Science, 10* (1), 95–101.

Quality Assurance Agency Scotland. Online, available at: www.enhancementthemes.ac.uk (accessed 21 December 2008).

Rich, M. & Smart, J. (n.d.). Win–win: the benefits of a successful collaboration for information professionals, teaching staff and students. Online, available from Higher Education Academy database at: www.ics.heacademy.ac.uk/italics/vol5iss4/rich-smart.pdf (accessed 21 December 2008).

Sachs, J. (2003). *The Activist Teaching Profession*. Buckingham, UK: Open University Press.

Smith, M. K. (2001). Community. Online, available from *The Encyclopedia of Informal Education* website at: www.infed.org/community/community.htm (accessed 21 December 2008).

Case Study

A Learning Community of University Teachers

An Exploration of the Scholarship of Teaching and Learning

JANE MACKENZIE
University of Glasgow

Context

In 2001–2002 a new category of academic staff – University Teacher – was introduced at the University of Glasgow, with an expectation that they would engage in scholarship rather than research. Scholarship, for the purposes of their contract, was then defined, in 2003, by the university's Human Resources department as 'maintaining and developing knowledge within an individual's specialism, and academic professional discipline, as necessary to fulfil an effective research-informed teaching role'.

The term 'scholarship of teaching' (now commonly termed 'scholarship of teaching and learning', SoTL) was introduced by Ernest Boyer (1990) in a report for the Carnegie Foundation entitled *Scholarship Reconsidered: Priorities of the Professoriate*. This report aimed to enhance the status afforded to teaching in universities. The apparently lower standing of teaching relative to research is a common and continuing concern sensed by many (Coate *et al.*, 2001; Harley, 2002), and since *Scholarship Reconsidered* there has been much debate around the issue of SoTL and its implications (Healey, 2000; Kreber, 2002a; Nicholls, 2004).

For many University Teachers, maintaining and developing knowledge in their academic professional discipline can be equated with engaging in SoTL. In 2006, SoTL was a relatively unfamiliar term in the institution, and the need to engage in, and provide evidence of, SoTL was causing anxiety among the University Teachers, as gauged through discussions at the institution's first SoTL symposium. I'm a University Teacher and I shared this anxiety. My first career was as a research biologist and I was therefore used to working in collaboration; most biological research takes place in research groups. By the time of this project I had already engaged in educational research but I had made a conscious effort to do this in collaboration with colleagues in other departments across the university, mainly in the Biology Faculty. This is where I felt and continue to feel comfortable: working in partnership with others. Therefore, being aware of and sharing the anxiety of University Teachers in the institution, I wished to support my colleagues in their SoTL efforts. To this end, in 2006 I set up and facilitated a learning community of University Teachers. This initiative was not a wholly altruistic one on my part; it was an attempt to become part of a network of academics all engaged in the same goal: an exploration of SoTL.

This particular learning community was based on a specific model drawn from the work of Milton Cox of Miami University, Ohio, and his idea of Faculty Learning Communities, whose purpose is to 'establish networks for those pursuing pedagogical issues, meet early-career faculty expectations for community, foster multidisciplinary curricula and begin to bring community to higher education' (Cox, 2004; see also the Faculty Learning Communities website, www.units.muohio.edu/flc/index.php). Membership of such a community at these institutions is used as evidence of teaching excellence, especially for the purposes of tenure and promotion. I had heard Milton talk about Faculty Learning Communities at a conference and decided it was a model that might work at my own institution. These communities normally consist of up to fifteen members of staff who work together on a shared area of interest for a period of twelve months and are either topic based (e.g. problem-based learning, online learning) or cohort based (i.e. groups of staff at a similar career stage coming together).

Formation of the Learning Community

Once funding had been obtained (from the university's Learning and Teaching Fund), all University Teachers then employed at the university were contacted by email and invited to apply. Twenty-two of a possible 142 applications were received (15.5 per cent), and the community was formed solely on the basis of availability for the preferred meeting times (Tuesday evenings); there was no selection process as such. The resulting community consisted of fourteen people, representing six of the nine faculties on campus. Two members left shortly after the formation for personal or professional reasons, but the remaining twelve members remained active throughout the year-long project. As well as coming from a range of disciplines, members also had a range of experience of teaching and/or research in higher education. Some had worked for many years as teaching staff (often termed teaching assistants or associate lecturers) and had been transferred to the new contract; others had come into their post from a research background. Some had experience of educational research; others had none.

Activities of the Learning Community

The Retreat

The community started with a retreat (as proposed in the Miami model) at a large self-catered house in rural Scotland. Small groups of members were responsible for the planning, shopping for and preparation of different meals. Thus, each member knew two or more others prior to arriving at the retreat. A number of activities were scheduled throughout the two days of the retreat, including discussions around what SoTL is and how it is distinct from excellent or expert teaching and educational research; how to evidence an engagement with SoTL; and the challenges and opportunities offered in being a University Teacher. The retreat was perceived as being highly successful in terms of building the community (Bell *et al.*, 2006).

Monthly Meetings

For the remainder of the year, the learning community came together for an evening meeting every month. At each meeting, light refreshments were provided and the meetings started with members sharing a meal and catching up on each other's news. Cox (2004) has stated that there should be a social element to Faculty Learning Communities, and this was provided by these informal 'chats'. The remainder of the meeting focused on an issue or aspect around SoTL. The topics for the programme of meetings had been negotiated during the retreat, and the facilitator designed each seminar either alone or in collaboration with other members. While there is much debate around what SoTL is, most scholars agree on three crucial elements (Martin *et al.*, 1999; Kreber, 2002b; Trigwell & Shale, 2004):

- engagement with the scholarly literature on teaching and learning;
- dissemination of aspects of the practitioner's scholarly practice;
- reflection on practice and student learning.

It was these three elements that shaped the activities of the learning community. Topics of monthly meetings included reflective practice, gathering student feedback and obtaining ethical approval for SoTL projects. At one of the early monthly meetings the community also made the decision to write a short paper disseminating early outcomes (Bell *et al.*, 2006).

Teaching Development Projects

In addition, each member proposed a Teaching Development Project that they worked on throughout the course of the year. To support this project, members were allocated to a mini-group of three or four individuals, and in addition to the monthly meetings these mini-groups met at various points throughout the year for the members to offer each other support and provide critical feedback on projects at various stages from proposal to implementation.

Evaluation of the Learning Community

One of the final regular meetings focused on discussing how best to evaluate the impact of the community; this design process continued over to a final one-day retreat. Using a negotiated methodology a range of data have been gathered to explore the impact of being a member; outcomes of this evaluation will be published elsewhere (MacKenzie *et al.*, manuscript in preparation). As part of this evaluation, members took part in small-group interviews recorded for research purposes. The clearest outcome of this evaluation was how positive the members were about the experience and that they valued the opportunity to be 'part of something', while the social aspects were seen as extremely important both during the year-long project and subsequently, and despite the feelings of work pressure, all twelve members attended the majority of meetings and were active participants to the end. There is also much evidence from our research that individual members changed in terms of confidence and engagement in the SoTL process and, while members reflected that some of these outputs would still have been produced without the existence of the learning community, they had been supported in their production by being a member; other outputs would not have happened without the learning community.

Facilitator's Reflections

As already mentioned, the social aspect of the learning community was seen as crucial. Certainly, the initial retreat exceeded my expectations in terms of participants' enthusiasm and levels of energy. The group would not have formed so rapidly and successfully without the retreat. I believe that simply being removed from their normal working environment and spending time with people with common interests allowed individuals to get to know each other and feel confident to talk about their SoTL endeavours with enthusiasm.

The social links that were made during the year of the learning community continue. Members continue to meet informally and have told me how pleasant it is to 'bump into another member and go for coffee'.

But was the learning community a collaborative venture? As described above, I had hoped to gain a network of colleagues who shared the same vision and who would support each other (myself included) in their SoTL endeavours. This was never fully achieved and, while I learned a lot during the year, I perhaps didn't gain the support I'd hoped for. I now realize that I made a number of errors of judgement. Believing that I could abdicate the leadership role was naïve. As an educational developer I was seen as 'expert', and that view was unshakeable. Initially I'd thought that members would embrace the idea of ownership of tasks and activities and that the processes for the year would be very participant driven; they became participant influenced (for instance in terms of the topics of our meetings), but as facilitator I remained very much in the driver's seat. I believe the issue of time was a major contributing factor. Members simply did not have the time or energy to take ownership of the activities.

I had also hoped that the learning community would lead to new collaborative SoTL projects between small groups of individuals; this did not happen to any great extent, and other members share my disappointment. Again, I believe that I made mistakes. If, as the facilitator, I had wanted members to initiate collaborative, interdisciplinary projects, then that should have been a focus of our activities. To expect such collaborations to occur spontaneously was, again, naïve.

The most collaborative aspect of the community was most certainly the sharing of and discussions around the Teaching Development Projects. The mini-groups met outside the monthly meetings (meaning that I had nothing to do with the meetings). Members report that it was within the mini-groups that they made the best contacts and friends. It is the mini-groups that continue to meet informally on campus; it was here that the most important links were made.

However, I would urge anyone who is considering setting up a learning community to consider very carefully its purpose and goals, and to design activities to support those goals; don't assume that your vision will come to fruition organically.

Acknowledgements

I would like to thank all the University Teachers who gave up their time and energy to be part of the Learning Community.

Case-Study References

Bell, S., Bohan, J., Brown, A., Burke, A., Cogdell, B., Jamieson, S., MacKenzie, J., McAdam, J., McKerlie, R., Morrow, L., Paschke, B., Rea, P. & Tierney, A. (2006). The scholarship of teaching and learning: a university teacher learning community's work in progress. *Practice and Evidence of the Scholarship of Teaching and Learning in Higher Education*, 1 (1). Online, available at: www.pestlhe.org.uk/index.php/pestlhe/article/view/8/13 (accessed 21 December 2008).

Boyer, E. L. (1990). *Scholarship Reconsidered: Priorities of the Professoriate*. Princeton, NJ: Carnegie Foundation for the Advancement of Teaching.

Coate, K., Barnett, R. & Williams, G. (2001). Relationships between teaching and research in higher education in England. *Higher Education Quarterly*, 55, 158–174.

Cox, M. (2004). Introductions to faculty learning communities. *New Directions for Teaching and Learning*, 97, 5–23.

Harley, S. (2002). The impact of research selectivity on academic work and identity in UK universities. *Studies in Higher Education*, 27 (2), 187–205.

Healey, M. (2000). Developing the scholarship of teaching in higher education: A discipline-based approach. *Higher Education Research and Development, 19*, 169–189.

Kreber, C. (2002a). Controversy and consensus on the scholarship of teaching. *Studies in Higher Education, 27*, 151–167.

Kreber, C. (2002b). Teaching excellence, teaching expertise, and the scholarship of teaching. *Innovative Higher Education, 27* (1), 5–23.

MacKenzie, J., McAdam, J., Bell, S., Rea, P., Bohan, J., Brown, A., Burke, A., Cogdell, B., Jamieson, S., MacKenzie, J., McAdam, J., McKerlie, R., Morrow, L., Paschke, B. & Tierney, A. (manuscript in preparation). 'Experiences of a learning community of University Teachers: A shared exploration of SoTL'.

Martin, E., Benjamin, J., Prosser, M. & Trigwell, K. (1999). Scholarship of teaching: A study of the approaches of academic staff. In C. Rust (ed.) *Improving Student Learning: Improving Student Learning Outcomes*, Proceedings of the 6th International Improving Student Learning Symposium, 1998. Oxford: Oxford Centre for Staff and Learning Development, Oxford Brookes University.

Nicholls, G. (2004). Scholarship in teaching as a core professional value: What does this mean to the academic? *Teaching in Higher Education, 9*, 29–42.

Trigwell, K. & Shale, S. (2004). Student learning and the scholarship of university teaching. *Studies in Higher Education, 29* (4), 523–536.

2

Theoretical Perspectives

The Collaborative Cocktail

> What is it that relies upon people's concepts but which
> they never fully know? What is it that depends upon
> action but never corresponds to the actions of even the
> most powerful?
>
> **(Archer, 1995: 165)**

Collaborative working can unfold in a myriad of ways. Take CERN, the European Organization for Nuclear Research, which involves half the world's particle physicists. This cooperative effort gave rise to the World Wide Web and the development of the grid concept of sharing distributed processing. Or take the personal collaborations forged by Paul Erdös, the Hungarian mathematician who wrote 1,500 journal papers with the help of 511 different collaborators. Mathematicians measure their prowess according to whether they have published joint papers with Erdös's collaborators or with the collaborators of these collaborators, and so on. Then there are alliances between institutions, informal collaborations between colleagues in the same department, degree programmes offered jointly by several institutions, consortium funding arrangements, and old-established bodies such as the Royal Society for the Encouragement of Arts, Manufactures and Commerce (RSA) or the Carnegie Foundation for the Advancement of Teaching. The scope of collaborative working within higher education is vast, according to the perspectives that we adopted in the previous chapter. How then can we expect to identify any underpinning characteristics? How can we expect to theorize processes of joint decision-making and action in the pursuit of academic goals?

Perhaps you have read Kingsley Amis's *Lucky Jim*, the classic novel set in a university in England? The new lecturer, Dixon, was keenly aware of the power of the Professor of History, Welch, over his immediate future. He couldn't quite work out how Welch had made it to professor, but he knew that he had to seem interested in concerts:

> Welsh was talking yet again about his concert. How had he become
> Professor of History, even at a place like this? By published work? No. By
> extra teaching? No in italics. Then how? As usual Dixon shelved this

question, telling himself that what mattered was that this man had decisive power over his future, at any rate until the next four or five weeks were up. Until then he must try to make Welch like him, and one way of doing that was, he supposed, to be present and conscious while Welch talked about concerts. Of course, Dixon would rather run along to the Staff Cloakroom with Welch, and plunge the too-small feet in their capless shoes into a lavatory basin, pulling the plug once, twice, and again, stuffing the mouth with toilet paper.

(Amis, 1954: 10)

The unique charms of life in a university certainly colour how collaboration unfolds. Hierarchies, for instance, are quite evidently associated with the academy in the popular mindset. Academic life may well involve one or two individuals holding sway over others, with a professor or Principal Investigator usually at the top of the pile. The exercise of power is alive and well in the university world – as are desires to flush colleagues down the toilet.

We could seek to build a body of theory by drawing together lessons from a wide range of case studies, not unlike the approach taken to develop theories of change management (Hunt *et al.*, 2006). Or alternatively, we could seek to rely more heavily on the extensive literature that prioritizes bibliometric analysis in understanding collaborative working within higher education. But given the seemingly all-pervasive nature of collaborative working, and the way in which it is so closely linked to what it means to live in this world, our view is that drawing on thinkers who have already theorized human activity at this core level offers the most realistic route for us in this chapter. We use case studies primarily to illustrate, and make sense of, the perspectives that we develop through this more fundamental stance. Our approach to theorizing collaborative working is thus two-pronged. While we draw on this context of too-small feet and capless shoes, we also rely on paradigmatic theorists. We explore both the nature of our work in the academy and the social basis for collaborative activity, while also taking into account the unique contributions from each individual involved. And as well as making space for both the group and the individual, the corporate dimension also looms increasingly large. In this we will see that our model for collaborative working in higher education introduced in the previous chapter is no mere cocktail concocted at random.

Plans and Surprises: Mission Impossible?

One of the most distinctive features of work in higher education is the way in which it occurs at the boundaries of what is possible. The complexity of building the world's largest and most complex scientific instrument defies belief: 27 kilometres of super-fluid helium. Planning and division of the workload entailed in this is clearly essential, with six distinct experiments and a distributed computing and data storage infrastructure that allows worldwide access to the vast reams of data streaming from the experiments. In seeking to manage the intellectual and practical challenges involved, we can gain from project management techniques (see, for instance, Davidson Frame 2003). There is clearly value in specifying work, setting schedules and apportioning responsibilities; or in establishing workflow systems and protocols for sharing information.

Technology allows further patterns of sharing, as with offering teaching resources through digital repositories or scientific workflows within virtual research environments. We see this in the iPlant collaborative, an initiative funded by the US National Science Foundation to foster mass-scale academic collaboration within the field of plant science, and involving the creation of a national cyber-infrastructure centre at the University of Arizona. Here technology is essential in coordinating the work of staff in remote locations as they work together on common problems; or in building up an infrastructure for analysing and manipulating data, looking towards the day when users of iPlant will be able to zoom in and out (as with Google Earth) at the various levels of plant biology, whether pertaining to the molecule, the organism or the entire ecosystem. With both CERN and iPlant there will need to be a clear focus on detailing the work involved.

Troublesome Activity

But work in higher education involves more than a complexity that can be addressed through efficient project management. Working at the boundaries of what is possible brings further challenges in its wake. Perkins (2006) talks of ways in which knowledge can be alien and hard to grasp, counter-intuitive and disquieting. It can clash with our everyday, ritualized notions of what to expect. The knowledge that our students have to deal with is certainly for them *troublesome*. But if this is true for students trying to make sense of a body of knowledge that is new to them, it is equally true for the researchers struggling to articulate knowledge in the first place. We can thus extend Perkins's notion of troublesome knowledge to take in wider aspects of life in higher education. We would suggest that someone struggling to conceptualize an entirely new domain of thought is engaged in troublesome *activity*, but so equally is a tutor looking to master a new teaching technique, especially when it clashes with their existing repertoire.

How indeed is it possible fully to plan for the creation of a new theory or to detail the ways in which someone should guide students into new intellectual territory? Carlo Rubbia, the Nobel Prize-winning one-time director-general of CERN, speaking at the Landau meeting in 2008, recognized that nature is smarter than physicists: 'Our experience of the past has demonstrated that in the world of the infinitely small it is extremely silly to make predictions as to where the next physics discovery will come from and what it will be' (http://public.web.cern.ch/public/; accessed 25 January 2009). There is no production line that can guarantee a Nobel Prize, or even an educated student. Of course, production lines are ideal for producing a single, clearly specified product. But what if we want to produce something that we cannot specify fully from the outset, or even until we see its final piece?

Collaborations in higher education are thus inherently open in their scope to realize unanticipated outcomes beyond that which was originally envisaged. We use the term 'emergent working' to describe those forms of collaborative work that cannot be substantively planned from the outset; and we contrast such a notion with 'planned working'. It is no surprise that there is overlap with notions of planned and emergent learning (Megginson, 1994), which involve either establishing at the outset the direction that future learning will take or taking advantage of opportunities for learning as they arise. We can say that collaboration in higher education requires both planning and the scope for emergence; but the priority given to emergence is one that distinguishes the academy from other contexts.

Social Relations for Emergent Working

If the pattern of work itself in the academy can lend itself to either planning or emergence, so equally can the way in which social relations are conducted. If a team of people interact with each other only on the basis of the immediate products they are working on, then the scope for new ideas and for change in direction is limited. We will all have experience of functional email contact with colleagues whom we barely know; but while this is efficient, it hardly provides much of a basis for developing a completely different way to approach the task involved.

Gustavsen (2001) talks of single-product events that are designed to create one single story or plan that can be shared by all. We might expect to see plenty of presentations in such an event, with little opportunity for discussion among the participants. There is relatively little need for those involved to know each other well, as long as they are all prepared (or can be induced) to sign up to one vision. By contrast, Gustavsen talks of relationship-building events that are designed to open up possibilities and a plurality of stories, and that enable us to find new partners and allies. He argues that what is needed for this to occur is for people to present themselves to each other, so that they can then join together on the basis of common interests. Gustavsen argues further that the scope for new ways forward is determined by the density and richness of one's relationships. Such thinking applies not only to events, but also to the way in which we interact with each other more broadly. Food and drink, corridor conversations and peer reviewing – these all provide space for the exchanges that trigger new understanding and ideas, as well as new alliances.

The environment in which the collaboration is conducted thus affects the extent to which emergence is possible. Imagine a building where each person enters by their own doorway, to an office located on its own floor. Contact with others is ruled out of court. Or imagine a working environment with a common area to which people return again and again during the day; for messages, mail, printing, meetings and refreshment. There is then a realistic basis for conversation or exchanges about work to occur, with Hagstrom (1965) earlier identifying such informality as a key factor in encouraging collaboration. Proximity and co-location similarly matter a great deal for the informal contacts that Katz & Martin (1997) identify as the basis for most research collaborations. And indeed this was the case even for Plato, with an olive grove near Athens giving way to a gymnasium, hence the phrase 'the groves of Academe'. It is no surprise, either, that Morrison *et al.* (2003) point to the way in which most collaborations occur within the same discipline or subdiscipline; attempts to develop interdisciplinary working also need to recognize the role that working in the same location plays in fostering the contacts that make collaboration a realistic possibility. And while common interests will account for much of this, there is no doubt that working alongside someone increases the possibility for discovering mutual interests, as we shall explore further in Chapter 6.

While these principles are all no doubt of interest, it remains a challenge to gauge the way in which our own attempts at collaborative working match up against them. It is easy to engage in wishful thinking in this area, or to fail to imagine how things could be different. It will help each of us to make a more concerted attempt to understand where our own collaborations sit in relation to planned and emergent working. The approach that Helsby & Saunders (1993) take is helpful here in suggesting that we look on indicators of performance essentially as foci for data collection, against which judgements can then be made. Such indicators can focus on different aspects of the collaboration – its products, the process involved, wider enabling factors, and the like – so that 'performance' is interpreted in a broad sense. Table 2.1 suggests a range of data

Table 2.1 Practice: Planning and emergence in work as indicators

Questions to identify data sources for the planning indicator	Questions to identify data sources for the emergence indicator
To what extent have tasks been specified, apportioned and scheduled, or other project management techniques employed? What management processes are in place to ensure that work is completed as agreed? How does the work relate to strategic planning processes (e.g. strategy formulation, goal-setting)? What outputs and deliverables are to result from the collaboration?	In what ways do meetings, events or social encounters lend themselves to the creation of multiple products or the building of relationships? What mechanisms or review strategies are in place to allow one to revise goals set for the collaboration? How does the physical or virtual working environment support relationship-building? What space is provided for identifying and achieving new goals?

sources to provide a basis for such an assessment. You might thus take a specific collaboration in which you are involved, and consider the extent to which you have scheduled the completion of different tasks; or consider the nature of the events that are associated with it, and whether they genuinely offer space for people to present themselves and their interests to each other.

The emergent forms of working that are characteristic of higher education take us beyond what is standard in commercial or industrial settings. One is reminded of the Skunk Works project within the aerospace firm Lockheed Martin. Back in the 1930s a secret group within the corporation was given freedom to develop a competitor to the Messerschmitt. The resulting P-38 fighter became one of the mainstays of the US Air Force, and Skunk Works entered engineering folklore. Such freedom is an exception within industry and yet commonplace in higher education. If we are to facilitate the development of others or discover new knowledge, then our patterns of working must respect the demands that these activities place upon us. We thus see planned and emergent working as essential ingredients of the model that we introduced in Chapter 1, helping to fill out the initial dimension 'practice'. And even at this stage we can see that such practice is particularly linked to the professional dialogues that are conducted within the collaboration, as it is such dialogue that in particular makes possible these emergent ways of working.

Digging Down to the Foundations

To what extent, though, do these somewhat pragmatic notions of planning and emergence relate to more fundamental notions of human activity? There is broad agreement across a range of social theorists and philosophers that an instrumental stance dominates much of modern life, one focused on efficient organization in pursuit of utilitarian ends. This is the technical mindset that delights in production, with thinkers such as Habermas, McIntyre and Taylor pointing out the consequences for our societies. There is, though, less agreement on the alternative stances to the technical mindset that vie for our attention. Habermas (1984), for instance, argues for the need to prioritize open and democratic forms of communication, with an interpretive stance that focuses on ensuring mutual understanding before pursuing goals in common. This may be seen partly in accepting a range of approaches or understandings, without attempting to judge which one is true or even most appropriate; although such relativism is by no means always seen to accompany interpretation. One might say that our analysis in the previous section displays a bias in the academy towards interpretation over production, even if we recognize that a place remains for efficient planning.

Other thinkers concentrate more directly on exposing the interests and displays of power that colour our approaches and understandings, and indeed they criticize those who prioritize interpretation as overly idealistic. While many such thinkers are more positive than Nietzsche as to our capacity to overcome self-interest, as with Marx, history nonetheless indicates that it remains a challenge to escape one form of oppression without succumbing to yet another – even in education. Part of the issue is that criticality does not itself always provide a clear direction of travel or provide a compelling reason to act, as Elliott (2005) argues. But in the face of such challenge, need our collaborations resort to serving instrumental ends alone?

We might remember that the pursuit of truth formed the original basis for university life as we now know it, with scholars coming together first of all as monks in monasteries, and then in more open schools also linked to the Church. Indeed, it should come as no surprise, after our above discussion on emergence, that such early forms of collaborative working in higher education included living and working together. One can see why the English colleges of Oxford and Cambridge provide a supportive environment for joint intellectual endeavour. Nowadays, of course, scepticism is directed at the idealistic notion that absolute truth is found in the knowledge that we produce in the academy. We all know that we have found better geometrical descriptions of the world in Einstein than in Euclid. But a critical realist reading of knowledge, whether relating to the natural or the social sciences, would still argue for the possibility of alethic truth. Bhaskar (1979) suggests that while our knowledge remains relative, it may still attain to ever closer approximations to realities that lie beyond the capacity of language or theory fully to express. Scientists, indeed, generally retain an outlook that is implicitly realist in seeking to describe or discover the workings of the natural world ever more faithfully; as Einstein yet provides a more satisfying account of space and time than Euclid. We suggest here, at least, that our collaborative working should be driven by more than utilitarian ends alone, and that we should widen our vision beyond an exclusive focus on technical production.

Groups and Grids

And if we can look to such theoretical positions for an understanding of academic work, then it is worth too giving further consideration to theories of social interaction. We turn first of all to Mary Douglas and social anthropology, linking to our round-table discussion in Chapter 8. Douglas picked out two key aspects of variation in our social interactions: group and grid, as Wildavsky (1998) outlines. The group dimension concerns the extent to which one's life is absorbed in and sustained by group membership. A high group rating comes when you spend a large proportion of your time within a single group, whereas a low score comes when your time is split between several different groups. The grid meanwhile refers to the extent to which one's social context is regulated and individuals are kept apart. Douglas thus argues that social interaction is characterized by four cultural biases: egalitarianism, fatalism, hierarchy and individualism. Egalitarian social relations involve strong group boundaries with minimal prescription or internal role differentiation. An individualistic social context results where there is little group incorporation and no prescribed roles. Hierarchical relations involve strong boundaries and clear roles. Finally, someone who is subject to binding prescriptions and excluded from group membership inhabits a fatalistic social context, with little or no control over what is going on (the classic learner situation!). It is clear in this that these patterns of interaction are determined in significant part by underpinning social structures, whether tribal customs or academic hierarchies.

Extensive experience of operating within a single such mode of interaction may also make it difficult to operate within other modes. We can thus speak of *orientations* to collaboration, on a similar basis to the orientations to educational development that Land (2004: 13) describes as

> analytical categories that include the attitudes, knowledge, aims and action tendencies . . . in relation to the contexts and challenges of their practice, but they are not innate personal characteristics . . . and are not fixed [but] imply a way of making sense of a given situation or set of tasks that subsequently informs and influences action.

One person may habitually look to avoid making any substantive contribution, effectively adopting a fatalistic orientation. If one is used to commanding others, then it may be difficult to shift into a mode where their contributions are valued, with a hierarchical mindset in evidence. We may find it shocking, as Gordon Roberts did in the case study in Chapter 6, when information only comes to us through a senior colleague. Or then again we may find that tensions result when one expects others to adopt an egalitarian orientation, and instead they display little concern for the group as a whole, adopting an individualistic orientation that is concerned primarily with their own interests. We can view this as a form of collaborative *dissonance*, one that emerges where one's own orientation to collaboration is challenged by the mindsets or approaches of others.

Complexity and Professional Dialogues

These theoretical considerations are relevant when we consider the complexity of academic work. A demanding task will almost inevitably mean that some division of workload is in order, with one or more individuals playing a role of coordination. With the iPlant Collaborative, for instance, we find a series of specialized teams, covering cyber-infrastructure, research synthesis, education and training, and social networks. We can thus expect to see a well-defined grid that is often in operation, with fully egalitarian modes of interaction evidently unrealistic. And indeed, the need for such a grid will be particularly impor-tant in mass-scale academic collaboration. But it is intriguing that academic collaborations are not typically driven by scale alone. There must be some fundamental way in which the scale allows one to address the complexity underlying the problem to be addressed. More of the same does not necessarily offer what is required. Scale might matter a great deal when creating a free online encyclopedia, enabling one to bring together a large number of people working independently of each other. But when working to tackle global challenges of sustaining the environment, feeding the world's population, preserving biodiversity or providing for our energy needs, then the iPlant initiative will require much more than modular patterns of working.

We can see this too in the case study involving collaborative research that we include at the end of this chapter. Gordon Roberts from a research-intensive university in the United Kingdom offers us a view of a collaborative research project in which he was involved. Rather than simply looking to have each member of the collaboration take on a different piece of work, the person driving the collaboration sought mainly to use the case-study author and a further colleague as a sounding board to ensure careful deliberation on ways forward:

> Keith and I essentially acted as a sounding board for Ben. We were very much hands-off, rather than always saying that you can't do this or that. Ben would say, 'Here it is, guys, what do you think?', and we'd make our comments. He was a good listener as well. He wasn't someone who would ignore everything you said. He had enormous respect for Keith because of his criminology background and the work he's done, and he would listen to me as a past tutor; well, I don't know. Alongside this I did manage to get out and do a bit of data collecting, because, as I said to Ben, 'If I don't do that I won't have a feel for what it's like.' So I went into a couple of primary schools and a couple of secondary schools. Keith himself never actually went out to collect data, but listened and joined in the meetings. And then Ben did all of this analysis, but he would come to us and say, 'How should I do this?'

We see that Roberts was keen to engage in some of the fieldwork himself, so that he would be able to contribute more fully to these discussions over breakfast that were at the heart of their collaboration. Indeed, the egalitarian nature of the relationships is clearly in evidence, with the most junior of the partners taking the lead in securing the funding and driving the research. He clearly gained cognitive authority from involving the others in the project, and yet was able to offer them a fascinating opportunity to discuss some challenging research issues. Indeed, it was clear that the professional dialogue centred on the most troublesome aspects of the research:

> We were presenting kids from ages 9 to 15 with a difficult questionnaire to complete in class, where the middle part was about dangers that they might encounter from strangers. Choosing words that are understandable by 9-year-olds and not too condescending for 15-year-olds is quite tricky.

Some of the questionnaire was easy to complete for the pupils, but the sexual nature of some the material was complicated. So we spent quite a lot of time chatting about what was needed.

It is certainly a challenge to undertake such research on one's own. Indeed, the theory of hermeneutics suggests that a richer vein of understanding is likely to result from engaging in dialogue with others around the ideas involved, as Gadamer (1989) argues. The challenge here is to identify different roles that pertain to the same piece of work, rather than simply split a task into different silos before pooling the results. And clearly when two or more professionals engage in a dialogue around an issue, then insight is unlikely to emerge if one of these parties orchestrates the entire proceedings. The troublesome nature of academic working thus ensures that significant space remains in collaborative working in higher education for egalitarian modes of working, where each of us can influence the entire outcome.

Where teaching is concerned, complexity stems, of course, from the intellectual challenge also; but perhaps more importantly, the issue is whether the teaching is genuinely collaborative or simply rather colleagues teaching alongside each other; modularity in teaching represents a weak although pervasive form of collaboration within the academy. Each member of the faculty may agree to teach a specific part of the curriculum, in their own manner of course, with the curriculum represented by the sum total of all these individual contributions. By contrast, imagine a situation where all of the faculty adopt a similar approach to teaching, as often occurs with problem-based learning or the use of online learning. Here the course content and the teaching methods are brought together within a single common approach – ruling out more individualistic notions of teaching. We are increasingly seeing such approaches to collaboration within the academy, as academics recognize the edge that comes with a common vision.

Difference and Professional Dialogue

One of Douglas's insights is that the character of social interaction shifts when those involved share relatively little. To what extent, then, does the incorporation of difference present a challenge to collaborative working? Almost by definition, a collaboration will involve working together across some form of difference, as we explore further in Chapter 5, whether national, cultural, institutional, subject or other; although clearly a collaboration among colleagues within the same subdiscipline and academic department is likely to involve a great deal in common.

Differences may manifest themselves in surprising ways, even beyond the familiar national worlds that we inhabit. One person may be used to working in fits and starts, while another paces themselves evenly. Matthew Taylor reminds us in the round-table discussion that government policymakers work on different timescales: while we have a week in politics, we have academic years. One might naturally expect there to be plenty of similarities in what constitutes evidence within different disciplines; but the case study from University College London in Chapter 5 springs several surprises here. We need to be aware of the limits of our own expertise, aware that it is *delimited*, whether this pertains to tracking the location of pathogens in wheat or isolating genes in a laboratory, as in our illustration in the final chapter. Such mutual understanding is essential for cohesive collaborations where individual agency comes to the fore, with the potential for creativity and innovation. In each of these cases we can, though, see scope for collaborative dissonance.

Modular approaches, where we each work within our own office, can hardly facilitate cohesion across such difference. We need mechanisms that promote sharing and mutual learning in order to ensure cohesion, just as much as we need mechanisms to deal with complexity. We will explore further in Chapter 6 ways in which physically coming together in an ongoing dialogue allows further ideas to emerge for yet more collaborative working. This was clearly also the case with Roberts and his colleagues:

> It could easily have been 'Finish project, get report in and that's the end of it.' But our breakfast meetings still go on, even long after the original project has finished; although not just the three of us. And I still play golf with Keith. Work together has also continued on a number of further papers. Ben was in a position that meant he always had to get the next grant or contract and as soon as that finished he's got to get another one to support himself in a way. So he would write up a research report, but not publish anywhere near as much as he could have. So I've had the opportunity to comment on and rework plenty of material. We've just actually had published the second paper relating to work that finished in about 1999 – although much of the delay on this one was down to a peculiar editor. And now Ben's put in for a PhD by publication, so I've again helped him for a little bit with comments about that. So I've been in a senior role, but not the lead; more like a mentor. I wouldn't be surprised to get an email soon saying, 'I've got the PhD!' (He just has.)

Levine & Moreland (2004) suggest further that trust is harder to achieve in larger groups, so that specific strategies are required to encourage the sharing of ideas. What chance does the iPlant collaborative face in solving key global challenges when working across agriculture, medicine, pharmacology, basic science and engineering unless it opens up spaces for learning across these subject boundaries?

Putnam (2000) further distinguishes between 'bonding' capital, which constitutes strong relationships within a group, and 'bridging' capital, which involves links across groups, complementing Douglas's ideas. Adapting Putnam's argument for an academic context, we can identify bonding as occurring when individuals work with others who are like them and from the same disciplinary 'tribe'. In this context, these bonds are likely to be strong and clearly understood, as language, conventions and approaches are shared. Nonetheless, while this may support a peaceable and close immediate working environment, it may not be the best recipe for new and more challenging collaborative working practices, practices that 'upset' the established social order. In order to achieve this, bonds with colleagues from other 'tribes' can be made through a different kind of social capital: 'bridging'. Examples of this connectivism across the disciplines can be seen through cohesive collaborations between systems and software engineers, and biologists, in the production of adaptive software solutions such as neural networks and genetic algorithms (*New Scientist*, 2007). It is also demonstrated later in this book in Chapter 5, in the case study from Paul Harrison and Mhairi Towler, where an art and science collaboration across disciplinary and tribal boundaries has created new representations and understandings of their work. These new collaborations for the twenty-first century can open doors to innovation and discovery and all that can be achieved in relation to emergent working.

If we look beyond the immediate sharing of information within a single collaboration, we can see also that the infrastructure of the academy exists in large part to facilitate the exchange of ideas. The Royal Society, for instance, was formed as an 'invisible college' of natural philosophers in the 1640s to discuss the ideas of Francis Bacon. The college was originally based around the weekly viewing and discussion of scientific experiments – around the sharing of insights. The academic publishing industry itself represents a vast mechanism for sharing knowledge. While there is clearly a commercial element to this industry, the contrast with other models of sharing ideas such as the patent system remains stark. Patents represent another model for the disseminating of ideas; they are designed in their very essence to restrict the open exploitation of intellectual ideas (and to ensure that appropriate commercial rewards flow to the creator of the idea). But instead we see here a huge range of journals that allow for ongoing debate around ideas, with conferences comprising another forum for exchange. And new trends are set to intensify this sharing of information with the creation of the Semantic Web, in which a common framework has been established to allow data to be shared and integrated across a range of formats, and the drive towards open-access journals. This is evident also in the requirement of the US National Institutes of Health for researchers to deposit copies of their publication in an open repository. We draw together insights from across all of the above sections on professional dialogue in Table 2.2. The character of the professional dialogues that emerges on any given collaboration is the result of a set of wider conditions that concern roles, locations, technology, intellectual habits, scholarly societies, and so on. We need to pay attention to these structural factors if our collaborative working is to be characterized by appropriate patterns of dialogue.

Table 2.2 Professional dialogues as an indicator

Questions to identify data sources for the professional dialogues indicator

To what extent are those involved making contributions to a holistic process rather than offering separate pieces of work that are then joined together?

What strategies or conditions are in place to promote the exchange of ideas, aspirations, memories and resources?

What strategies or conditions are in place to encourage the involvement of a range of perspectives or contributors, whether on the periphery or as an integral aspect of the work?

In what ways does the physical environment or the use of technology promote a range of different contacts?

Explaining the Erdös Factor

So far we have focused primarily on the social aspects of collaborative work, and indeed many theorists in this area go little further. The work of Giddens (e.g. 1991) prioritizes social structure when considering what determines the actions of the individual. Wenger (1998) argues that his own work with Lave around communities of practice similarly places significant emphasis on the social structures that shape human action. Indeed, the very wording of the term 'communities of practice' gives priority to the social structure of community, with the phrase 'of practice' serving to qualify the nature of this social structure. Foucault (1970), meanwhile, dissolves the individual within the discourse.

While such perspectives offer significant scope to demonstrate, for instance, the way in which power is exercised in social situations, we have already noted that the main purpose of this book is to assist readers in understanding and shaping their collaborative work within the academy, at whatever level they operate. We are less immediately concerned with looking to target inequalities, rather looking to help create spaces for those more immediately involved to take the initiative. Clearly, there is a danger that this subsequent action will not take place – but we would suggest that putting in place a process that gives greater voice to all those involved still represents an important shift that may then allow those individuals to judge what is most appropriate. But the troublesome nature of academic work suggests that significant space remains for the agency of individuals within this field. Were there no need for academic staff to make a significant contribution to the direction of their work – as might possibly be the case for a worker on a production line – then we might be able to dismiss the notion that the agency of the individual matters much. Given the egalitarian edge we have identified in academic work, even if this is moderated with a good dose of both hierarchy and individualism, we can hardly avoid such discussion. Many of the collaborations in higher education are forged between individuals, as we see with our concluding case study in this chapter. This is the stuff of academic life. And we all know that some individuals pull their weight while others do not. Students, certainly, are keenly aware when one of their number is taking a free ride, securing good grades on the back of other people's work!

Concerns and Ideals

We thus do need to address what we can call the Erdös factor quite explicitly. How can we understand, and catalyse, the personal contributions that drive practice in higher education? How is it that individuals react differently even in the face of the same social influences? It thus makes sense to draw on theories that take the agency of academics into due account, rather than theories that expect social contexts to hand out individual fates. Archer (2007), for instance, has explored ways in which an individual will pursue different concrete courses of action, based on interactions between their own concerns and the social contexts within which they must live. Indeed, Archer argues that one's configuration of concerns provides a primary locus for identity, determining as this configuration of concerns does the projects that one embarks upon, and the stable practices and habits that result.

Personal interests do play an important part in determining the collaborations in which we get entangled. We see in the case study at the end of this chapter that latent interests in researching both criminology and children led Roberts to join the collaborative research venture:

> Then much later on he approached me in relation to a bid on stranger danger. He'd done a lot of work with the police, and was interested in comparing police records with what happens from the children's point of view. So he came up to me, and said, 'Would you be interested?' I found the idea for the research fascinating, given that it involved researching children and linking up with the police.

But our concerns are also driven by more than intellectual considerations; the chances of gaining promotion or receiving recognition for one's work may well also be relevant. Archer (2007) further traces differences in the ways in which we think about our social lives, and thereby seek to direct them. While some colleagues are driven in significant part by a concern to maximize their performance or climb the career ladder, others are driven by social ideals. Yet others still deliberate on future courses of action primarily through discussion with others. Perhaps there are relatively few academics who find it impossible to deliberate on future actions at all.

Collaborative working adds further complexity to the way in which such concerns influence our actions, as in relation to issues of recognition. Working with others may involve one setting aside one's own concerns, putting the priorities of others before one's own. In such a case one may be unwilling to offer the additional commitment that might enable the collaboration to flourish. If one consistently interacts with others in this fashion, then a *subjugation* of self may effectively be present. Indeed, it is clear that a number of representations of self are at stake in a collaboration, whether pertaining to authenticity, role or authorship. If we allow others to dominate the dialogue within a collaboration, for instance, we may find that our own contribution is less authentically ours. Charles Taylor (1992) argues that we find authentic identity in defending our ideas in our dialogue with others, crystallizing our views on what we believe is important. Or there may be issues related to acknowledging the various contributions that those involved make to a project. Patterns of working that acknowledge the contributions of others are essential – as a matter of ingrained habit. This is true whether acknowledging or quoting someone's name in a lecture or journal paper, or whether talking informally to other partners. The promotion of others need by no means involve the subjugation of self. Rather, 'others-promotion' involves explicitly recognizing, and paying attention to, the contribution that others make to achieving the common goals. Such an approach may be essential when working with others for whom concerns related to recognition and esteem are central to their actions.

Roles to Legitimize Action

The roles that are undertaken in collaborative work also determine one's scope to pursue concerns through joint action. A role can legitimate our initiative, or render it all but impossible. We do not primarily have in mind here the widely employed roles that Belbin (2004) advocates, whether completer-finisher, shaper or leader; or general dogsbody. Such roles seem too generic or unac-knowledged to legitimize initiative, but rather we need explicit responsibilities for aspects of work or for facilitating social interaction. If no one takes on the role of social secretary, then we may find that the group rarely engages in social events. And without informal or more personal contact between the group members, the scope for emergent patterns of work dries up. It is wishful thinking to imagine that evaluation will occur unless someone has taken on the role of evaluator; academic life is far too pressed to expect it to be otherwise. And if no one suggests new goals that might form a basis for joint action, then the collaboration may well fade away.

Archer (2000) argues also that roles provide an important means of contact between social structures and the agency of the individual. We do not catalyse agency by hoping that someone will become concerned about something – but we can increase the odds through handing over responsibility. Joint process thus does not necessarily lend itself to a straightforwardly egalitarian model where all carry out the same function, but rather to one where those involved make substantial contributions to shaping the process. We can carve out specific roles for ourselves, and encourage others to take on particular roles.

Capacity for Joint Action

But even with a collaboration that articulates with someone's concerns and within which they have a role that legitimizes action, we are all well aware that individual capacities count for a great deal. Knowledge, experience and expertise all reside significantly within individuals – and if they are missing when they should be there, huge problems in collaborative working can arise. But a concern for joint action suggests also that it is important to address our capacity for working alongside others regardless of expertise focused on the work itself.

If we are prone to play up our own contribution to a collaboration, we may find that others are less willing to include us in their plans. Character makes a difference in our ability to work together, but McIntyre (1984) is clear that we cannot generate qualities such as truthfulness and courage simply by wishing them upon ourselves or by spelling out an ideal set of personal qualities to which we should all subscribe. Rather, he argues that certain conditions need to be in place for virtue to thrive. We need stable forms of communal life and working, where we can agree together over the longer term on what patterns of behaviour are desirable. Dialogue around the personal qualities needed to work in common is thus essential, stimulated by the perplexing challenges that we face each day in our academic work. What we see here is that part of the content of our professional dialogue should stem from the troublesome nature of academic work. We would argue, for instance, that persistence is essential in the face of the hurdles that are almost inevitable with troublesome activity. Dweck (1999) is clear that self-efficacy makes a huge difference; we need a willingness to persist in the face of difficulty. But such persistence will be made possible partly through participation in a stable context that values this quality and that allows scope for dialogue around specific ways in which one might actually persist.

We see a fascinating interplay between our own willingness to commit ourselves to actions, our capacity to persist in the face of perplexity or difficulty, and the conditions that help to make such persistence possible, whether stemming from stable social contexts or the quality of our conversations as professionals. Such interplay may account for a good deal of our fascination with collaborative working. We know that we can influence proceedings, and that others can too; and that there are constraints that affect our influence. It thus makes sense, as we do in Table 2.3, to draw out specific ways in which our collaborative working supports the engagement of all those involved. And if the Erdös factor needs exploring in this interplay, so also does the corporate dimension.

Institutional Collaborations

When we think of higher education institutions, competition may come more naturally to mind than collaboration. Universities are typically keen on climbing the league tables, at the expense, obviously, of their competitors. We vie for

Table 2.3 Personal engagement as an indicator

Questions to identify data sources for the personal engagement indicator

---

In what ways do the goals for the work together align with the interests and priorities of those involved? To what extent are these goals focused on performance in relation to productivity, communication with others or social ideals?

What space is given within collaborative working to encourage those involved to deliberate on the initiatives that they themselves might initiate?

What roles are present within the collaboration that allow scope for those involved to take the initiative?

In what ways are the personal capacities of those involved being developed alongside the collaborative effort, whether in relation to specialist expertise or the ability to engage in collaborative working?

---

students and research funds, and for staff with Nobel Prizes or journal papers to their name. Collaboration is indeed most likely to occur between organizations that are not directly competing against each other, or in niche areas where the gains from collaboration outweigh any loss of competitive advantage, although the concept of 'competitive collaboration' is something that we explore further in Chapter 9. But securing research funds provides an immediate way in which collaboration may be encouraged between otherwise competing institutions. We see increasing collaboration globally, as institutions in different countries work together to carve out their own stake in the increasing flow of students moving country to study, with a rise in joint degrees, campuses and even institutions that straddle two or more countries. The development of a single European zone for higher education, with common standards and systems, also fuels this drive towards collaborative working in Europe. And we further see collaboration with partners beyond the university sector, involving schools, community colleges or further education, and industry.

It is clear, though, that the characteristics of collaborative working shift quite markedly when the collaboration occurs between organizations rather than individuals, as Ron Barnett reminds us in the round-table discussion. What we see here comprises its own strata of social reality, with its own complexities. Katz & Martin (1997) similarly question whether collaboration between individuals is the same as between groups or organizations, or indeed sectors and nations. The case studies in Part II provide several examples of this collaborative working, putting flesh on the bones of this introduction. We thus see in Whaley's story of commercial collaboration that account needs to be taken at this institutional level of staff changes and reassignment of work within teams, and of the value to the institution from this work opening up further possibilities for institutional partnerships. And with the case study of academic development in New Zealand by Stefani we see that management processes play a key role in facilitating collaborative working. In all of this, institutional commitment thus matters a great deal, seen in terms of senior management attention, and provision of staffing and resources. So, the university makes a decision, commits resources, adopts an impressive bargaining position and, hey presto, a successful collaboration is in place. But is this enough? While one will need to turn to the literature on strategic partnerships for a more substantive discussion, it is important also to consider the interplay between the corporate factors and the contribution that individuals must make for such a collaboration to flourish. Bailey & Koney (2000) suggest that a collaboration between organizations is still rooted in individual relationships, and Kanter (1994) argues that establishing many interpersonal relationships between partners helps resolve small conflicts before they escalate.

One of us spent a period of time facilitating a partnership between two universities in the United Kingdom. But where did it go? While initiated and undertaken at the highest of levels, the original intentions for the partnership have yet to be realized at the time of writing. Part of this stemmed from an inability fully to engage the agency of individual academics in each institution. Greater rewards for engagement might have made a difference, if the partnership really mattered quite so much – as might a less competitive international student market. But institutional cultures also played their part. The challenge in fostering collaboration across boundaries remains as real for institutions as it does for individuals or groups, as we explore further in the case studies included within Chapter 5. Thus, in the case study by Holmes, Haigh and Naidoo we see that an effort was required to ensure that all of those who had initially signed up to the collaboration remained engaged. And cohesiveness was also an issue for this collaboration that one of us facilitated earlier. If two institutions are located in different regions, then how does one arrange for the informal contacts that open up the possibilities for action? An extensive use of social networking software might have made a difference, enabling staff across two institutions to connect with each other and identify common academic goals, but in the absence of such action it is only too easy to drift into strategic rhetoric. We need more than fatalistic interactions to identify and achieve common academic goals.

Our next indicator thus concerns this corporate dimension, as we outline in Table 2.4. The challenge again is to identify concrete ways in which corporate engagement is fostered, so that we can reach beyond rhetoric and affect reality on the ground.

Towards a Synthesis: The Collaborative Cocktail

Collaborative working in higher education unfolds for us in this chapter as a complex phenomenon, but one that we can still appreciate if we attend to its fundamental aspects. In this the multilayered basis for collaborative working stands out. The work itself constitutes the most visible aspect of a collaboration,

Table 2.4 Corporate engagement as an indicator

Questions to identify data sources for the corporate engagement indicator

To what extent is the institution committed to the venture, through allocating staffing, resources, rewards and the attention of senior managers?

In what ways does the collaboration involve a range of personal contacts and relationships across the relevant part or parts of the organizations, whether linked to immediate priorities in achieving common goals or in wider ways?

How do the respective institutional cultures and missions influence the concerns and capabilities of the staff?

as carried out within a given context, providing as it does the main reason to come together; and this is reflected in the relative positioning of 'practice' at the forefront of our model in Figure 2.1. It quickly becomes apparent, though, whether the individuals involved are actually engaged in what is going on, and taking initiative rather than simply exhibiting a fatalistic orientation to collaborative working. And indeed it becomes apparent relatively quickly too whether an organization is ready to commit resources and attention to a partnership. But one of the main challenges in writing this book is to expose the way in which collaborative working depends on further layers.

There is a depth to collaborative working that extends beyond parcelling out bits of work to individuals. In including shading within this model, we suggest that there are aspects of collaborative working that are less apparent, extending as they do beyond the dominant technical-rational mentality of the modern age. Dialogues do indeed support the patterns of emergent working that we have seen as central to the troublesome activity of the academy, even if it remains a challenge to quantify this connection. Underlying social structures meanwhile might at first seem less than relevant to the conduct of our collaborative working. But it is the social vehicle that provides stability across a set of social interactions, and that enables dialogue, engagement and action over the longer term. We thus use the term 'social vehicle' to help surface these more fundamental aspects of collaborative working; with the term 'vehicle' suggesting that the structure exists in order to accomplish something, as we noted in Chapter 1.

We can further think of a social vehicle as a characteristic network of social relations (Outhwaite, 1998). This network may be manifested in a range of ways, through habitual patterns of interaction, roles, stable practices, agreements, events, meetings, and so on. Thus, a committee will have a title, a designated function, terms of reference, a pattern of meeting, a chair and secretary, and so on. Or a team or working group may meet regularly over an extended period of time in order to carry out an agreed programme of activity. We thus see in the case study which now follows that a regular pattern of meeting in an informal setting was involved. While the notion of a social vehicle may remain somewhat elusive despite such manifestations, the effects of different social vehicles are

Figure 2.1 A *stratified* model for collaborative working in higher education.

nonetheless influential in shaping collaborative working as it unfolds on all the further levels that we consider in Figure 2.1. Our model thus draws directly on Bhaskar's notions of stratification in social reality (1979), a stratification that takes in individuals, social interactions, social structures and corporate bodies. Clearly, much of the complexity of collaborative working stems from the interactions between these layers, as evident in our use of overlapping circles, within the given context of higher education. This is an aspect of our model that we will explore across the rest of the book, as social structures facilitate dialogue or as practice provides a focus for people to come together and to engage with each other (as Wenger (1998: 72–73) argues in relation to communities of practice) – although here we would suggest that operating with a wider notion such a social vehicle, rather than focusing on the narrower concept of a community of practice, provides a more effective underpinning to the broad notion represented by collaborative working itself. In any case, the complexity that is evident here in turn helps to ensure that collaborative working often remains a riddle to us, as Archer (1995) is aware, even when we are able to focus on the different social structures that underpin a collaboration, as we do in Table 2.5.

Table 2.5 Social vehicles as an indicator

Questions to identify data sources for the social vehicles indicator

What working practices, relationships, roles, events and agreements are embedded within the collaboration? In what ways do these different characteristics help to establish a stable network of social relations between those collaborating with each other?

How is the collaboration linked to further social vehicles that might support the collaboration, whether by strengthening its underlying social vehicle or through facilitating collaborative working at the other levels of our model?

We can now take this understanding of emergence and closure, differentiation and cohesiveness, as well as agency and social structure, into the more practical business of establishing and sustaining collaborative working; and also into our analysis of specific case studies and thinking for the future. The ideas and indicators discussed in this chapter provide a helpful basis for the actual business of working with others. Indeed, you might begin already to assess an existing collaboration in which you are involved against these ideas and indicators. But one more immediate effect of our analysis in this chapter is, we would claim, the establishment of a rationale to underpin our model for collaborative working in higher education.

References

Amis, K. (1954). *Lucky Jim*. London: Victor Gollancz.

Archer, M. (1995). *Realist Social Theory*. Cambridge: Cambridge University Press.

Archer, M. (2000). *Being Human: The Problem of Agency*. Cambridge: Cambridge University Press.

Archer, M. (2007). *Making Our Way through the World: Human Reflexivity and Social Mobility*. Cambridge: Cambridge University Press.

Bailey, D. & Koney, K. (2000). *Strategic Alliances among Health and Human Services Organizations*. London: Sage.

Belbin, R. M. (2004) *Management Teams: Why They Succeed or Fail*, 2nd edn. Oxford: Butterworth Heinemann.

Bhaskar, R. (1979). *The Possibility of Naturalism*. Brighton: Harvester.

Davidson Frame, J. (2003). *Managing Projects in Organizations: How to Make the Best use of Time, Techniques, and People*, 3rd edn. San Francisco: Jossey-Bass.

Dweck, C. S. (1999). *Self-Theories: Their Role in Motivation, Personality and Development*. Philadelphia: Psychology Press.

Elliott, J. (2005). Becoming critical: the failure to connect. *Educational Action Research, 13* (3), 359–374.

Foucault, M. (1970). *The Archaeology of Knowledge*. New York: Pantheon.

Gadamer, H.-G. (1989). *Truth and Method*, 2nd edn, trans. J. Weinsheimer & D. G. Marshall. New York: Crossroad.

Giddens, A. (1991). *Modernity and Self-Identity: Self and Society in the Late Modern Age*. Stanford, CA: Stanford University Press.

Gustavsen, B. (2001). Theory and practice: the mediating discourse. In P. Reason & H. Bradbury (eds) *Handbook of Action Research*. London: Sage.

Habermas, J. (1984). *The Theory of Communicative Action: Reason and the Rationalization of Society*, vol. 1, trans. T. McCarthy. Boston: Beacon Press.

Hagstrom, W. O. (1965). *The Scientific Community*. New York: Basic Books.

Helsby, G. & Saunders, M. (1993). Taylorism, Tylerism and performance indicators: defending the indefensible? *Educational Studies, 19*, 55–77.

Hunt, L., Bromage, A. & Tomkinson, B. (eds) (2006). *The Realities of Change in Higher Education: Interventions to Promote Learning and Teaching*. London: Routledge.

Kanter, R. M. (1994). Collaborative advantage: the art of alliances. *Harvard Business Review, 4*, 96–108.

Katz, J. & Martin, B. (1997). What is research collaboration? *Research Policy, 26*, 1–18.

Land, R. (2004). *Educational Development: Discourse, Identity and Practice*. Maidenhead, UK: Society for Research into Higher Education/Open University Press.

Levine, J. & Moreland, R. (2004). Collaboration: the social context of theory development. *Personality and Social Psychology Review, 8*, 164–172.

McIntyre, A. (1984). *After Virtue: A Study in Moral Theory*, 2nd edn. Notre Dame, IN: University of Notre Dame Press.

Megginson, D. (1994). Planned and emergent learning. *Executive Development, 7*, 29–34.

Morrison, P., Dobbie, G. & McDonald, F. (2003). Research collaboration amongst university scientists. *Higher Education Research and Development, 22* (3), 275–296.

New Scientist (2007). Intelligent collaboration, *2591*, 21.

Outhwaite, W. (1998). Realism and social science. In M. Archer, R. Bhaskar, A. Collier, T. Lawson & A. Norrie (eds) *Critical Realism: Essential Readings*. London: Routledge.

Perkins, D. (2006). Constructivism and troublesome knowledge. In J. H. F. Meyer and R. Land (eds) *Overcoming Barriers To Student Understanding: Threshold Concepts and Troublesome Knowledge*. Abingdon, UK: Routledge.

Putnam, R. D. (2000). *Bowling Alone: The Collapse and Revival of American Community*. New York: Simon & Schuster.

Taylor, C. (1992). *The Ethics of Authenticity*. Cambridge, MA: Harvard University Press.

Wenger, E. (1998). *Communities of Practice: Learning, Meaning and Identity*. Cambridge: Cambridge University Press.

Wildavsky, A. (1998). *Culture and Social Theory*, ed. S. Chai & B. Swedlow. New Brunswick, NJ: Transaction Publishers.

Case Study

Discussing Research over Breakfast in the Conservatory

GORDON ROBERTS *(a pseudonym)*
The Russell Group in the United Kingdom

The Principal Investigator was a chap who had originally been a student of mine in the late 1970s, Ben. He was a geography–geology student who somehow got into crime – the geography of crime, not crime itself. I met him again at a conference that had an element of the geography of crime in it. I found that he'd got a job here at the university working in social policy. We chatted, and had lunch or something. We then bumped into each other from time to time when he was working in the library, and we'd have coffee and chat about work. Then much later on he approached me in relation to a bid on stranger danger. He'd done a lot of work with the police, and was interested in comparing police records with what happens from the children's point of view. So he came up to me, and said, 'Would you be interested?' I found the idea for the research fascinating, given that it involved researching children and linking up with the police.

He put in the bid with myself and with a professor from social policy, Keith, a criminologist who had gone to another institution. The opportunity of working alongside Keith was another attraction. And getting both of us involved probably made a big difference to getting the grant. Keith's name was extremely well thought of in criminology; he's one of those rare people who always put their name on the end of what's written, even though he's the key writer. And having a geographer involved would have added an edge, given the geographical dimensions to the bid. So, the three of us got on with this, with Ben, very much Ben, doing the work with the help of research assistants.

A Sounding Board

Given that we were all based in different parts of the country, we met regularly in a garden centre that was equidistant from all of us. We met for breakfast in the conservatory. The meetings were interesting, partly because of the sorts of issues that came up in relation to researching stranger danger. The first few meetings involved setting up some protocols so that Ben could go into schools. We were presenting kids from ages 9 to 15 with a difficult questionnaire to complete in class, where the middle part was about dangers that they might encounter from strangers. Choosing words that are understandable by 9-year-olds and not too condescending for 15-year-olds is quite tricky. Some of the questionnaire was easy to complete for the pupils, but the sexual nature of some the material was complicated. So we spent quite a lot of time chatting about what was needed.

Keith and I essentially acted as a sounding board for Ben. We were very much hands-off, rather than always saying that you can't do this or that. Ben would say, 'Here it is, guys, what do you think?', and we'd make our comments. He was a good listener as well. He wasn't someone who would ignore everything you said. He had enormous respect for Keith because of his criminology background and the work he's done, and he would listen to me as a past tutor; well, I don't know. Alongside this I did manage to get out and do a bit of data collecting, because, as I said to Ben, 'If I don't do that, I won't have a feel for what it's like.' So I went into a couple of primary schools and a couple of secondary schools. Keith himself never actually went out to collect data, but listened and joined in the meetings. And then Ben did all of this analysis, but he would come to us and say, 'How should I do this?'

Attending to the Challenges of the Research Process

Or then we would discuss drafts of papers and reports together, or go through comments from an editor or referee on a paper. The final report was one case where both Keith and I were concerned that it was initially too descriptive, because Ben hadn't got to the point where he'd unpacked it all. We spent a good amount of time on the research design. The structure that we used for this design was partly mine, because I suggested that he interview some of the people who had indicated an experience of a stranger-danger incident. He interviewed the kids and the parents; that was his idea. He was trying to look at the background that the kids came from, and their behaviour and any parental controls of various kinds. And I suggested also that if you're going to do that, then you really need a control group of interviews with people who haven't had anything happen, and to talk about their behaviour. If they're exactly the same, it's nothing to do with that. So, trying to pair off people in a control group was what he tried to do – by age, gender, etc.

We did try to make a more direct contribution to the research on one occasion, when Keith and I did get together. I thought it was going to be for a morning, but it turned out to be for an entire day. We were trying to work out probabilities of certain things happening, because what we had was information on the last experience that someone had encountered. 'Clearly, if you're 15 years old you've got a greater chance of actually having experienced an incident involving stranger danger than if you're 9, and we tried to work out probabilities of events occurring, but it all got too complicated.'

The Personal Dynamics

One thing that made a huge difference in sustaining all of this was how well we get on together – something that I knew would be the case right from the outset. Keith would always have a full breakfast and chomp away. In those days I had my bacon butty, which I'm not even allowed to have now. Before his fiftieth birthday party, Ben's wife called me and said, 'Gordon, I'd like to put on a surprise party. Who should I invite from the university world?' My wife was away so I was on my own – off in the States. I went to it, and I didn't realize that Ben had seven or eight brothers or sisters. It was lovely; packed, one of those surprise parties: 'Is he coming? No, he's not.' Keith said he'd come and didn't, and when I talked to Ben he said, 'Oh, Keith phoned up and apologized, and said he'd forgotten all about it, but he hadn't, he didn't like that sort of thing.' So Ben obviously knows him very well.

It could easily have been 'Finish project, get report in and that's the end of it.' But our breakfast meetings still go on, even long after the original project has finished; although not just the three of us. And I still play golf with Keith. Work together has also continued on a number of further papers. Ben was in a position that meant he always had to get the next grant or contract and as soon as that finished he's got to get another one to support himself in a way. So he would write up a research report, but not publish anywhere near as much as he could have. So I've had the opportunity to comment on and rework plenty of material. We've just actually had published the second paper relating to work that finished in about 1999 – although much of the delay on this one was down to a peculiar editor. And now Ben's put in for a PhD by publication, so I've again helped him for a little bit with comments about that. So I've been in a senior role, but not the lead; more like a mentor. I wouldn't be surprised to get an email soon saying, 'I've got the PhD!' (He just has.)

3
Establishing and Sustaining Collaborations

> Successful partnerships manage the relationship, not just the deal.
>
> **(Kanter, 1994: 96)**

A collaboration may last little longer than a passing dream, or it may endure for a lifetime and beyond. The guilds of craftsmen in medieval Europe were one set of social structures that lasted a fair time. Guilds were designed to ensure high standards of work and mutual support among the members, but they effectively also operated as a cartel, excluding open access to the trade. Guilds have similarly operated in other societies as well, as, for example, in India during the Gupta period or with the *warraqeen* system of publishing knowledge in the Islamic world. The medieval guilds, of course, largely died out as wider shifts in society rendered them obsolete – as people sought free trade and business innovation. But some guilds still outlived others. The Guild of Saint Luke for painters in Antwerp, for instance, ceased to operate only in 1795, after a decision by the local government to destroy its monopoly.

There will evidently be a range of reasons as to why a collaboration similarly might outlive many of its counterparts, or indeed never quite make it in the first place. (And it is, of course, quite possible to see the academy itself as a restrictive guild.) Any social structure depends on the ongoing activity of individuals, or else it passes with time, as Bhaskar (1979) reminds us. Part of the challenge is for us to adopt a mindset which recognizes that it is important to pay attention to the social aspects of collaboration, and not simply look at what a partnership is producing. It is easy, for instance, as a member of a group to leave it to others to take responsibility for the interactions; one does find this with students, but it can equally be true with colleagues. One challenge in this chapter is to help us find ways to actually take responsibility for establishing and sustaining our collaborative endeavours, rather than to leave this to others.

We will, of course, in this look to the theoretical perspectives articulated in the previous chapter. We retain a place for both productivity and emergence as to the way in which we embark on collaborative working, while also respecting the need for professional dialogues. And interactions with other strata of social reality will affect proceedings, whether the contribution of the individual or the organization. But the twists and turns that come from the actual business of making something happen provide much of our immediate concern in this chapter. What makes for an interesting focus for collaborative work? How can we piggyback on existing social structures, rather than start from scratch every time we want to achieve goals that are best advanced through collaboration? What of the actual decision to get something off the ground, how we make sense of a collaboration as it unfolds, or the challenges involved in breathing new life into a sluggish collaboration?

Finding a Focus for Collaborative Working

How do you find a compelling focus for collaborative work? There is of course little substitute for living and breathing your field day and night, as it were. But we also see that sources of ideas are often social in nature, even if the light bulb needs an individual to turn it on. A vibrant academic culture will include plenty of exchanges with colleagues around issues of common interest. Our own partnership in writing this book stemmed from participation in a short residential course offered by the Staff and Educational Development Association in the United Kingdom. But it will help also to be aware of the different sorts of collaborative working in which colleagues now routinely engage. If we are to establish stable patterns of collaborative working, then a more detailed under-standing of the collaborative landscape is essential. And with this landscape comes further understanding of why someone might collaborate, drawing out some of the drivers for collaboration that we identified in Chapter 1.

Teaching Together

We can look first of all at collective practices for teaching and learning. Typically, colleagues come together to design programmes of study, and in testing or assessing students. Collaborative working is clearly involved in these standard practices, with committee meetings providing a stable way to ensure that agreement is reached and that everyone completes their own tasks. These practices are at the heart of life in the academy, but they can be designed in ways that leave colleagues to then go off and do their own things, or that require them to work together in an ongoing fashion. Take programme design. Given competition among institutions to attract and retain students while still maximizing fee income, there is an increasing awareness of the need to project the distinctive characteristics of the education that students are to encounter: 'If you come to this department, you will learn in this unique fashion.' 'We employ problem-based learning across our entire provision.' In such cases the tutors on the programme need to sign up to the same pattern of teaching; whereas traditionally the classroom has been one's own private domain as a tutor. There would need to be a substantive reason for faculty to give up long-cherished freedoms in how they teach their students, not to mention the need to develop expertise in what might be a new manner of teaching. The survival of the department might be at stake, and one would rarely see this happening in practice without the exercise of clear leadership.

But other drivers are at work too. One of these is technology, as the classroom may be a virtual one. Asynchronous discussion via a virtual learning environment offers plenty of scope for several colleagues to work together, especially when there is a large group of students involved. And yet another driver is interprofessional learning, with each tutor contributing from a particular perspective. Funding arrangements may provide a further reason, especially where innovations in learning and teaching are concerned. An innovation may benefit from road testing in a range of locations or disciplines. One of us helped to lead a regional project that sought to develop capacity to engage in inquiry-based learning. Those involved needed to understand how to support students in directing their own lines of inquiry; and it was evident that such understanding emerged in significant part from seeing one's colleagues implement their own approaches. And indeed students can be drawn into such work too, as occurs at the University of Glasgow in Scotland with students employed over the summer to assist lecturers in introducing inquiry-based learning into further modules.

When we look for collaborative teaching across institutions we need a clear sense that value is added in some way. Two institutions may be able to pool their expertise or achieve a greater scale in order to make a new degree programme viable. Or viability for the programme may come from the greater scope for student mobility. We see this with the Master's in Environmental Sciences, Policy and Management – from the University of Lund in Sweden, the University of Manchester in England and the Central European University in Budapest, Hungary. In this case the requirement to move between institutions constitutes a fundamental aspect of the programme. Environmental policy is very much an international affair, with postgraduate education needing to respond accordingly. Of course, the situation is further eased when a collaboration attracts funding. In this case the joint Master's degree is supported by the European Union (and with money from the financier George Soros also in evidence). Such educational collaborations are also assisted in the European Union (EU) with the development of a common regulatory framework through the Bologna process, and to the ongoing moves towards integration within the EU.

Collaborative Research

We see similar, if not greater, scope evident for collaboration on research. The day is yet to come when half of the world's particle physicists teach on the same degree programme. In some ways the requirements of quality assurance and the institutional competition over the income streams associated with teaching make it difficult for colleagues to collaborate around teaching. But the way in which research is funded in significant part by grant-making bodies offers huge scope for collaborative working across a range of otherwise insurmountable boundaries. One programme of research funding after the next is looking to capitalize on collaboration. Take, as it were at random, one of the programme areas at the US National Science Foundation (NSF). International collaboration is the very first heading that comes up in relation to the programme in Social, Behavioral & Economic Sciences. Then, in the funding programme for the 2008 competition in Human and Social Dynamics, we see an emphasis on multi-disciplinary teams with the intention to bring together researchers from fields of research not previously known for working together. Should one, then, be surprised that typing the word 'collaboration' into the search engine on the NSF website yields 25,000 hits? Not surprisingly, clear guidance is provided on how to present bids that involve several organizations or international partners. And indeed, international collaboration is a particular focus. A recent report has found in the United Kingdom that almost all universities explicitly confirm that they are seeking as a matter of policy to expand their extent of collaboration with international partners on research activity (UK Higher Education International Unit and Universities UK, 2008).

Morrison *et al.* (2003) argue that if we take into account the processes involved, and not simply the number of names on the paper, then collaborative research is now the most common way in which research is conducted in the sciences, whether experimental or theoretical. Zukerman & Merton (1973) earlier saw evidence for an increasing dominance of collaboration within the social sciences, with Lariviere *et al.* (2006) now suggesting that patterns of collaborative working for researchers in the social sciences are closer to those of the natural sciences and engineering than to those of the humanities. Even in the arts and humanities, the traditional domain of the lone scholar at work in the archive or library, we see new patterns emerging. The Stanford Humanities Lab constitutes a collaboration among the faculty in Stanford's School of Arts and Sciences that looks to adopt a Big Humanities/Arts approach modelled on the lines of Big Science. Their aim is to address questions that they believe transcend the boundaries between arts, sciences and humanities, or between the academy and industry. New media, collaborative research, public exhibitions and interactive archives are all involved in this. While the lab is predicated primarily around research, it also provides a focus for projects that involve students, with research outputs feeding into teaching, and education that breeds humanities-savvy techies and techie-savvy scholars in the humanities. Such shifts are partly down to funding regimes and institutional agendas, of course, but the emergence of new disciplines depends on thinking across established academic divides.

And Beyond

While research and teaching take the lion's share of our attention in this book, the collaborative scene within higher education also includes other areas, such as administration and outreach activity within the locality of a university, or beyond. Efficiency gains may drive the establishment of a purchasing consortium or the development of common information technology infrastructure. And we see university and national libraries working together to ensure that low-use printed journals can be made easily available to the academic community, again resulting in capital savings each year. But collaboration may also be driven more directly by wider academic goals, as with those that relate to social justice or community engagement, in working together with local schools and colleges. Universities in this way can play a role in promoting greater social inclusion within our societies.

The challenge in part is to ensure a focus that will genuinely be worthwhile, and thus catalyse the engagement of others or the commitment of the institution. Of course, there is a counterpart to this also, in that the ambition present within many academic goals can place quite exceptional demands on others. If a goal involves plenty of change on the part of other people's attitudes, then clearly there will be many challenges on the way. This affects the extent to which you can actually rely on their engagement, or indeed their opposition. Changing established practice is as much a form of troublesome activity as inventing new knowledge is. In this case the difficulties arise in part from challenges to identity and not simply knowledge, as change can lead to uncertainties and anxieties over one's role or familiar practice. D'Andrea & Gosling (2005: 59) indeed suggest that 'people do not have one identity, but several. . . . Identities are social constructions involving reflexive awareness. They have a symbolic significance that enables us to give meaning to what we do.'

Standing on the Shoulders of Giants, or Starting from Scratch?

Part of the issue in deciding whether or not to establish a collaboration is to size up whether the additional investment of coordination is justified. It is not simply a question of settling on a suitable academic goal, but rather also of assessing a good way to achieve the goal (and perhaps others as well). The extent to which infrastructure already exists that might support a collaboration is thus a key issue, given the significant investment required from those involved.

This is true first of all in relation to any social vehicles that underpin the collaboration. While we can say that the collaboration itself incorporates one or more social vehicles as an integral element, through embedded structures and social practices, there may be further social vehicles linked to the collaboration. The extent of these will affect the extent to which you will be able to work together in a cohesive fashion from the outset. If you see each other on a regular basis, then trust is likely to have been established already. We can in effect dispense with some of the 'forming', 'norming', 'storming' and 'performing' that Tuckman (1965) identified as accompanying the establishment of a new group. You have a real advantage when you have worked with someone else before, in knowing the extent to which they are likely to deliver on what they promise. Think about your own practice. Are there ways in which you can build on the basis of existing social groupings? How can you tap into ways in which your colleagues already come together in your field or institution?

The Infrastructure for Collaboration

One of the most pervasive social vehicles likely to be involved concerns the university department or other formal unit of organization. But the members of an academic department may find very little opportunity to collaborate together on substantive pieces of academic work, as opposed to carrying out work alongside each other rather than together with each other. Committees, for instance, may account for many of the occasions on which staff come together in a department, but primarily involve joint decision-making rather than joint working as such. The presence or absence of a place to socialize as a department can make a significant difference to the extent to which collaboration is possible, as we saw in the previous chapter. The staff common room exists for more reasons than a convenient cup of coffee. But if this is absent, for instance, then the basis for collaborative working may well be weak.

One of us was working recently with a group of academics who were taking a qualification in learning and teaching. Each of them was looking to introduce a change within their practice that would involve the cooperation of others. But it was clear that there were very few social vehicles in place to support them in this process, beyond the overall department within which they operated. In one case there was an admissions team in operation, and in another case a working group was responsible for agreeing problem-based learning scenarios. Being part of the same department, however, need not mean that one is ready to carry out work in common with others in this context. An annual visit from a peer reviewer cannot replace the daily discussions that are needed to develop a common mind on ways to teach with others in an innovative fashion. While research groups are present within the university world, quite generally there are few social vehicles that have been developed to support teaching, beyond departments and committees. Programme or course teams may in theory exist, but in practice they may never operate together, except perhaps in the context of a committee. But unless teaching is carried out on a mutual basis it is hard to see why staff would need to pull together in this area, in ways that go beyond arrangements for quality assurance. We may find that the social vehicles underpinning a collaboration are hardly established at all, with there being no durable structure or features to support us in achieving the academic goals of the collaboration.

But the infrastructure for collaborative working usually does run deeper than this, especially in relation to research. Research groups increasingly constitute part of the accepted academic infrastructure, as do the professional and scholarly societies based around disciplines. Indeed, we may also be able to find ways in which teaching can benefit from these social vehicles based around research. This is especially evident in relation to postgraduate teaching, where a research group can provide a focus for the education of research students; but there are many other possibilities. We see one of these in a recent collaboration between Computer Science at Brown University and the Illustration Department at Rhode Island School of Design, where students from design and computer science work with each other to create scientific software in Brown's 'Cave', an immersive virtual environment. This initiative was made possible in part through a discussion group that involved several colleagues from the same research group at Brown's (Laidlaw, 2003). Alongside this we see different fora for professional dialogues within traditions of collaborative inquiry, such as peer-reviewed journals, edited texts, conferences, blogs, and so on. These intellectual fora provide an occasion for establishing trust with specific individuals, or for developing common language with which to speak about one's work. We need to explore ways in which collaboration around teaching might draw on the more extensive social capital apparent within the domain of research.

Established academic organizations and professional associations also play an important role in their national settings, whether the Royal Society in the United Kingdom and Commonwealth, the Japan Academy or the Australian Academy of Science. These organizations invest significant resources in establishing networks from which collaborations of a significant scale can then be built. They form part of the collaborative capacity of higher education. We see this, for instance, in the establishment of the Carnegie Initiative on the Doctorate. This initiative was a five-year project that worked with doctoral-granting departments committed to restructuring their programmes to better prepare graduates. Founded over 100 years ago, the Carnegie Foundation for the Advancement of Teaching is an independent policy and research centre with a primary mission 'to do and perform all things necessary to encourage, uphold, and dignify the profession of the teacher and the cause of higher education'. Collaboration does take additional effort – and the existence of bodies whose primary purpose is to advance the cause of higher education is thus a key advantage. What would there be in it for a single institution to organize such a collaboration as the one envisaged here?

There are further elements to the collaborative infrastructure of the academy. If you need to secure further partners, then the strength of your network of contacts in the given area will make a significant difference. In our earlier work together (Kahn & Walsh, 2006) we introduce a continuum that spans from networking to collaboration. A network of contacts provides a starting point for collaboration with which we can hardly dispense, allowing the possibility for work in common or ongoing contact. And we can also consider in this the contacts of our contacts, especially where an institution maintains a facility to link one up with potential partners. Such a facility is clearly essential in securing funding from the European Union, given its general approach to require collaborative work across the union.

Without such an infrastructure in place, significant time must be devoted to establishing environments, systems and technology that support the collaboration. Time will be required to establish common agreements, trust and mutual understanding. Coming to understand the nature of the differences between those involved, and the effect that they have on the work and interactions between those involved in the collaboration, is clearly an essential feature of this initial stage. But this time may still be worth investing, particularly if you are looking to establish a new area of research. In this case the focus of your attention can be on establishing the infrastructure as much as on carrying out the work. One of us is currently moving into a new line of research, but before looking to invest energy in bidding for research funding, the intention is to secure funds first of all that will allow for the development of a wider set of contacts in the field. Such contacts can of course also come from putting together a proposal and drawing others into the proceedings, but then one must also recognize the additional effort that will have to be expended by moving more directly into pulling together a collaboration when only a relatively modest infrastructure is in place to support it.

Ready, Steady, . . . Collaborate?

But even if you are relying on the use of existing social vehicles, a collaboration with others will typically involve a significant contribution from those involved. Risk is inherent in this. We may find that a collaboration represents academic espionage rather than a joint endeavour; or, perhaps more commonly, one or more of those involved will look to take a ride on the back of our work, gaining undue recognition as a result. Clearly, risk is reduced where funds are secured from an outside body, offering an often compelling reason to engage. We see this in the case study that concludes this chapter in which Connolly, Jones and Lydon outline a collaboration between higher education institutions and further education colleges (e.g. community colleges) in Wales:

> The aim of the First Campus Collaborative Project is to engage further with schools to raise the awareness of progression routes into higher education for pupils, encouraging the notion that learning is fun, and that university is an option for all. The strategy was underpinned by the assumption that making university facilities available to young people raises their educational aspirations and achievements, and hopefully encourages them to progress to higher levels of learning.

It was clear that external funding helped to ensure that this was a relatively low-risk collaboration. It appears that the dynamics of funding (resources), the political and socio-economic environment and the nature of the activities were the most significant factors in establishing the case-study collaboration. The 'contextual incentives' identified by Gray (1996: 59) – the limited government funding for widening access, coupled with pressure for collaboration, 'declining growth rate and increasing competitive pressures' and 'differing perceptions of environmental risk' – were significant elements underlying the dynamics of this collaboration.

But other issues may still arise. The collaboration may involve crossing too many barriers, whether from working at a distance from each other or failing to share a common language – or indeed from a lack of shared history of prior collaborative activity. So it makes sense at the outset to step back and assess the odds on success, and the gains that are to be had from working together. It is easy to be swept up into a collaboration that you are only half-interested in joining, simply from the force of circumstances, as Gordon Roberts found when working with a senior colleague in his own research in the case study in Chapter 6.

Putting in Place the Initial Arrangements

In judging whether or not to go ahead with a collaboration, it may help to engage in exploratory work to start with, in order to test the waters or to help build commitment among others. Appreciative inquiry represents one approach to this. An inquiry begins with a positive question that 'guides inquiry agendas and focuses attention towards the most life-giving, life-sustaining aspects of organisational existence' (Ludema *et al.*, 2001: 189). Initial work would then lead to dreams and plans for new possibilities, while drawing others into the cycle. The theory is that growth occurs where we focus our attention, and that people are more attracted to joining an initiative that is working well than to joining one that is riven with the relentless criticism that is often found in higher education. This also provides a way to test whether the collaboration really does resonate with the concerns and priorities that others hold.

If the involvement of others is a precursor to establishing a new collaboration, then one of the most important steps to take before looking to launch a collaboration is to bring people together, as we saw in the case study on learning communities in Chapter 1 and as is the situation with the curriculum development work at the University of Aberdeen in Chapter 4. In and of itself this may change the direction that the collaboration is set to take, at least if this coming together occurs on a sufficiently open basis. The nature of the event thus makes a difference; if the idea is simply for you to convince others that your idea should be pursued, then it can hardly be a surprise when others fail to agree. It is worth looking to build in the openness to multiple products and relationships that Gustavsen (2001) argues are essential for generating, and taking forward, ideas for development. The reactions that others bring with them thus provide further feedback on the advisability of running with something.

The way in which you establish things in the first place sets the agenda for the collaboration as it unfolds; after all, we are creatures of habit. In investigating strategic alliances between firms, Doz (1996) suggests that the early stages of cooperation have a disproportionate impact on the long-term evolution of the alliance; and we can see also that the different moments of collaboration that we consider in the round-table discussion in Chapter 8 will influence the mentality that determines these initial stages, whether in a defensive or opportunistic fashion, or with short- or long-term ends in mind. Such early stages include the initial conditions of task definition, partners' organizational routines, interface structure and partners' expectations. But rather than a collaboration simply resulting in a working out of these conditions, Doz suggests that the early stages can help to block subsequent learning and adaptation, or foster it. Kezar (2005) similarly picks out issues that should be addressed at an early stage when considering collaborations within higher education, as we have already seen in Table 1.2. Her stress on the importance of learning fits well with Doz's findings on what counts during the early stages of a collaboration, but a role is also evident for compelling reasons to work together, compatibility of priorities and social networks.

We can, though, further view this initial basis in terms of our model for collaborative working in higher education. One of us was involved recently in a project to review literature on the use of reflective practice within programmes for new faculty. We can see how this collaboration was planned in relation to our model for collaborative working:

- *Practice*: the resources allocated from the funding body came with a demanding timescale and an extensive report to complete. Almost inevitably, we were required to have a clear set of project management techniques, including the ubiquitous steering group, and to employ a series of protocols to shape the actual core work of reviewing the literature. Scope was present for emergent patterns of working, principally as a result of the face-to-face meetings planned into the proceedings.
- *Professional dialogues*: the work was essentially carried out by peers – who were thus inclined from the outset to exchange frank views on the progress of work. But the project also included an evaluator whose role was to investigate the conduct of the project. Her contribution to the dialogue within the team subsequently provoked a greater under-standing of the underlying academic basis for the review.
- *Engagement*: flexibility was built in to allow variation in the extent to which those involved were to engage, whether in simply completing a core set of reviewing work, or taking on further roles in writing journal

papers. Given that all but two of the participants were based in different institutions and that the project budget was small, it is hard to see how a project leader could have forced individuals to engage when they were not willing. While this did allow significant variation in the amount of effort expended by those involved, and cause a certain measure of frustration in the final stages, it now seems a small price to pay, given the resulting academic outcomes (see, for example, Kahn *et al.*, 2008), which could not have been attained alone.

- *Social vehicles*: the team was built around common membership of a network of programme leaders, as well as on some long-established personal connections, thus providing a certain measure of cohesiveness from the outset. And the project itself was planned in a regular pattern of interaction, with clear roles for project coordination.

We thus outline in Table 3.1 some key elements of initial planning, spelled out in relation to our model for collaborative working in higher education, enabling you to consider whether your initial basis will ensure the creation of suitable outputs, dialogues among professionals, engagement across the board and supportive social vehicles. Plans, and even formal agreements, are relevant across the whole of our model, rather than simply in relation to project management. We shall see, for instance, that the collaboration across engineering departments in Chapter 7 incorporated a clear agreement between

Table 3.1 Issues for initial planning in relation to the model for collaborative working in higher education

Practice	Planned working: project management techniques, workflow processes, specification of outputs, links to strategic agendas, funding and resources
	Emergent working: events, encounters and environments favouring multiple products and relationships, spaces or strategies to enable one to adjust collaborative goals
Engagement	Personal engagement: roles to allow scope for initiative-taking, articulation with concerns of those involved, spaces for deliberative thinking, strategies to reward engagement and discourage passivity, capacity-building
	Corporate engagement: expressions of institutional commitment, alignment of institutional cultures, development of social networks that span both institutions
Professional dialogues	Strategies to promote exchanges between those involved, including those across areas of expertise or other forms of difference, or to ensure the inclusion of those with alternative perspectives or contributions to make
Social vehicles	Instigation of stable patterns of social interaction, as through practices, relationships, roles, events and agreements; connections to further social vehicles

those involved, while accord was reached on the uses for the virtual research environment in the collaboration among educational researchers outlined in Chapter 6. Unless we pay attention to these issues, the likelihood is that key elements of what is required for collaborative working will simply be left unaddressed, although the scale and formality of the planning will vary. Otherwise, the dominant modes of thinking and working in society may simply take over, focusing only on efficiency in achieving predefined goals. The stratum of social reality represented by geo-historical trends can impinge more than we would like on our ways of working collaboratively in higher education. We need to do more than merely pay lip service to those aspects of collaborative working that are simply valued too little in the realms beyond the troublesome work of higher education.

And we further suggest that one way to help formalize this initial agreement is to frame a collaborative protocol. One might even expect to see funders or institutions requiring that such wider dimensions of collaborative working are addressed as a condition of funding. We have in mind a protocol for collaboration rather than one for carrying out the work per se, one that covers each of the aspects of our model for collaborative working. Each situation is unique, but a formal agreement is often more necessary than we realize, given the need to establish mutual understanding across the different perspectives represented within the collaboration. Thus, one might see a range of practical elements included within such a protocol:

- the use of social software, or periodic working in a common location, to ensure that discussion and networking occur on a wider basis than simply that required to complete predefined tasks;
- regular review points included within meetings to discuss the social dimension to the collaboration, or to articulate concerns held by the individuals involved;
- roles and responsibilities to facilitate exchanges across areas of professional expertise or to ensure the development of further expertise or capacity among those involved.

We see that it is essential here to address a range of actual processes and structures to ensure that our collaborative working is actually characterized by these aspects of our model. As we saw in Chapter 1, Kezar (2005) also identifies a range of formal processes and structures that were evident in successful collaborations, whether computing systems, regular meetings, rewards and incentives, or the creation of new social networks or organizational units. We see this quite clearly also in the First Campus case study:

It might have been anticipated that, given the tensions resulting from some of the failed collaborative ventures described above, First Campus might well have had problems. However, one of the interesting features of higher education is the range of networks – formal, quasi-formal and informal –

that exist and have been developed at the operational level. The genesis of this collaboration originated from a small number of key individuals operating in the widening access/educational development field in two of the partner universities, a number of whom had developed contacts over a number of years and who were deeply committed to increased access.

Alongside such formal elements, Kezar also stresses the importance of informal elements, pertaining to such factors as an ethos of innovation and an egalitarian ethic, although such aspects are harder to address quite so directly through a protocol and need to be supported in emerging from the aspects of that protocol, such as regular discussion, networking and freedom to share ideas in a supportive environment. Sargent & Waters (2004) also stress the importance of such informal elements in their analysis of collaborative working, involving such issues as the climate, support, trust and mutual attraction.

Sustaining Collaborations

We may have a tendency to assume that once a collaboration is off the ground, it will carry forward with its own momentum, whether or not we do much to support it. But Bhaskar (1979) further emphasizes that while physical reality remains there whether we like it or not, the social world depends on our own contribution. Social realities are thus inherently transformable, more so indeed than the natural world around us. We thus need to take concern for the nature of this transformation, whether it involves a collaboration flourishing or withering. One of the keys to our capacity to sustain a collaboration is to realize that there is a close connection between our contribution and the way that the collaboration unfolds. Many people never bother to vote in elections, but without a sufficient number of individual citizens going out to the polling booth, democracy would grind to a halt. Part of the issue is that when so many people are involved, we find it hard to see what difference our own contribution has made. The rest of this chapter in many ways constitutes a series of strategies to help us keep our eye on the progress of the collaboration. We start by looking at some ways to understand the characteristics of the collaboration as it unfolds.

Securing Insight

There is a need for reflexivity in relation to our collaborative working, so that we each begin to perceive this connection between our own actions, or the actions of others, and shifts in collaboration. We can only too easily jump to conclusions about why someone else has acted in a certain way, or forever hold it against them, but without our conclusions actually being rooted in any robust process of discernment. Such insight is essential if we are to avoid a collaboration stagnating, or succumbing to collaborative inertia, described by Huxham (1996: 4) as a situation where 'the apparent rate of work output from a collaboration is slowed down considerably compared to what a casual observer might expect it to be able to achieve'. The development of such a condition can be the result of a range of factors, including poor communication, unresolved (or as yet undiscovered) differences in culture, lack of agreed direction, or real or perceived power differentials or tensions within the partnership – many of which could have been resolved, or at least addressed, through the negotiation and establishment of collaborative protocols.

Marshall (2006) suggests that the focus of our attention plays an important role as we try to make sense of our practice. She directs what she calls inner arcs of attention at her own actions, noticing the way in which she herself operates. Note-taking plays an important role for her in capturing this inner world. But of greater relevance in our context are the outer arcs of attention of which Marshall also speaks. An outer arc of attention involves reaching out beyond oneself, asking a question of others or raising an issue with someone. One could also take notes in relation to the reactions and views of others, enabling one to appreciate aspects of the practice involved from the viewpoints of others. Palmer (1998) indeed argues that insight into what is going on inside ourselves is the most powerful thing that we can achieve in any kind of work. But we would argue further that there is a need for *mutual* arcs of attention, whereby all of those involved take common responsibility for throwing out questions to the group or raising issues with each other, discerning together the issues that need to be addressed as a result, and thus the future direction of the collaboration. We would suggest that *mutual* insight into what is going on in a collaboration is as powerful as the personal insight of which Palmer speaks. In this way we can see expansive learning develop within the collaboration, as Engeström (1994) suggests – whereby a group or community transforms itself through a process of redefining its own practices, social structures and tools.

We thus suggest that dialogue should play an important role in reflection on collaborative working. Brockbank & McGill (2007) indeed suggest that dialogue with others should form an integral aspect of all reflective learning, with the paper stemming from the aforementioned review of reflective practice (Kahn *et al.*, 2008) reaching a similar conclusion. But we would suggest here that such dialogue is essential for genuinely collaborative working, so that emergent patterns of working to which all can agree really do arise. If we are to avoid wishful thinking or working that is almost entirely driven by a preset agenda, then we need to establish patterns of communication that reveal and synthesize different perspectives on the functioning of the group. And such reflexive dialogue can also involve outsiders with some knowledge of our collaboration or other stakeholders, to stimulate yet further insights into the working of the group – even students. We need to build in habits and strategies that legitimize such reflection, whether within a collaborative protocol or after discussion among those involved. It is interesting that the success of this literature review on reflective practice stemmed also from the readiness to adapt the initially agreed basis in the light of the issues emerging from our discussions together about our struggles with the work involved. The egalitarian approach to our interactions with each other certainly helped in surfacing these struggles, with the academic basis for the review and the frequency of meetings shifting in the light of dialogue within the project team.

Monitoring and Evaluation

There is a role also for more formal monitoring and evaluation of collaborative working, especially where the collaboration is on a large scale. Clearly, it is relatively easy to establish targets in relation to what the collaboration will produce. And if you are simply looking to convince a funding body that your collaboration is worth pursuing or to persuade a management team to keep you in employment, then this may well be sufficient. It is relatively easy to track your outputs or the extent to which these are taken up by others, but identifying impact on student learning or research outcomes is hard to ascertain. Thus, if you are looking for more substantive insight into the extent to which your work is characterized by emergence, engagement or cohesion, then you need to think outside the box. Scriven's (1973) notion of 'goal-free evaluation' fits with this agenda. This approach involves the use of critical incidents, allowing scope to explore unanticipated findings. The long-standing illuminative approach to evaluation of Partlett & Hamilton (1972) similarly offers a helpful way forward, as does our earlier use of the indicators that Helsby & Saunders (1993) advocate.

But we can further learn from the participatory research perspectives of collaborative action research (e.g. Reason & Bradbury, 2001). We can see such a participatory approach also in Gajda's 'Collaboration Baseline Data Report' (2004), which assesses the extent of the collaboration that is going on in the given situation. The approach here is to bring key people together in a workshop and ask them to engage in a form of social network analysis. In a more formal sense this involves mapping of relationships (modelled by links) between individuals or groups (modelled by nodes). One can look at the number of connections that one node has with other nodes, ascertaining whether the node is central to the network or one of its branches, and so on. Modelling the changes in the network over time can provide one indication of the progress of a collaboration. In this, one could incorporate a measure of the character of the communication involved, as indicated in Table 3.2. Such analyses provide us with ways to analyse the social capital that Putnam (1995) argues forms part of the collective value of a social network, although the extent to which two individuals actually trust each other is clearly harder to assess. But one can then ascertain the way in which the relationships that form the basis for the collaboration shift as it unfolds. A collaborative approach to collating such data would then be complemented by a collaborative approach to the analysis of those data.

Table 3.2 Indices for the degree of communication between a group of professionals

1	No direct communication	No opportunity to meet or communicate information to each other.
2	Brief communication	Encounters or communication of information, but no meaningful interaction.
3	Substantive communication	Encounters or correspondence that includes transferring substantive information or opinions.
4	Communication around a task	Participation on a common task or tasks, regularly exchanging information and issues that directly support the progress of that task.
5	Collaborative communication	Participation on a common task or tasks, regularly exchanging information and issues that both support the progress of that task and address issues that extend beyond it.

Source: Adapted from Gregson *et al.* (1992) as reported by Leathard (2003).

Making It Happen

We can of course see the way that things are, but think that they will never change. Carol Dweck calls this the fixed mindset (1999), where we think that personal qualities are carved in stone, susceptible to a little chipping away but not much else. The growth mindset meanwhile acknowledges that we can change our basic qualities through our own efforts or the assistance of others. If we expect the relationships involved in a collaboration to require little or no work on our part, then we are likely to give up when difficulties hit. But if we are looking to understand each other and find how best things work together, then the collaboration has a future. It is thus clear that self-efficacy, the willingness to persist in the face of difficulty (see, for instance, Bandura, 1997), can make a huge difference when applied to collaborative working. We see this in Lee and Ouellet's story, in Chapter 7, of the Professional and Organizational Development Network in the United States, where there is an evident need for persistence in maintaining a common ethos as new members with different outlooks arrive. We can thus expect to see shifts in the personal qualities of those involved, although such self-efficacy will need to be well informed to be effective, given, for instance, our earlier discussion on McIntyre's (1984) stress on the conditions that make virtue a possibility.

But we can also look for shifts in the expertise of those involved. The troublesome activity of higher education may well make it hard for some colleagues to contribute. Students certainly find plenty of challenges when, say, analysing data for the first time, or actually writing a dissertation. But similar issues arise when working at the borders of knowledge, or when straining to extend one's own capacities, as may be the case when struggling to draft a journal paper. We indeed work with a range of challenging artefacts and tools in higher education, whether in laboratories or archives. Activity theory recognizes that this adds a further layer of complexity to the systems within which we work (see, for instance, Engeström, 1994). If a colleague seems unable to contribute fully, we may respond in a range of ways. We might hope that the problem will go away, or perhaps look to close down the collaboration (although in any case an exit strategy will often be helpful). But another option may be to support the colleague in developing the missing capacities. In taking this forward we may find it helpful to explore such options as mentoring and action learning, where capacity-building is directly tailored to the given professional context. A further option may be to look for alternative work for the colleague to undertake on the project – perhaps work that involves less independent action and a greater degree of work on common tasks. And yet problems of unreliability in the work of colleagues may stem from further factors too, whether from the pressure on their time or through according the collaborative work a relatively low priority in their wider workload. Different strategies may be required in this case to ensure openness about the extent to which their contribution is a realistic possibility. We need to find spaces within the academy where we can help others to develop their capacities. Morrell (1990: 51–64) points out that 'the university laboratory provided for science an equivalent of the Renaissance artist's studio, in that it offered to apprentices induction into the scientific guild through pupilage in practical skills under a master-practitioner'. This involves organizing our activity partly on the basis of whether this will allow others to develop their expertise. The aim in this way is to develop more extended notions of what it means to be a professional, as Hoyle (1975) also argues. Such approaches will clearly take additional time or require adjustments to the collaboration in the short term, but they may all help to establish a culture that remains supportive and that encourages the engagement of all those involved.

When It All Goes Wrong . . .

Collaborations, though, do usually end at some point in time. Levine & Moreland (2004) identify dissolution as an almost inevitable stage in collaborative working, as the market wanes for the creative products of this group or as conflict arises over goals or the ownership of ideas. While strategies such as horizon scanning or emergent patterns of working can help to ensure that a market remains for one's creative products, we still need to face head-on the possibility of failure. There is certainly a tendency (even in our own writing) to play up the advantages that stem from collaboration. But we are aware also that collaborations can easily fail to live up to their initial promise.

One of the classic examples of a failed collaboration within the United Kingdom concerns the online university, UKeU. This initiative, which involved a collaboration between the UK government, universities in the United Kingdom and private partners such as Sun Microsystems UK Ltd, was wound down after the expending of £62 million of public funding. The project was initially intended to help develop the infrastructure within the United Kingdom for e-learning, and to further embed e-learning programmes in UK universities; but only 900 students immediately benefited – at great expense to UK taxpayers. The official investigation into UKeU's failure concluded that the business model was supply driven rather than demand led, and that insufficient market research had been conducted. But this investigation recognized also that the decision to establish a completely new e-learning platform had placed considerable strain on the initiative. In terms of our analysis of collaborative working, we would suggest that the challenge of building mutual understanding across boundaries seems not to have been squarely faced. While staff at the UKeU were convinced that the way forward was to base teaching solely within a virtual learning environment, much of the rest of the e-learning community preferred to mix and match both online and face-to-face modes in a blended approach. A focus too early on the e-learning platform may well also have prevented the emergence of alternative models of delivery, and also the development of social networks with possible providers of programmes across higher education or particular constituencies of potential students.

All manner of things can evidently go wrong in collaborative working, whatever the scale of the activity entailed. We will indeed see ways in the case studies that now follow in Part II as to how collaborations failed in some respects, for a number of reasons, at least to live up to the hopes of those involved – although we also see that this may provide a stimulus for yet further activity, as with Jan Parker's case study of 'writing in the disciplines'. While we can influence the processes of a collaborative venture, we must accept also that this influence is by no means complete; and that others too are involved and affect the outcome.

Conclusion

Our main concern in this chapter has been to find ways to increase our influence on the manner in which collaborative working unfolds. If we are to stand a realistic chance of establishing and sustaining thriving expressions of collaborative working in higher education, then we clearly need to pay direct attention to the processes involved. We need to concern ourselves with the relationships and not just the deal, as Kanter (1994) argues. We need to ensure that this attention is paid up front to the initial basis for the collaboration, and that our collaborative working includes attention to generating insight into its progress, so that a realistic basis is provided for joint decision-making as well as for joint activity. And in this insight generation there is little substitute for approaches that are genuinely mutual.

References

Bandura, A. (1997). *Self-Efficacy: The Exercise of Control.* New York: W. H. Freeman.

Bhaskar, R. (1979). *The Possibility of Naturalism.* Brighton: Harvester.

Brockbank, A. & McGill, I. (2007). *Facilitating Reflective Learning in Higher Education,* 2nd edn. Maidenhead, UK: Open University Press.

D'Andrea, V. & Gosling, D. (2005). *Improving Teaching and Learning in Higher Education: A Whole Institution Approach.* Maidenhead, UK: Open University Press.

Doz, Y. (1996). The evolution of cooperation in strategic alliances: Initial conditions or learning processes? *Strategic Management Journal, 17,* 55–83.

Dweck, C. S. (1999). *Self-Theories: Their Role in Motivation, Personality and Development.* Philadelphia, PA: Psychology Press.

Engeström, Y. (1994). *Training for Change.* Geneva: International Labour Office.

Gajda, R. (2004). Utilizing collaboration theory to evaluate strategic alliances. *American Journal of Evaluation, 25,* 65–77.

Gray, B. (1996). Cross-sectoral partners: Collaborative alliances among business, government and communities. In C. Huxham (ed.) *Creating Collaborative Advantage.* London: Sage.

Gregson, B. A., Cartlidge, A. M. & Bond, J. (1992). Development of a measure of professional collaboration in primary health care. *Journal of Epidemiology and Community Health, 46,* 48–53.

Gustavsen, B. (2001). Theory and practice: The mediating discourse. In P. Reason & H. Bradbury (eds) *Handbook of Action Research.* London: Sage.

Helsby, G. & Saunders, M. (1993). Taylorism, Tylerism and performance indicators: Defending the indefensible? *Educational Studies, 19,* 55–77.

Hoyle, E. (1975). Professionality, professionalism and control in teaching. In V. Houghton, R. McHugh & C. Morgan (eds) *Management in Education: The Management of Organisations and Individuals.* London: Ward Lock Educational.

Huxham, C. (ed.) (1996). *Creating Collaborative Advantage.* London: Sage.

Kahn, P. E. & Walsh, L. (2006). *Developing Your Teaching: Ideas, Insights and Action.* Abingdon, UK: Routledge.

Kahn, P. E., Young, R., Grace, S., Pilkington, R., Rush, L., Tomkinson, C. B. & Willis, I. (2008). A practitioner review of reflective practice within programmes for new academic staff: Theory and legitimacy in professional education. *International Journal for Academic Development, 13,* 161–173.

Kanter, R. M. (1994). Collaborative advantage: The art of alliances. *Harvard Business Review, 4,* 96–108.

Kezar, A. (2005). Redesigning for collaboration within higher education institutions: An exploration into the developmental process. *Research in Higher Education, 46* (7), 831–860.

Laidlaw, D. (2003). Collaborative classroom teaching of art/computation/science. *The Teaching Exchange, 7.2.* Providence, RI: The Harriet W. Sheridan Center for Teaching and Learning.

Lariviere, V., Gingras, Y. & Archambault, E. (2006). Canadian collaboration networks: A comparative analysis of the natural sciences, social sciences and the humanities. *Scientometrics, 68,* 519–533.

Leathard, A. (2003). *Interprofessional Collaboration: From Policy to Practice in Health and Social Care.* London: Routledge.

Levine, J. & Moreland, R. (2004). Collaboration: The social context of theory development. *Personality and Social Psychology Review, 8,* 164–172.

Ludema, J., Cooperrider, D. & Barrett, F. (2001). Appreciative inquiry: The power of the unconditional positive question. In P. Reason & H. Bradbury (eds) *Handbook of Action Research.* London: Sage.

McIntyre, A. (1984). *After Virtue: A Study in Moral Theory,* 2nd edn. Notre Dame, IN: University of Notre Dame Press.

Marshall, J. (2006). Self-reflective inquiry practices. In P. Reason & H. Bradbury (eds) *Handbook of Action Research.* London: Sage.

Morrell, J. B. (1990). Science in the universities: Some reconsiderations. In T. Fränsmyr (ed.) *Solomon's House Revisited: The Organization and Institutionalization of Science.* Canton: Watson Publishing International.

Morrison, P., Dobbie, G. & McDonald, F. (2003). Research collaboration amongst university scientists. *Higher Education Research and Development, 22* (3), 275–296.

Palmer, P. (1998). *Courage to Teach.* San Francisco: Jossey-Bass.

Partlett, M. & Hamilton, D. (1972). *Evaluation as Illumination.* Edinburgh: Centre for Research in the Educational Sciences, University of Edinburgh.

Putnam, R. D. (1995). Bowling alone: America's declining social capital. *Journal of Democracy, 6,* 65–78.

Reason, P. & Bradbury, H. (2006). *Handbook of Action Research.* London: Sage.

Sargent, L. & Waters, L. (2004). Careers and academic research collaborations: An inductive process framework for understanding successful collaborations. *Journal of Vocational Behavior, 64* (2), 308–319.

Scriven, M. (1973). Goal free evaluation. In E. House (ed.) *School Evaluation.* Berkeley, CA: McCutchan.

Tuckman, B. (1965). Developmental sequence in small groups. *Psychological Bulletin, 63* (6), 384–399.

UK Higher Education International Unit and Universities UK (2008). *International Research Collaboration: Opportunities for the UK Higher Education Sector.* London: UK Higher Education International Unit.

Zuckerman, H. & Merton, R. K. (1973). Age, aging, and age structure in science. In R. K. Merton (ed.) *The Sociology of Science: Theoretical and Empirical Investigations.* Chicago: University of Chicago Press.

Case Study

Collaboration among Welsh Educational Institutions

First Campus

MICHAEL CONNOLLY, NORAH JONES AND
JULIE LYDON
University of Glamorgan, Wales

Context

First Campus is a collaborative partnership originally involving the six higher education institutions[1] and seven further education colleges[2] in south-east Wales. The collaboration was established in 2002 in response to the funding opportunity from the Higher Education Funding Council for Wales (HEFCW) to support widening access initiatives to meet the targets set by the Welsh Assembly government. The Assembly, as part of the devolution settlement, has secured a range of powers for education and health, powers it has used to generate policies that are distinct from those in England.

The structure of higher education in Wales has particular characteristics. It is a small country (with 5 per cent of the UK population), but with a geography that inhibits face-to-face communication. Further, the main population centres are along the coasts, especially the south coast. All of this has contributed to the structure for higher education involving a number of comparatively small institutions, Cardiff and Glamorgan being the exceptions. Hence, a number of these institutions have faced challenges in terms of sustainability. The various institutions – with the exception of the University of Glamorgan – have been part of the federal University of Wales, though for a series of reasons this arrangement has shown signs of wear and tear in recent years and a number of the more prominent members have sought their own degree-awarding powers. The period of the partnership was additionally one of considerable turbulence for the higher education sector: there were the Rees (Welsh Assembly Government, 2005) and Graham (National Assembly of Wales, 2006) reviews, with the resultant specific Welsh responses to fee changes; and reconfigurations, alliances and mergers, some of which were realized and some which failed.

Given this structure and the various pressures, not surprisingly the Assembly has had a long-standing agenda to promote not only collaboration, but also mergers and alliances in higher education across Wales. However, while a number of proposals were initiated, few were successful. At the time of inception of the project there were detailed merger discussions between two of the post-1992 institutions, but these failed during 2004; two pre-1992 institutions merged in 2004–2005; and a small elite college merged with a post-1992 institution in 2007. Hence, the Assembly, working through HEFCW, continues to promote collaboration. This has been facilitated by European convergence (objective 1) funding from 2007 to 2010.

How the Collaboration was Established and Sustained

In addition to the characteristics described above, Wales has had long-standing issues of poverty. For example, it has the highest rate of unemployment of any region within the United Kingdom. This has of course led to a number of related issues in education, including comparatively low achievement in secondary schools and participation in higher education.

The Assembly has recognized these issues in a number of important policy statements, particularly *The Learning Country* (National Assembly of Wales, 2001), which identified, inter alia, a phenomenon of underachievement at ages 11–14 in secondary schools. This initiative, from the HEFCW, provided for additional funds to be available to geographically based regional consortia covering different regions of Wales. The overall project is referred to as the Reaching Wider scheme, but each consortium developed proposals for specific activities that were designed to complement and enhance the existing widening access work of the higher education institutions. The First Campus consortium – the only one to be branded – is, then, a sub-project of the broader pan-Wales project and is focused on the institutions in south-east Wales. The original bid was for a period of three years (academic years 2003–2006); additional funding enabled the partnerships to continue for a further two years to the end of the 2007–2008 academic year.

The aim of the First Campus Collaborative Project is to engage further with schools to raise the awareness of progression routes into higher education for pupils, encouraging the notion that learning is fun and that university is an option for all. The strategy was underpinned by the assumption that making university facilities available to young people raises their educational aspirations and achievements, and hopefully encourages them to progress to higher levels of learning. The Assembly commitment to the First Campus project was underlined by Jane Davison AM, then Minister for Education at the National Assembly for Wales, who officially launched it.

Since the inception of the collaboration, First Campus has engaged with four main groups of people of all ages who are currently under-represented in higher education:

- people living in Communities First areas;
- people from black and ethnic minority communities;
- people who wish to study through the medium of Welsh;
- disabled people.

Targets have been identified for the above groups by the Assembly. Thus, for example, the Communities First catchment areas of all schools in the partnership have been identified. First Campus has consolidated its involvement with schools and communities to interact with large numbers of young people, their families and adults, primarily in Communities First areas and the Heads of the Valleys, and those in disadvantaged neighbourhoods. First Campus will contribute to Reaching Wider targets, which seek to motivate and raise the aspirations of school students to work towards ensuring that

> [t]he percentage of all full-time and part-time Welsh domiciled under-graduate new entrants to Higher Education courses at UK Higher Education Institutes (HEIs) and Further Education Institutes who are domiciled in economically disadvantaged areas [will] rise from 8.9% to 11.4% by 2010.
> (Retrieved on 11 February 2009 from www.firstcampus.org/targets/)

First Campus at the time of writing was in its fourth year of operation, and concentrating on all four Reaching Wider targets for all four groups identified above. The programme of events was reviewed and a slightly different approach was adopted for 2006–2008, with activities being focused on development and progression, allowing pupils to access higher education institutions (HEIs) a number of times throughout the year. There were some one-off events, which tended to be larger-scale and high-impact; these were focused on schools from all three hubs across our target area.

The arrangements for the operation of the partnership were based on three hubs: in the valleys, Cardiff and Newport respectively. Management of the project occurs at two levels, strategic and operational. The lead organization provided overall strategic coordination under the guidance of a steering group which included representation at a senior level from each of the HEIs and other key stakeholders. The steering group negotiates with HEFCW on projects and plays a pivotal role in allocating moneys, ensuring in essence that all the HEIs involved receive 'some of the cake', as someone involved expressed it. Three of the HEIs appointed First Campus coordinators, the others embedding the project into existing arrangements, for example, the marketing unit. Operational meetings occur regularly – approximately once per month – between the coordinators and those holding equivalent posts in each of the HEIs involved. In addition, ad hoc meetings take place involving, for example, the lead co-ordinator and First Campus coordinators in HEIs, as well as meetings in which contact is maintained between HEIs and further education institutions (FEIs) and schools. Inevitably a number of initiatives take place involving one HEI, but there are a number of initiatives, for example, a science initiative, that draw on all the HEIs.

Key Characteristics of the Collaboration

It might have been anticipated that, given the tensions resulting from some of the failed collaborative ventures described above, First Campus would have had problems. However, one of the interesting features of higher education is the range of networks – formal, quasi-formal and informal – that exist and have been developed at the operational level. The genesis of this collaboration originated from a small number of key individuals operating in the widening access/educational development field in two of the partner universities, a number of whom had developed contacts over a number of years and who were deeply committed to increased access. In addition to these networks, we can identify a series of pull-and-push factors driving the project. The 'pull' factors include:

- the continuance and expansion of widening access activities;
- building and enhancement of the academic reputation of one partner's work in student mentoring;
- the unlocking of additional funding streams.

The 'push' factors were:

- the political expectation of collaboration and merger from the Welsh Assembly government;
- the targets for widening access set for the higher education sector;
- the chronic social and economic decline of the region (notably the Welsh valleys);
- the commitment by a number of key actors to address the associated difficulties in terms of educational achievement and low participation.

In essence this is what might be described as a low-risk collaborative project, in that moneys were supplied externally and all partners involved had a prior interest in the material outcomes (more students). The project had a number of characteristics that encouraged success. These characteristics include the following:

- An appropriate sphere of activity was selected, which avoided encroaching on the competitive ground between some of the partners while being different from, and complementary to, other widening access initiatives.
- The project provided benefit for each partner in financial, reputational and professional domains.
- It addressed the political agenda set by the Welsh Assembly government, in terms of widening access targets and in demonstrating collaboration between the HEIs in south-east Wales.

- There was clarity in terms of the project's purpose, governance and organizational arrangements.

As a result, there were unanticipated developments as the project progressed. For example, the HEIs grew to exploit cross-HEI expertise and to promote genuine collaboration around specific initiatives. Further, as some new players became involved, due, for example, to staff retirements and new appointments, the project reflected critically on its mode of operation and encouraged new ideas and initiatives.

Learning Points

It appears that the dynamics of funding (resources), the political and socio-economic environment and the nature of the activities were the most significant factors in establishing the case-study collaboration. The 'contextual incentives' identified by Gray (1996) – the limited government funding for widening access coupled with pressure for collaboration, 'declining growth rate and increasing competitive pressures' and 'differing perceptions of environmental risk' – were significant elements underlying the dynamics of this collaboration.

Without the impetus of additional funding that required collaboration, it is doubtful whether the parties contributing to the partnership would have collaborated in this field of activity at that time. The complexity of the number of partners, the diversity of the partners' missions and institutional contexts, and the mistrust created by failed mergers and competition were factors countering collaboration. The additional resources provided balanced the demands and costs of working collaboratively; this enabled all partners to pay more than lip service to the government edict of collaboration.

In addition, the project owed something to the dynamics of existing informal networks among a number of individuals who had been working on increasing participation over a number of years. A number of these, including the lead coordinator, had levels of trust in each other, trust that was enhanced by the attitude and skill of the lead coordinator, as well as other coordinators.

How Readers Can Take Forward Their Own Practice

Three suggestions that readers may find helpful emerge from this case study. First, it is important to separate policy or strategic-level matters from operational ones. Institutions will wish to be confident that their interests are protected and that financial probity is secure. But equally, those tasked with undertaking the operational initiatives need to feel they have the independence (within guidelines) to work with colleagues in other HEIs and institutions. Second, and following from that, the appointment of coordinators, especially the lead coordinator, is crucial. Their relationship with each other and within their own institution is central, and those appointed need to have the skills to maintain and develop the necessary relationships. Finally, being accountable to the funding body through set targets encourages clarity of thinking around selection of projects and promotes collaborative behaviour.

Case-Study Notes

1. The higher education institutions are the University of Cardiff (which the University of Wales College of Medicine merged with in 2004); the University of Wales Institute, Cardiff; the University College of Wales, Newport (the current name dates from 2005); and the University of Glamorgan (which now includes the Royal Welsh College of Music and Drama following completion of a strategic alliance in 2007).
2. The colleges are Glan Hafren, Gwent, Bridgend, Morgannwg, Ystrad Mynach, Barry and Merthyr Tydfil. Merthyr Tydfil College was merged with the University of Glamorgan in May 2006.

Case-Study References

Gray, B. (1996). Cross-sectoral partners: Collaborative alliances among business, government and communities. In C. Huxham (ed.) *Creating Collaborative Advantage*. London: Sage.

National Assembly of Wales (2001). *The Learning Country: A Comprehensive Education and Lifelong Learning Programme to 2010 in Wales*. Cardiff: National Assembly of Wales.

National Assembly of Wales (2006). *The Independent Review of Part Time Higher Education Study in Wales* (the Graham Review, Final Report and Recommendations). Cardiff: National Assembly of Wales.

Welsh Assembly Government (2005). *An Independent Study into the Devolution of the Student Support System and Tuition Fee Regime in Wales* (the Rees Review, Progress Report). Cardiff: Welsh Assembly Government.

Part II

Case Studies in Collaboration

4
Brokers of Collaboration

Brokers of collaborations can play as important a role in joint partnership working as the agents of collaboration; indeed, some brokers may be part of the collaboration themselves but will also have a pivotal role to play in introducing partners to each other, and in maintaining relationships and connections. Brokering collaborative working is a key way to bridge divides and to draw in resources, insights and contacts from an alternative context. An approach such as this is of particular importance in the academy, where the troublesome nature of work in higher education can make it difficult to access the ideas and resources within anther context without a more direct personal involvement. Particularly important in development contexts, brokers can act to support collaborations between individuals and institutions looking to extend the ways in which they engage in academic working, at a variety of levels.

Role of the Broker

In the three case studies presented in this chapter we see collaborative brokers working across both institutions and continents. In two cases the brokers are individuals and in the other case the main broker is the vehicle provided by a national organization – although to reduce the collaborative process to a single individual or organization is to under-represent the complexities of any such process. When an institution acts as a broker, then clearly the broker may be able to connect a range of different individuals or groups. The Royal Society for the Encouragement of Arts, Manufactures and Commerce (RSA), for instance, is an example of an organization that takes on this role: 'we kind of foster collaboration . . . in which we're seeking to produce useful work which will change the world' (Matthew Taylor, Chief Executive, RSA, as cited in Chapter 8). And we see also that the characteristics of our model for collaborative working again emerge in this brokering role – with opportunities to catalyse the engagement of others in these bridging activities; social structures to underpin their work, whether an event or pattern of events to draw people together; and so on.

Creating Cohesive Collaborations

In the first example, from the University of Auckland, Lorraine Stefani shares her experiences of restructuring within her institution and the benefits gained through collaborative approaches. This case study provides a clear example of the importance of consideration of all aspects of our model for collaborative working in higher education: the reconstruction of *practice*, the need for *engagement* from both individuals and groups, the use of several *social vehicles* as exemplified through the new social and work-based groupings, and the resulting enhanced *professional dialogue* across the institution. The challenge to personal orientations to collaboration and the associated dissonant expertise experienced by some individuals is acknowledged by Stefani and discussed in her commentary on handling change in order to create cohesive collaborations.

Sharing Cognitive Authority

The second case study, from Bates and Baume, provides evidence of a striking collaboration across cultures and continents, where Imelda Bates' collaborative work with medical practitioners and students in Ghana has provided for empowerment and also personal, professional and societal development and successes for her Ghanaian colleagues, as well as a range of opportunities for her own institution in Liverpool. The 'cognitive authority' gained by them in their early collaboration with Bates has developed through emergent working into independence and enhancement through collaboration. The importance of trust, a central element of the collaborative process in higher education, is significant in this experience, further reflecting the power of individual engagement as a key factor in sustaining and supporting successful collaborative working.

Partnership Working with an External Agency

Our final case study in this chapter comes from the United Kingdom, where a national organization, the Higher Education Academy, can be seen as the broker in a collaboration between institutionally based colleagues in England, Scotland and Wales and the Higher Education Academy's Subject Centre for English, with illustrative examples drawn from the University of Aberdeen. Focused around an area of practice – curriculum development – the collaboration supported the academics in engaging with the Higher Education Academy Subject Centre around these issues and also promoted and supported the agency of individual academics within the partnership in order to give them ownership of the process. Helen King takes us through the stages of the collaboration and draws out the elements of the joint working (as indicated in Figure 4.1) including suggested collaborative protocols for effective working between an external agency and an academic department.

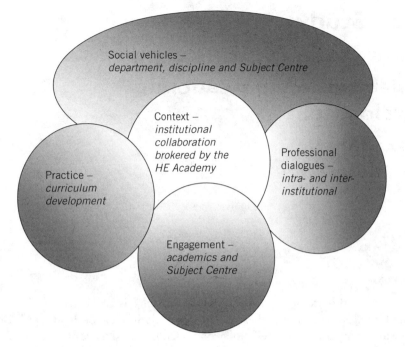

Figure 4.1 Model for collaborative working in higher education applied to the King case study.

Developing Genuine Professional Dialogues

This chapter focuses on the key points of overlap within our model, whereby the interplay between its different aspects is made manifest. Collaborative brokers act as a point of contact across these aspects, operating in the intersections between practice, engagement, construction of professional dialogues and mobilization of effort through social vehicles. In taking on a facilitative role that provides individuals or organizations with opportunities to engage with one another; it is the engagement of the brokers that counts. This is especially so in relation to their capacity to help establish social structures that ensure interaction between the parties involved, and to help translate categories and perspectives from across the different contexts, so that a genuine dialogue between professionals can be realized.

Case Study

Creating the Conditions for Collaboration in Academic Development

LORRAINE STEFANI
University of Auckland

Context

The setting for this example of collaborative working is the University of Auckland, the top-performing research-led university in New Zealand. Until 2006 the university had a dispersed model of academic and educational support for staff and students. There were three key autonomous centres with potentially overlapping and complementary remits, namely the Centre for Professional Development (CPD), responsible for providing development opportunities for both general and academic staff; the Centre for Flexible and Distance Learning, with responsibility for building e-learning capacity across the university; and the Student Learning Centre, with a remit to provide a range of learning support services for all students, including undergraduate, postgraduate and international students. When I took up my position as Director of the CPD in 2003, this Centre was definitely flagging, even though there were some excellent, dedicated and highly skilled staff members. The Centre was inward-looking, overly attached to outdated models for provision of professional development opportunities, and lacking in visibility and positive advocacy. There were some fundamental issues with the Centre for Flexible and Distance Learning that acted as barriers to its efforts to gain traction and recognition across the university. The staff were dedicated and committed, and produced online modules of stunning quality; however, as I have said, the Centre was inward-looking instead of working proactively in partnership with staff within their disciplines, and there were issues over ownership of the work. The Student Learning Centre was also inward-looking, working on the basis of a 1980s-style 'remedial' approach to providing learning support for students.

My working ethos is to promote collaborative working as much as possible. At the beginning of 2006 I was appointed to the position of Director of the new Centre for Academic Development (CAD), and I believed we could develop stronger, more meaningful, sustainable collaborative partnerships with other service centres such as the Library and the School of Graduate Studies. Managing the restructure to embed a collaborative approach was not easy, as so many of the staff were unaccustomed to collaborative models. However, the situation was handled through a number of strategies. First, change management processes such as those outlined by Kotter & Cohen (2002) were deployed. For example, working on a vision and mission for the new Centre with staff members, supporting the building of teams with particular areas of responsibility and expertise, and empowering staff were strategies key to team-building. Leading by example in ways of working in partnership with our target client groups was a further strategic move, and ensuring that the vision and mission for the Centre were well aligned with the institutional strategic plan gave the Centre more credibility with senior management. A highly significant strategy was to develop a distributive model of leadership (Gill, 2006), providing opportunities for staff to enhance their personal profiles and creating conditions for building leadership capacity within the Centre.

The Centre now encompasses five significant teams:

- the Administrative Team, which is a major hub, enabling the streamlining of internal policies, guidelines and protocols essential to the smooth operation of the Centre;
- the Academic Practice Group, responsible for providing support to academic staff on teaching, learning, assessment, curriculum design, research writing and supervision as well as managing the CAD Postgraduate Certificate in Academic Practice programme;
- the e-Learning Design and Development Group, with a wide remit in enhancing the use of technology in teaching and learning and in research;
- the Photography and Television Group, which works closely with the e-learning group providing multi-media input where required, in addition to working with staff across the university and the Student Learning Centre, which provides learning support for all students.

Examples of Collaborative Strategies in Action

In setting up the Centre for Academic Development with a distributive leadership mode of management, an important consideration was to ensure that the teams and functional divisions within CAD did not become autonomous units feeling no real connection with the 'bigger picture' of CAD as an entity, or CAD's vision and mission. To circumvent this possibility, CAD has a management committee, comprising the Director and the five team leaders, which meets monthly. The electronic version of the minutes of the meetings is posted on the internal CAD shared drive so that all staff are kept informed of CAD's progress against its annual plan. Particular collaborations between CAD and other sections of the institution include the following:

- a Doctoral Skills Programme, which comes within the remit of the University Board of Graduate Studies and spans all faculties in its scope;
- an e-Learning Network, which spans CAD, several faculties and departments;
- collaborative work between the Academic Practice Group and faculty members.

The next section of the case study will provide details on key aspects of these collaborations and how they are sustained.

Doctoral Skills Programme

One of the goals set by the University of Auckland is to achieve a target number of 500 doctoral completions per year by 2012 (University of Auckland Strategic Plan 2007–2012). The University Board of Graduate Studies has responded to research which indicates that 'universities need to admit that "practical skills" are required to negotiate the world of competitive research' (Morris, 1998) by developing a Doctoral Skills Programme. This programme is a collaborative venture by the School of Graduate Studies, the Centre for Academic Development, the Postgraduate Career Service and the Library. The programme is administered through the Graduate Centre and coordinated by a governance group comprising representatives from the 'centres' named above and the University Quality Office. The Graduate Centre could not offer the Doctoral Skills Programme without the input of CAD and the other central services. The CAD staff members are drawn primarily from the Student Learning Centre and the Academic Practice divisions of CAD. Since staff members team-teach on key components of the programme, it has been instrumental in bringing them together.

The Student Learning Centre was the most resistant part of CAD to the changes that arose out of the restructuring, but a positive spin-off of the Doctoral Skills Programme is that CAD staff members, particularly those from the Student Learning Centre, are collaborating in a more constructive way with the Library. There was overlap between what the Library provides and what the Student Learning Centre provides, which was often confusing for students, but what we have achieved through the programme is a service-level agreement between the Student Learning Centre and the Library, with staff now team-teaching on key workshops. Staff and students are benefiting from this arrangement.

An e-Learning Network

The CAD e-Learning Design and Development Group was established in 2006. The leader of the group instigated a review of performance indicators, project processes and evaluation reports from work carried out previously by the Centre for Flexible and Distance Learning to inform subsequent implementation of an e-learning capacity development strategy. Sustainability aspects of individual and departmentally driven e-learning initiatives, applied research to inform practice, and engagement with all sectors of the university community were priority goals for a new strategy. A call for project proposals from departments across the institution was disseminated, resulting in eighteen submissions to the e-learning team. Perceptions and expectations, both within the team and externally, required careful management, as the services offered to projects were significantly different from previous practice.

In addition to managing projects in a way that builds collaborative partnerships between staff within their disciplinary area and members of the e-Learning Design and Development Group, there was a significant change in how the e-learning group members engaged with academic and related staff. In very simplistic terms the change was one of 'doing with' rather than 'doing for'. As the e-learning team members work with disciplinary-based staff, a key input is enabling staff to develop the skills to use software tools in such a way that they could carry out more of the instructional design work themselves – in other words, building e-learning skills capacity. The team, through the Team Leader, is proactively developing relationships with key committees and groups of staff, including those from other learning technology units across the university, helping to promote the services of CAD across the wider institution. This level of integration into the university community is a key element of the capacity development strategy, the success of which is dependent upon the collaborative approach.

Because the Centre for Academic Development is still in its infancy, extensive evaluation data are not yet available. However, there are clear indications that staff are very pleased with the new collaborative, capacity-building strategy and feel that they have more of a sense of ownership over their projects. Academic and professional development are occurring in a subtle manner – the 'traffic' between CAD and the wider university has increased considerably – and the research outputs in partnership between members of the e-learning team and discipline-based staff are also growing.

Collaboration between the CAD Academic Practice Group and Faculties and Departments

The Academic Practice Group has a wide remit that involves internal collaboration with other CAD groups and external collaboration with faculty. It is rare now for the Academic Practice Group to facilitate generic workshops. Rather, the group members work with staff within the disciplinary base. What this means in practice is that CAD staff embrace a scholarly approach, being open to learning more about the culture of any particular disciplinary area and working in partnership with faculty to contextualize pedagogical principles to the needs of disciplinary-based staff. There is no question but that this mode of working has enhanced the visibility and credibility of CAD overall.

Examples of partnership in action become explicit during high-profile activities such as the mandatory three-day Introduction to Teaching and Learning Programme, where Teaching Excellence Award winners present keynote lectures, and staff with particular expertise from across the wider university facilitate workshops in partnerships with CAD staff. The University of Auckland postgraduate Certificate in Academic Practice is a flagship programme within CAD. We initiated faculty fellowships in academic practice whereby CAD provides one fellowship per faculty, which comes with a monetary award to support buy-out of time for an individual chosen by the dean of a faculty on the premise of building leadership capacity relating to learning and teaching. Some deans are now matching the CAD award with further incentives to support participants on the programme.

The Academic Practice Group has responsibility for providing academic development opportunities that align with the institutional obligations under the Treaty of Waitangi. A lectureship position specifically relating to Maori academic development was established in 2006. Particular activities in this area include:

- the establishment of an informal advisory group (with three senior Maori academic staff, including the Pro-Vice-Chancellor Maori) to provide guidance to the Maori academic adviser in the provision of services for Maori staff;
- collaboration with the Equal Opportunities Office to prepare a proposal for a Maori Advancement Programme, including a hui (gathering) and a workshop for Maori academic staff on the institutional academic promotions process;
- collaboration to develop a website for Maori academics to provide a mechanism for wider and more accessible dissemination of information relevant to Maori academic development and to enable and encourage online discussion of related topics.

Overcoming Resistance to Change

Managing major change and restructuring is not a task for the faint-hearted. The major barrier to effective change is generally the attitudes of staff members, particularly those who have created a niche or a comfort zone for themselves over a long period of time. Dealing with 'difficult people' is a skill that needs much more attention within organizations and institutions because change is inevitable in present times. In this scenario a positive signal was given out to staff by creating new leadership positions, developing the new leaders and making their roles meaningful. Where possible, incentives were deployed, such as promoting professional development opportunities for staff who were previously marginalized in this respect; creating a transparent and fair process for applications from staff to attend national and international conferences, where previously decisions had been on an ad hoc basis in some areas; signalling to staff that changes in practice would not be immediate but would be phased in over a period of time; and creating conditions for collaboration through research clusters, projects and so on.

In some cases where resistance to change was particularly problematic, engaging with staff on an individual basis was helpful. For example, carrying out the performance reviews of staff members personally and raising awareness that, as Director, I was cultivating an environment for staff to thrive personally and professionally. The intention was to create a critical mass of individuals who would begin to see the benefits of the change rather than only receiving negative propaganda from staff unhappy with the change. In extreme cases, however, it was necessary to isolate the 'ringleaders of resistance', putting the focus and energies on staff who were 'pushing the boat out' to make the new structure a success – and taking every opportunity to flag up and disseminate successes. The resistors generally came on board or recognized that they needed to move on.

One cannot be a lone ranger throughout major change. There is a need to deploy whatever support mechanisms are available within the institution. A major factor in 'success' was keeping senior management informed as to the goals being set and achieved, keeping the relevant line manager of the Centre on board with us, and not being afraid to articulate the problems and difficulties to be resolved.

Summary

The examples of partnerships provided above are selected from a wide range of collaborative arrangements that have become possible only because of the restructuring described earlier and a constant promotion of a collaborative ethos within CAD. While much of the work previously carried out by the autonomous units has been built upon as opposed to being completely discarded, the most difficult aspect of change management is undoubtedly changing the attitudes of staff. However, success leads to more success, and, as CAD staff have come to realize, the value of collaboration far exceeds the value of inward-looking protectionism of space, resources and, particularly, knowledge and skills.

Case-Study References

Gill, R. (2006). *Theory and Practice of Leadership*. London: Sage.

Kotter, J. P. & Cohen, S. (2002). *The Heart of Change*. Boston: Harvard Business School Press.

Morris, M. (1998). Publishing perils and how to survive them: A guide for graduate students. *Cultural Studies, 12* (4), 498–512.

University of Auckland Strategic Plan 2007–2012. Online, available at: www.auckland.ac.nz/uoa/about/uoa/publications/strategic_plan.cfm (accessed 22 April 2008).

Case Study

A Collaboration in Medical Education and Development between the United Kingdom and Ghana

IMELDA BATES
Liverpool School of Tropical Medicine

DAVID BAUME
Higher Education Consultant

Context

In 1986 the major and urgent educational requirement at the new Medical School and Teaching Hospital, in Kumasi, Ghana, was to fill the large training and qualifications gap between the newly qualified junior doctors and the senior hospital consultants, who had been trained outside Ghana and were due to retire during the next few years. Imelda Bates, a doctor at St George's Hospital London, was appointed to a three-year post. Her training was for the most part one-to-one, at the bedside, on the job and indeed in the job, conducted alongside a large amount of medical practice and working closely with medical, nursing and management staff. Professional relationships were formed. The work was judged to have been successful. Imelda found it immensely rewarding. Some eighteen months later a need was identified in Ghana for training for medical lab staff. A small travel grant was obtained from a UK charity and used to do some initial training, which, being successful, then fed successful larger applications, including to the Ghanaian Department of Health.

'Difference is a success factor here'

This has continued. Imelda has typically made two visits each year, on a succession of funded projects – a collaboration approaching in total fifty visits since 1986, around 100 weeks in Kumasi. The traffic has been two-way, with staff from Kumasi contacting Imelda and visiting her in the United Kingdom, consulting on research grants or PhD supervision questions, and a steady flow of Ghanaians working for a Liverpool PhD, with Imelda helping to find appropriate supervision. Why so many visits to this one location? 'Because people asked me to come back. They knew I could help.'

The relationships developed during the first three years have been sustained but they have also changed, with many of Imelda's early collaborators now in senior positions, including the Dean of the Medical School. The observer sees the warmth and the respect with which these former students greet Imelda on a working visit to Kumasi – 'Our teacher,' they say, with a hug – and these early relationships have provided a basis for continued collaboration, through a variety of roles and joint projects. There is at least one more layer of collaboration here. Very junior staff, and medical students, saw both how Imelda collaborated with hospital staff and how these staff valued Imelda's medical and educational expertise. Current participants in Liverpool School of Tropical Medicine (LSTM) programmes in Kumasi are, in professional terms, from the third generation of Ghanaian medics with whom Imelda has worked.

What made the collaboration work? A direct link between one individual in each country was initially important. Imelda provides a first point of contact for anyone in LSTM interested in Ghana, for example. The relationship has broadened considerably over the years, with many contacts at each end; but the strong central axis between LSTM and Kumasi remains. Imelda and her Kumasi counterpart are both very well networked into their national health and health education systems; each can usually find, in one or two steps, a person or some expertise that someone at the other end needs.

Watching Imelda work with staff from medicine and medical education across Ghana offers further clues as to how the collaboration has been sustained for so long and so productively. In Kumasi, Imelda is an outsider – white, UK educated and UK qualified, and now based in the United Kingdom. But Imelda is also an insider – a member of the medical profession, of the medical education profession, and, again, highly respected by these professions and by many individuals at all levels in these professions in Ghana. Sometimes Imelda is (and is encouraged to act) the outsider, asking challenging questions that might not be apparent to or comfortable for an insider, bringing perspectives from elsewhere in Africa, from the United Kingdom and from around the world; being an authority, and having her authority accepted. Sometimes in exactly the same moment, Imelda is also the insider, showing a respect for, and comfort and fluency in, the very open, participative, supportive style of debate, sometimes to an uneducated English eye rather circuitous, which enables good and – a vital part of good – acceptable conclusions to be reached and decisions to be made; decisions that have a good chance of being implemented.

Reflecting on the implications of this for teaching and working in higher education, one can point out that many of us work across communities and cultures. These communities and cultures may be variously defined, and to various degrees distinct. We are encouraged to be culturally aware, culturally respectful. Cultural awareness, cultural respect are important, but are only the start. The very effective and sustained collaboration being described here also shows cultural competence. But behind and beneath that cultural competence lie both a high level of enthusiasm for a particular culture and the ability to stand outside it, critique it, play in it and with it. To be clear: in the particular collaborative setting being described and analysed here, this is as true for the Ghanaian medics and medical educators as it is for their visitor from Liverpool. Difference is a success factor here.

Future Directions

Courses and programmes are continuing elements of the collaboration, starting with the training of laboratory staff, which began in the early 1990s and led to a national qualification in Ghana for medical laboratory technicians by the late 1990s. The major current collaborative programme, and the focus of the rest of this case study, is the Diploma in Project Design and Management. This is a Liverpool course run in Kumasi, which has been transformed over the (six) years since it first ran. The story of its transformation over that time captures much of the approach to collaboration being considered.

The initial request from Kumasi was for a course that would give qualified doctors who wished to become consultants the necessary research skills to undertake successfully the research project which was a requirement for registration – a later version of the reason for Imelda's first visit in 1986. This course was first taught by Imelda on visits from the United Kingdom; but this was not sustainable. It would be very expensive when external funding stopped. Nor, in Imelda's view, was it ethical as it failed to develop local capacity; and it encouraged continued dependence on the United Kingdom. Success, for Imelda, would mean Kumasi progressively taking over and running the course. There was no great enthusiasm for this change from Kumasi. The course was taught well. Everyone liked it. Why change? And how to get this change to happen? 'I'm not going to run this course for ever. I'm just not going to do it.'

Imelda's declaration of Kumasi's impending educational independence was initially not well received. 'They kept saying to each other, "When Imelda comes back next year . . ." and I had to keep saying, "I'm not coming back next year to do this!"

'I knew they could do it – they just didn't think they could. A lot of my work – on a lot of the projects, come to think of it – is about building competence, and then building confidence on the back of that competence, when they see they really can do things.'

How did Imelda know they could do it?

'I believe that – with enough of the right kind of support – everyone can always do it!'

Wow!

The reaction of the Kumasi people when Imelda first told them they would take over the running of the course was: 'We hadn't a clue how we would do it. Not a clue. [Pause] But, because it was you, we trusted that it was all going to be all right in the end.'

Fortunately for Imelda (by her own report), they didn't say this to her at the time. 'The pressure would have been so great I would probably have picked up my bag and left.' A long process of collaboration leading to such trust – including this referred trust, this trust in another's trust – is a substantial achievement. Such mutual trust both results from and leads to judgements of character. It is nourished by a hundred smaller moments of trust, trust that was not broken. And by some larger ones; there was some substantial risk-taking, for example, making requests of very senior figures at the request of a collaborator without necessarily knowing all the politics. Or, indeed, as another example, agreeing to run a prestigious course without knowing that you could. Trust and risk led to partnership led to collaboration.

Realizing Cognitive Authority

The shift of primary responsibility from Liverpool to Kumasi happened over three years. First, Kumasi facilitated some and then all of the course, then assessed it, subject to oversight from Liverpool. An early stage in the handover was Imelda running workshops in facilitation for Kumasi. The predominant teaching style in Ghanaian medical education is didactic, and this was a big stretch. But, as students whose learning had previously been facilitated by Imelda on previous runs of the course, they knew they liked this approach, and were keen to facilitate its spread.

The first year they facilitated, they were nervous, unnatural, asking my help a lot. One year later, when I (D.B.) next visited, they were serious professional facilitators, as good as any I had seen. In just twelve months. It was a huge leap. And they had learned these skills alongside more than full-time medical jobs.

Here, effective collaboration, effective development, were best served by leaving people alone – or, more precisely, without their previous expert support, as in reality they were not alone, being part of a close team, all learning to facilitate and facilitating together, which was of immense importance.

They didn't know how good they were. I asked them how they had got so much better so quickly. It turned out, in conversation, that they had been doing most or all of their teaching in the intervening year by facilitation, though they hadn't realized this until I asked them the question. They had all had many, many hours of practice at facilitating. One had been facilitating Sunday school!

And they're not worried about things going wrong; they just own up, learn from it and move on.

Members of the Kumasi team have moved from a very conscious incompetence to an equally high level of unconscious competence in facilitation without moving through the allegedly necessary intermediate stage of conscious competence. We may debate whether Imelda's questioning took them back to conscious competence (probably not), or forward into consciousness *of* competence (not the same thing at all) and/or on into what may be called 'reflective competence' (Wikipedia, n.d.)[1]

The collaboration continues. The centre of gravity is shifting towards Ghana, and the next stage is the roll-out of this programme across the country, for which modest funding is being sought. As well as a model of education and a model of educational dissemination, we also see here a model of collaboration, a dynamic model, in this case aiming at empowerment and also at economy but capable of being used towards other goals, such as dissemination through facilitated collaborative local reinvention, perhaps.

Case-Study Note

1. Wikipedia is used as the source because 'reflective competence' is my own coining and because I have failed to find a published source for the four-step model of competence on which this builds.

Case-Study Reference

'Four stages of competence'. Online, available at: http://en.wikipedia.org/wiki/Four_stages_ of_competence (accessed 3 December 2008).

Case Study

Collaborative Working for Curriculum and Professional Development

HELEN KING
Higher Education Consultant

Context

This case study describes a programme of collaborative work facilitated by a national organization. The scope, aims and outcomes are such, however, that a similar approach could be taken by colleagues locally (for example, through an educational development unit). Professional development for learning and teaching is facilitated through discussions and a programme of activity that take place within an academic department and around a key curriculum issue. Momentum for the development is provided by an external (to the department) facilitator.

The Higher Education Academy Subject Centre for Geography, Earth and Environmental Sciences (GEES) is one of twenty-four such Subject Centres in the United Kingdom. Its remit is to support the professional development of staff and the enhancement of student learning in the disciplines named in its title. The Subject Centre's activities include national conferences; departmental workshops; an annual event for new lecturers; funding for learning and teaching projects; an online resource database; publications, including a biannual magazine, *Planet*; and much more, including an inquiry service, email discussion lists and newsletters.

From 2006 to 2008 the Subject Centre undertook a pilot study to explore a new approach to professional development: providing longitudinal support for a focused set of activities within individual academic departments. Working with three departments, the Subject Centre sought to facilitate collaborative support for curriculum development, involving all teaching staff, the local educational development units, students and other key stakeholders at the institutions concerned.

There is a literature which indicates that activities at the departmental or programme level may have a significant impact. For example, Knight (1998) suggests that focusing professional development within the departmental 'activity system' and around specific curriculum development issues may help to support continuous professional learning. In their extensive review, Prebble *et al.* (2005) propose that, on balance, the research indicates that 'The academic work group is generally an effective setting for developing the complex knowledge, attitudes and skills involved in teaching'. They also suggest that a variety of approaches to academic development 'offer the best prospects for widespread change and improvement'. To this end, the Subject Centre decided to maintain its existing diversity of activities while piloting a more in-depth approach to working within specific departments.

The 'Departmental Activity' Programme

The three departments were selected to ensure representation across the United Kingdom (England, Scotland and Wales), across different types of institutions (from an old, research-oriented university to a more teaching-focused, newer university) and among the disciplines supported by the Subject Centre. In addition, as this was to be a pilot exercise, departments were chosen that had already had significant contact and participation with the GEES Subject Centre and that included individuals with whom there were well-established relationships. The departmental contacts were initially approached and they then took the idea to their head of department and/or teaching committee for agreement.

Examples of activity with the School of Geosciences at the University of Aberdeen are used in this case study to illustrate the processes. The programme of work had two main components: (1) an initial phase of discussion and negotiation around the theme and agreement of potential activities; and (2) the activities themselves and other ongoing support. With hindsight, it was the first component that was the more important in that it allowed for the establishment of rapport with the academic staff and gave them a forum for discussion of curriculum issues. The second phase acted to ensure that the momentum was maintained and that the individuals tasked with carrying the work forward felt valued and supported.

In order to establish the theme for the work, initial contact was made with the head of school, who produced a memorandum for staff identifying potential directions. At Aberdeen this included recruitment and retention, use of different forms of assessment, enhancing fieldwork, and improving school-wide identity (across the constituent departments of Geography & Environment and Geology & Petroleum Geology), encouraging alignment of teaching across the various disciplines and preparing for the internal teaching review in 2009. A discussion meeting was then arranged with members of the teaching staff in order to develop the activity agenda.

Approximately thirty colleagues from the school attended the discussion meeting, which was facilitated by two members of staff from the GEES Subject Centre and 'chaired' by one of the lecturers. The aims of the meeting were to:

- identify and agree the department's chosen theme;
- discuss the key issues for staff and students relating to this theme;
- identify and agree the department's goals for the year;
- brainstorm ways in which the Subject Centre might support the department in achieving these goals.

In order to 'win hearts and minds' and ensure ownership of the process, the meeting began with an opportunity for all participants to share their thoughts on current curriculum issues and what they would like to get out of the support programme. This was conducted in small groups as a 'SOAR' (as opposed to SWOT – strengths, weaknesses, opportunities and threats) analysis. Participants were asked to discuss their school's Strengths, the Opportunities currently available, their Aspirations and the Results they would like to see – all in terms of enhancing learning and teaching. This positive approach helped to move the discussion swiftly on from highlighting barriers and constraints to a more forward-looking, dynamic view.

This SOAR analysis and the discussion that followed indicated that assessment was a key issue for the school. Although there was much experience, ideas and innovative practice in assessment, what it seemed to be missing at that time was a forum for the sharing of that experience and practice and for the 'passing on' of information and methodologies between more experienced practitioners and newer members of staff. As well as an opportunity for staff and curriculum development, the school also saw its involvement in this pilot programme as a chance to demonstrate its expertise to other institutions (by contributing to Subject Centre activities). The Subject Centre's external viewpoint could help the school to identify its own innovative practice, examples of others' work, methods of integration and embedding of assessment, and a chance to collect and analyse its own data. All these activities would sit well with the Subject Centre's research-led and evidence-based approach to learning and teaching.

Finally, as part of the activity-planning process, colleagues were asked to identify other potential sources of support, both internally and externally, to supplement the provision from the Subject Centre (and to ensure the sustainability of the programme of work). These included the Centre for Learning and Teaching, the Careers Service, professional bodies and the Scottish Earth Science Education Forum.

This initial discussion meeting was very successful. As it was driven by the head of school, there was a good level of attendance. The facilitators and chairperson met beforehand to discuss the schedule of the event. Each discussion activity was led by the (external) Subject Centre facilitators but the use of an internal chair ensured that any decisions made came from the participants and that the school (and its individual members) retained ownership of the process. The use of educational jargon was avoided, and this was welcomed by the participants. In addition, the facilitators' familiarity with the subjects taught in the school, together with information gathered from discussions with the departmental contact prior to the event, ensured that they were able to support the conversations from a sympathetic perspective. This helped to develop the mood of collaboration and to dispel any sense of one organization coming in to stamp its change on another.

Before the meeting it was agreed with the head of school that the initial contact person should be maintained as the focal point for communication with the Subject Centre and to drive forward the programme of work internally. Following the meeting, a formal report was written by the Subject Centre staff, capturing the discussion points and listing the notes from the SOAR analysis. A draft outline of activities was drawn up based on the school's needs and the Subject Centre's known resources (including funding and time). This activity part of the programme was intended to take advantage of the vast repository of skills, knowledge, information and resources that the Subject Centre had (and as indeed have most educational development units) accumulated over the years. Rather than providing a prescriptive list of activities from which departments could choose, after the discussion meeting the Subject Centre staff used their experience to select and suggest the most appropriate resources and activities to suit the departments' particular needs. Potential activities might include workshops on specific topics; funding for departmental team away-days; and provision of a consultant to help with, for example, curriculum development, provision of resources, and case studies.

In the case of the School of Geoscience at the University of Aberdeen, the activities were designed to be very flexible: rather than propose a full schedule of support, it was felt that the school would benefit from a staged process beginning with an opportunity to take a step back, collect and share information, and look at what was useful. It was suggested that this might be achieved through an audit and/or the setting up of a learning and teaching seminar programme. In addition, it was suggested that the school might investigate student objectives, aspirations and issues with respect to assessment, retention and progression. Resources, in the form of funding for staff time, an external mentor or other advice mechanism could be provided by the Subject Centre for such a study. Finally, it was recommended that the school set up a coordination group to oversee this work, comprising colleagues from across the school and including new and experienced lecturers, a colleague from the Centre for Learning and Teaching, and student representatives. After this first stage had been undertaken, the Subject Centre would then discuss with the school (via the contact person) where the focus might be for the remainder of the project.

These activities were then agreed with the school as guidelines for forthcoming work, rather than as a definitive list of actions. This flexibility allowed an iterative approach to the development of activity and the ability to respond to changes in aim as the programme progressed. It was felt that such changes should be seen as a positive rather than something to fight against.

This flexibility proved both a negative and a positive. On the downside the provisional nature of the programme meant that it lacked authority, such that there was no comeback if the school failed to undertake a particular activity (hence making progress hard to monitor, particularly from a distance). The considerable positives were that the school had the ability (and the moral support) to direct the project itself, and to identify and make the most of new opportunities. For example, as a result of the discussions, colleagues successfully bid for funding from the local Centre for Learning and Teaching to undertake a mini-research project.

Lessons Learned

At the time of writing, this programme of activity was still in progress and had not yet been fully evaluated. However, it is still valuable to capture the Subject Centre's experience and lessons learned.

In theory, this approach has a lot of potential for engaging staff in learning and teaching development. In practice, the wider context of the department, including other priorities, research, changing staff and so on, means that the originally planned schedule of activity may not come to fruition. As previously suggested, this is not necessarily a negative outcome but rather an illustration of the complexity of the process and the influence of many other priorities and factors outside of the Subject Centre's (or, in some cases, the department's) control. Regular contact was maintained with the key member of staff at the institution, and some interesting and productive conversations were had. In addition, the Subject Centre offered facilitation of a student focus group, provision of resources relevant to assessment and fieldwork, brainstorming/ discussion and general moral support. It is hoped that a final activity will be a thematic workshop for the school, including a follow-up discussion meeting to share experiences and showcase the outcomes. This would provide an opportunity for the project to re-engage a wider selection of colleagues and to boost the momentum of the activities in the longer term.

An example of a specific outcome of the activity so far is the award of two grants to the school from the university's Centre for Learning and Teaching, as described by the project contact:

Good news: we got both awards. In fact, there were only [seven awards] for the whole university, so we got 36 per cent of the total fund. . . . From the point of view of GEES impact, this is a major concrete achievement for the collaboration. Without the inspiration from GEES, I don't think we'd have considered putting bids in at all, and it's the practical help that got us both awards. . . . Some informal feedback I got from the Centre's director was that our proposals were just better written and more aware of pedagogic issues and good practice elsewhere than most of the others. And this is largely down to GEES – talking with yourselves, getting stuff from the good-practice database and going to the conferences.

The complexity of academic life means that the process is unlikely to be straightforward. However, the Subject Centre does consider the programme of activity worthwhile in terms of developing relationships and enabling departments to move forward on key curriculum development agendas. In summary, these pieces of advice are offered to colleagues considering a similar approach:

- Ensure you have support from the head of school or department.
- Identify a key contact with whom to liaise (not necessarily the head).
- Adopt a facilitative approach based on discussion and negotiation (though the facilitators must be mindful of the need to conclude discussions and to pin down specific outcomes and activities).
- Enable department-led development around a pre-existing issue (i.e. something the department would have to work on even without the additional support).
- Be inclusive of all relevant members of staff (and, where possible, students).
- Be prepared to have a flexible agenda.
- Be prepared for unexpected or hidden outcomes.
- Recognize that the process of the collaborative engagement and conversations are perhaps more important than tangible outcomes.

This way of working with academic departments around key learning and teaching issues can be extremely valuable and exciting but also somewhat frustrating. As Knight & Trowler (2000) suggest, 'Desirable change is most likely to be achieved in collective and collaborative ways, which means that change processes are contingent and contextualised, and that outcomes are unpredictable and fuzzy.' Perhaps the most valuable aspect of the process is that it enables and facilitates productive conversations that might not otherwise happen.

Case-Study References and Further Information

Higher Education Academy Subject Centre Network. Online, available at: www.heacademy.ac. uk/ourwork/networks/subjectcentres (accessed 21 December 2008).

Higher Education Academy Subject Centre for Geography, Earth and Environmental Sciences. Online, available at: www.gees.ac.uk (accessed 21 December 2008).

Knight, T. P. (1998). Professional obsolescence and continuing professional development in higher education. *Innovations in Education and Teaching International*, 35 (3), 248–256.

Knight, T. P. & Trowler, P. R. (2000). Department-level cultures and the improvement of learning and teaching. *Studies in Higher Education*, 25 (1), 69–83.

Prebble, T., Hargraves, H., Leach, L., Naidoo, K., Suddaby, G. & Zepke, N. (2005). *Impact of Student Support Services and Academic Development Programmes on Student Outcomes in Undergraduate Tertiary Study: A Synthesis of the Research.* Report to the New Zealand Ministry of Education. Massey University College of Education. Online, available at: www.education counts.govt.nz/publications/tertiary_education/5519 (accessed 22 December 2008).

5
Crossing Boundaries in Collaboration

Boundaries can present barriers; or they can provide opportunities. In collaborative working in higher education, practice is often situated at the forefront of knowledge development, with collaborations pushing at the limits of cognition. Boundaries can be found in all areas of academic work, whether they be constructed around discipline, technology or geography; but breaking through boundaries can provide creative spaces for innovative practice and for collaborative working beyond the academy. And if we look beyond the confines of our own university, working with partners based in other educational sectors, the wider community, industry or internationally, then we can potentially gain impetus and new insights. Boundaries are encountered and crossed in all collaborations. In this chapter we look at four case studies where the experiences of the authors illuminate three examples of such crossings: of sector, institution and discipline.

Linking Industry and Academia

Some of these collaborations are breaking completely new ground, in that the joint working is sponsoring new directions in collaborative practice, with a resulting impact on the wider sector. Hannah Whaley's collaboration with Blackboard and the development of a new tool for use within the virtual learning environment 'created a new example for commercial e-learning companies to engage with educational institutions, and vice versa', and produced a product that can be adopted and utilized by colleagues across the sector. The process of collaboration in this case also resulted in emergent learning for both the institutional and the industrial partner, engaging with different professional languages, taking account of varied geographical time zones and different approaches to staffing resources as the project unfolded. There promise to be long-lasting effects for both partners, in addition to the benefits of informing future ventures and potentially saving valuable time and resources at an early stage, as a result of the professional dialogues that have been opened up by this collaboration.

'The *messiness* of academics "speaking across the disciplines"'

In the second case study, Jason Davies examines the complexities of a pro-gramme involving several disciplines. This is a collaboration that at one level represents a crossing of disciplinary boundaries, but the depth and richness of engagements and understanding that emerged from the professional dialogues, initiated and supported through these academic exchanges, have also spanned many other boundaries. Some of these were immediately obvious, such as disciplinary languages, but others only surfaced as a result of the engagement within the collaborative discussion:

> . . but a crucial qualitative difference should be emphasized: it is very different for an 'undisciplined' student to learn than it is for someone *already* expert in a discipline.

Collaborative activity can bring to the surface such 'hidden boundaries', which have the potential to enervate or to engage participants within any collaborative project.

Science Meets Art

A further example of a collaboration across disciplinary boundaries is provided by Paul Harrison and Mhairi Towler. The Designs for Life project was conceived with the intention of providing a framework for a series of collaborations that would explore the process of visualization of laboratory data relating to aspects of cell and gene research. This project went on to span several other boundaries, beyond the art and science interface, as seen in the numerous additional projects that have developed from the initial collaboration. The striking artwork created as a result of the project represents a challenge to personal boundaries created by our own perceptions and assumptions about disciplinary knowledge and output. What is science; and what is art? We must cross the boundaries of our own understanding in order to continue to nurture the professional dialogues that are created by such innovative practice.

Engaging Institutions

The fourth and final case study in this chapter originates in New Zealand and examines the boundaries created by cross-institutional working. But as with the Davies case study, there are also hidden boundaries that emerge only through the joint working practices of the participants.

For example, the apparent unwillingness of one teacher participant to share the work of the project with anyone else in his department does not challenge the overarching project but it does make the sharing of good or effective practice a more significant task for the home team. Conversely, the desire of the teacher participants not to do further iterations of the intervention, but rather to do something substantially different, is really good for the teacher participants in improving their practices, but not ideal for the overarching project.

The unfolding of practice within the joint working process erected boundaries, creating spaces for some which may be positive, but to the potential detriment of the experience for others. Emergent working can lead to a number of potential outcomes, some of which may not only be unanticipated, but perhaps also not entirely desirable. It is in situations such as these where different approaches to, or interpretations of, practice pose challenges to the collaborative process that strength needs to be drawn from the other elements of the collaborative model: the development and strengthening of *professional dialogues*, the *engagement* of individuals and particularly, perhaps, the *social vehicles*. In this example, these structures were sound ('One aspect of the collaboration which helps retain its vibrancy, a sign of true and honest collaboration, is the feeling of safety experienced within the team'). And with this in place, as Holmes *et al.* go on to comment, such emergent working can also stimulate new thinking: 'Such situations however, have also prompted us to revisit our original assumptions and concepts and to allow for emergent research questions and changes or shifts in the interventions.'

Collaborative versus Bounded Working

The balance between different facets of collaboration depends also on the context within higher education: with different disciplines (arts and humanities versus the sciences) and institutional or departmental cultures; and also on the market nature of higher education (links with industry and the drive for product development) versus the role of the academy to educate. And if the focus is on working together, then our understanding must also incorporate a more explicit place for another opposite to collaborative working: what we can call *bounded* working. In this chapter we can thus view our model from the perspective of working across boundaries, rather than from the perspective of working together within a single collaborative space. Such a perspective is essential if we are to see the collaborative space for what it is: a coming together of individuals, and indeed social entities, from *different* perspectives. We need engagement from those on both sides of a boundary, as well as dialogues that can be understood by all the parties involved. Within this the identification, development and support of the variety of social vehicles that can be utilized have a key role to play. And we need humility and trust to recognize that those on the other side of the boundary have a contribution to make from their own perspectives, resources and expertise. This is an integral aspect of all collaboration.

Case Study
Commercial Collaboration

HANNAH WHALEY
University of Dundee

Context

E-learning has emerged as a growing field in UK higher education in recent years. Trends show a continued rise in the adoption of enterprise-level educational technology such as virtual learning environments (VLEs) and an increasingly central role for learning technology specialists within the learning and teaching landscape. While some institutions choose to use an open-source or 'home-grown' VLE, the dominant choice is for commercial systems, with Blackboard holding the leading market share.

Connecting Learning and Teaching and Commerce

In 2007, learning technologists at the University of Dundee collaborated with Blackboard to commercialize a learning and teaching system developed in Dundee. In doing so, the University of Dundee was recognized as the first academic institution to partner with Blackboard to create a significant development within its core platform, and Blackboard delivered a system to a global client base derived from sound teaching principles refined within a client institution. The result of this collaboration is a new Self and Peer Assessment System that engages students in reflective learning, and the process of the collaboration has created a new example for commercial e-learning companies to engage with educational institutions, and vice versa.

This collaboration represents a change from common practice of universities. Learning and teaching initiatives used to be shared freely among academic staff internally and externally to create best practice within subject areas. Developments in e-learning continue to arise from the best practice of academic staff but are often coordinated centrally by learning technology staff and can involve the creation of a tangible asset such as a piece of software or an electronic course. Harsh financial times and an increased awareness within institutions that products of this nature can hold a value (monetary or reputation enhancement) have led many to be more careful about how they release them to the community. Openly sharing successful initiatives clearly fosters future collaboration and helps build communities of practice, while generating revenue can allow projects to be furthered and clearly identify institutions that will be committed to collaborating. Both paths have proved to be fraught with difficulties that are not easy to resolve.

Software developed to suit the needs of one institution will require substantive changes to become generic enough to be applicable to any institution. Managing the marketing and distribution of a project can present challenges, but the bigger issues lie in support and maintenance. Initial support is required for institutions deploying the software, and inevitably there are requests for modifications, customizations and enhancements. Issues are more likely to arise when the software is being used in different environments and for different purposes as compared with those originally anticipated. For other universities to use the software there has to be some commitment to maintaining it so as to overcome the problems that arise, and as time goes on this becomes exponentially more difficult as new releases cause backward compatibility issues. It has not been uncommon for the time required for this to escalate to a level where a project becomes unsustainable. Once this has happened, it is unlikely that the initiative will be successful or gain widespread adoption.

Educational technology companies appear eager to see new advancements continue to develop from the bottom up, and have worked to assist universities to innovate and collaborate. The main VLE providers have open-source communities that surround them, and have encouraged this by providing funding for collaborative or community projects, running conferences and events, providing online methods of releasing developments and, primarily, by making their products extensible in the first place. To use Blackboard as an example, Blackboard runs a Building Block programme that allows clients to develop enhancements that integrate with their products. A Developers' Network has been established to provide guidance, support and best-practice examples. The self- and peer-assessment project was developed as a direct result of access to this open architecture, and the collaboration formed because of a desire on both sides to find a sustainable way to release it to a wider community.

Benefits of the Collaborative Approach

This collaboration therefore found a way to further existing practices for both partners in the collaboration. Blackboard enabled a project that began in the community to reach all its clients, and the University of Dundee was able to see its work become sustained and widely used. The institution contributed its experience of developing systems through user-centred design and genuine involvement of academic staff and students, and the commercial partner added its understanding of a vast range of institutional and educational perspectives and commitment to professional support and future development. The key benefits were as follows:

- The project was made available to a wider community.
- The original creators were still credited with the project's development.
- The original development was driven by pedagogy and academic experience.
- The project was extensively trialled in a genuine university context prior to release.
- The product was made more generic and suitable for a wider audience.
- The product was supported and maintained professionally.
- The future of the product and backward compatibility were assured.
- There were opportunities for future collaborations and development of best practice.

There were key differences in the characteristics of the collaborators in this scenario, and this influenced the methods used to communicate and work together. There is a large geographical distance between Scotland and the United States, which meant differences in culture and time zones. Different internal structures and working practices were apparent between a university and a commercial company, with the latter being much more versed in intellectual property and legal matters. The boundaries of the collaboration were therefore initially defined by the legal representatives on each side before work began on the project and practices could evolve to suit those that were actively involved. Numerous different methods of interaction were utilized:

- identifying relevant contacts within each party;
- working with legal representatives;
- compliance with industry standards;
- web conferencing (for presentations and demonstrations);
- phone conferences (for meetings and updates);
- face to face (meeting at conferences, and working in the United States);
- an ongoing project group to resolve issues.

Each of these elements had the potential to exacerbate the differences between the two collaborating parties rather than ameliorate them, so it was important to keep focused on attaining the shared goal. For example, complying with standards for notation and documenting is an established procedure within software engineering companies, but is not commonly used in university work. However, ensuring that a common language could be used and understood equally was one way to combat cultural differences. Likewise, it is commonplace for collaborating research teams in universities to travel to meet at each other's institutions, yet it is not common for companies to open their doors to external clients. Doing so greatly enhanced the nature of the collaboration by increasing mutual understanding of working practices, and strengthened the partnership greatly.

Measuring Success

How can success be measured? One way is to acknowledge the successful completion of the project. In January 2008, a year after the collaboration began, Blackboard released version 8.0 of its Learning Environment, which incorporated the new self- and peer-assessment system, to over 3,600 global clients. The system allows an instructor to create an exercise, composed of one or more questions, and define the marking criteria. Students answer the questions online before proceeding to mark their own and others' work against the criteria set by the instructor. It can be used within any discipline or subject area, with small and large class sizes, for a variety of learning purposes. The system is ideal for engaging with students and enhancing their reflective learning practices. They learn about criterion-based reference marking, and develop the skills of providing constructive feedback. They benefit from reviewing their colleagues' work as they potentially assess work that is both better and worse than their own. Since the system has been released, many academic staff around the world have been able to innovate and extend their assessment practices because of the access they now have to this pedagogic approach. This was the core aim of everyone involved in the collaboration, and is definitely a successful outcome.

A second way to measure the effectiveness of the collaboration strategy is to reflect on what was learned from it. The changes and optimizations made along the way demonstrate that the collaboration methods evolved in order to ensure success. These improvements would be incorporated into the strategy for any similar project. The first of these would be to put a greater emphasis in the early days on establishing common language and terminology to prevent any early misunderstandings or delays that related to differences in industry as against university culture, or differences between British and American English. One example was a fundamental difference in the terminology used for grading work (evaluating work) – important in a project based on assessment software! Over time, practices evolved to rely on more formal documentation, ensuring understanding on both sides. Taking time to understand the backgrounds of the people involved would also have allowed for early discussions to be more focused, and planning for the possibility of staff changes in the project would have been beneficial. Turnover of staff in a software engineering company appears higher than that in a university, partly as a result of a more project-focused approach, meaning more reassignment of work between teams depending on workload. We have also been able to continue to collaborate on issues after the release of the software, but this had not originally been scheduled. This flexibility has helped ensure success, and what has been learned from it could easily be formalized into the structure of any future collaboration.

The final way in which I can highlight the benefit of the collaboration strategy is to look to the future. This work has opened a number of doors and allowed the University of Dundee to make new contacts within other institutions, creating discussions about new projects and collaborations, such as working with other early adopters to produce guidance and examples of best practice. For a university, the opportunity to create further work and find new academic partners is an ideal ending to any project.

Summary

As a final summary, this collaboration crossed a boundary between higher education and commercial enterprise, and in doing so has provided a case-study scenario that others can use to assess the potential benefits of doing the same. In any situation it is difficult to judge whether the collaboration worked well because of the individuals involved or whether a repeatable formula has been created. At the very least, the successful outcome of the work has paved the way for others to experiment, and delivered an exciting new teaching tool to many educational institutions in the process.

Case Study

'The *messiness* of academics "speaking across the disciplines"'

JASON DAVIES
University College London (UCL)

Context

One exchange from the Evidence e-mail list. A physiologist wrote, 'I don't have patience for arguments from the Chinese Room experiment, because as a physiologist I consider the human brain to be a machine.' A historian responded, 'Who makes that judgement – the brain? How does the brain do so? Automatically, presumably, if we keep to the logic of your position? On what grounds then does your judgement have any meaning, since it's simply the universe technologically noting its own existence as another function of a machine? Or are you implicitly distinguishing "brain" from "self"?' And a pharmacologist continued privately to that historian, 'If the brain is not a machine, then what is it? The only other possibility seems to be to start talking about souls or some other form of mysticism. I'd prefer not to do that myself.'

Interdisciplinary Beginnings

The preceding (heavily edited) exchanges come from the email list of the interdisciplinary UCL Evidence programme, which ran from 2004 to 2008. what follows is an attempt to elucidate *some* of what is evoked in this inconclusive exchange. The temptation (and indeed, what I was asked for) when narrating such a programme is to provide the reader with an 'accessible overview', starting with a general framework, then veering towards particulars before 'retrieving' a 'concluding overview' – a bird's-eye view that 'makes sense'. I have resisted this temptation for a particular reason: it would not represent the epistemological experience of the programme that I wish to emphasize. Before I can describe the programme in *any* way, I must at least briefly engage with the issue of what validates the type of description I intend to use and confess its partiality – its positionedness.

Offering a deliberately enigmatic narrative is a risky business because it is (frankly) annoying when one expects 'sense' and gets rather too much mystery.

Nonetheless, I retain a little epistemological disruption on strictly metho-
dological (rather than lazy or self-indulgently iconoclastic) grounds: the
programme *was* disruptive to its participants and I would be doing a disservice
to my readers to spare them *all* of the perplexity. When fundamental disciplinary assumptions and frameworks (the academic sense-making systems)
are suddenly, almost impossibly, swept away, how (exactly) does one speak? Can
we 'drop' to a more general level of shared understanding? Often we thought so
– until the illusion was shattered by the realization that this was precisely what
we were doing: few claims to general applicability are as vacuous as the one
enshrined in 'common sense', and my opening exchange shows what often
happened as scholars of different disciplines struggled to discuss something
beyond the banal.

What was lacking was not information or evidence: it was 'a "sensible" place
to stand', a point of reference for deciding what was relevant and what was not.
Any choice of explanatory position was, at best, pragmatic and had to be aligned
with explicit purposes. My purpose here is therefore to evoke the difficulties that
participants of the Evidence programme encountered: not just a mix of 'sense'
and 'non-sense' but – crucially – no consensual way to move items from the
latter to the former category. The very processes of 'sense-making' threatened,
at times, to break down in this interdisciplinary setting, and *that* was what we
(the interdisciplinary project within the programme) found most interesting.

In this emphasis, we are not contributing to an orthodoxy about cross-
disciplinary work, but, rather, going in a different direction from much of that
scholarship: multidisciplinary projects are often framed as 'synthetic' and
'unifying', and aimed at solving 'real-world problems' (see, among many others,
Klein, 1990, 1996, 2005; Klein *et al.*, 2001). As such, the terms 'multidisciplinary'
and 'interdisciplinary' are usually treated as virtually synonymous, but here I
examine something a synthetic study would discard: the *messiness* of academics
'speaking across the disciplines'.

In line with this emphasis, I propose that 'interdisciplinary' be clearly
distinguished here (at least) from 'multidisciplinary' to refer to an examination
of '(mis)communication and process' rather than 'results and outcomes' (on
this see Rowland, 2006: 87–103). This account therefore evokes processes rather
than formal structures, and should emphatically be read as *one possible* account.
(For those who nonetheless wish for a 'bird's-eye view', the full set of seminars,
papers and activities over the four-year period January 2004 to December 2007
can be seen at www.evidencescience.org.)

Welcome to the Programme

In summer 2003 the Leverhulme Trust offered funding for an 'Interdisciplinary
Study of Evidence'. To add to a growing focus on 'evidence' in academia
(medicine and education in particular), 'evidence' had shot to media fame in the

wake of the terrorist bombings, the search for weapons of mass destruction, the investigations and recriminations after 9/11. We found ourselves deep in media- and government-driven debates about who should know what, and how, and whom they should tell; evidence (at least temporarily) was an urgent question both within and beyond academia.

Led by Professor Philip Dawid (a statistician), preliminary meetings were held in UCL which would become the UCL Evidence programme (some funding was also procured from the Economic and Social Research Council). A number of projects emerged: not all disciplines were represented (the centre of gravity was the 'harder' social sciences, especially Statistics). Nor were all the projects mapped directly onto academic disciplines, but the disciplinary centre of gravity of the relevant staff is approximated here in parentheses with the named projects:

- *Formal Tools for Handling Evidence* (Legal/Forensic)
- *Model-Contingent Interpretation of Evidence* (Economics)
- *Historical Evidence* (Ancient History)
- *Human Attitudes to Evidence* (Psychology)
- *Synthesis of Complex Evidence Practice and Policy Making* (Primary Health Care/Computer Science)
- *Evidence in Natural Sciences* (Philosophy of Science)
- *Evidence: A Case Study of Interdisciplinarity* (Education)
- *Inquiry and Detection* (Crime Science)
- *Towards an Integrated Concept of Evidence* (Statistics/Law)

There were also informal participants from Classics, Anthropology, History (later periods), Pharmacology, Physiology, Archaeology, Comparative Literature and others, but very little input from the 'hard' sciences or the more relativistic disciplines (such as History of Art).

The programme initially hosted open presentations (which rapidly became 'the Causality series'): speakers gave introductions to their discipline and methods of working. At this stage the audience frequently felt they had a good enough grasp of a topic to contribute suggestions and interesting (frequently 'guiding') questions; there was confidence and optimism. If these early stages were to be characterized briefly, it would be as 'a search for consensus'. No particular theme was imposed beyond a general emergent interest in causality; speakers framed their own agenda, and discussion alluded to our soon 'getting on with' the task of finding common ground, to allow us to proceed to the 'greater' task of exploring a common understanding of evidence (as per most thinking about multidisciplinary work, which emphasizes problem-solving and synthesis).

But from the outset, another process that was to become familiar appeared: a suggestion would be made and the speaker would explain why it was not appropriate or could not be answered. Or speakers might find themselves mired in an ever-spiralling retreat from 'their real point' ('Could you talk us through that equation?' – 'Thanks, but what does that symbol *mean*, the one you read out?'). Audiences increasingly faced the choice of abandoning any detailed understanding (thus being left only with the – often counter-intuitive – concluding assertions) or bringing the speaker to a point of frustration where they did not know what they could say without 'retreating' to 'explaining the basics first'. This kind of situation created a recurring dilemma between respecting the disciplinary expertise of the speaker and bewilderment about even where to begin to make a statement meaningful. This occurred particularly with subjects like economics and statistics because of unmistakably unfamiliar (to some) mathematical representations: it *appeared* that some disciplines were more obscure than others.

What emerged only over time was the opaqueness of disciplines that *appeared* to use everyday language. For instance, as a historian of religion I asserted that 'belief is not a useful concept for studying religion', which makes *superficial* sense – the words form a syntactically intelligible sentence – but its implications extend into perplexity on closer examination. Apart from anthropologists, furiously nodding, no one could find a meaningful context for this counter-intuitive statement. If anything, the use of 'everyday words' simply created the extra difficulty of their specificity and richness being not just impenetrable but also *masked*. Explaining the rich (but confusing) implications of 'belief' required explaining the rich (and, in this case, equally treacherous) implications of 'religion', and this in its turn required the clarification of the very terms used to explain; the explanation process threatened to be an infinite regress.

Our opening quotes implicate this process neatly: the discipline-specific framing of 'the brain' as a 'machine' was explicitly the reason for impatience with a particular set of arguments from the field of artificial intelligence. The impatience was (I surmise) linked to the fact that these arguments (which run, in violent brevity, that a machine that processes language – Chinese in this case – so convincingly that someone might think they were talking to a human can still not be said to 'understand' the language) make physiology basically very difficult, to put it mildly. The historian, however, innocent of the implications for physiology, saw a different set of difficulties, based broadly on his disciplinary habits, where 'brain' is largely irrelevant, but *people* (and particularly the self) matter much more. Finally, the pharmacologist signalled that there was yet another disciplinary aspect involved, that of (legitimate) disciplinary limits; his science simply has no framework for going beyond the notion of a brain as a machine. It should be stressed that I do not seek to adjudicate claims here; rather, I wish to evoke the difficulties of discussing something apparently familiar in mixed disciplinary surroundings. Should one or another prevail in an interdisciplinary setting (and why)? If so, how would we agree on which one? With reference to 'facts'? (What exactly is a 'machine', anyway? How should we 'treat' machines? Are such implications relevant to our discussion?)

Thus, much broader questions arose as to what constituted 'understanding' and 'explanation', and these too moved from being 'clearly understandable' terms to a yawning abyss. Did 'understanding' mean someone could themselves now explain the difficulties or merely that they could pass on the news that 'belief is a difficult term for studying religion'? Some thought these were philosophical questions – but why privilege philosophy? The infinite regress was ever at our shoulders; as each idea was discussed, the terms used to discuss it would (necessarily) become problematized. There usually emerged a point at which, despite travelling quite some way with the speaker, we were ultimately reduced to 'taking someone's word for it'.

There were other issues. A perception that 'generalizability' and 'universality' were the 'favoured modes' in the programme, combined with the short-term existence of 'B-list projects' whose funding had not yet been secured, gave rise to what became known as the 'Narrative Group'. This group shared a perception (which may or may not have been fair) that the programme had a great deal of momentum towards 'reductionist and universalizing' modes of thinking. The participants of the Narrative Group instead had an intense interest in contextualized persuasion, rhetoric and narrative.

These divergences came to a head in 'the Schum Challenge': the work of Professor David Schum had been suggested as a starting point for collaboration, and he had already given presentations to the programme. These presentations were perceived as rather reductionist. (In fact, it became apparent later that his publications were far more nuanced and even anti-reductionist, but this was not clear at the time.) A one-day seminar was held, essentially framed around the participants of the Narrative Group putting their case for a different agenda. This day, and the e-mail interchanges that followed, revealed a great deal of previously concealed misunderstanding: typically, someone would say that *now* they had *begun* to realize that when they had thought they understood something earlier, actually they had not – but it took lengthy discussion before familiar (and therefore overlooked) assumptions were subjected to an inquiring gaze. This process was to repeat over and over, in a spiral – not of greater knowledge, but of greater sensitivity to *participants' own* modes of understanding.

At this point, the programme 'naturally' ('instinctively'?) moved towards subgroups where common interest had 'spontaneously' emerged: what had been the general Causality Seminar Series became the 'Causality Triangle', where statistical modes predominated – and other series and groups also arose around common themes or interests.

Thus, in what we might call its 'middle phase', the Evidence programme moved from being an apparently unified group aspiring to consensus to a self-selecting, more focused (but still overlapping) series of subgroups that could cooperate beyond the banal and introductory. Sometimes these groups were reasonably formalized (such as a seminar) but at other times they were ad hoc sets of participants on the e-mail list discussing a particular issue from contingent frameworks. Other threads on the list, however, served to demonstrate the extent to which *any* (disciplinary? 'informed'?) judgement requires disciplinary assumptions – and these do not travel well.

Nonetheless, rather than being the moment when people abandoned communicating, this point is better thought of as the moment that the texture and landscape (so to speak) of the interdisciplinary spaces came more into focus. Different ways of interacting evolved: most people continued to participate in different threads of the programme, which laid the basis for the 'final phase'. As time went by, and conversations continued in a wide range of contexts (seminars, e-mail lists, corridors, etc.), a mature awareness emerged among participants of the profundities of talking across the disciplines. This became visible in a cycle of presentations by the individual projects to the programme as a whole.

Thus, when the final conferences were held, with a mixture of long-term participants and outsiders, the 'insiders', we assert, had changed noticeably since the beginning: there was a different mode of questioning and listening. They (to use an antiquarian word) *suffered* more ambiguity, with more humility regarding their own level of understanding. There was also a more sophisticated mode of engaging with discipline-specific modes of reference (which were often assumed to be transparent by people new to interdisciplinary work). Such a qualitative change is extremely difficult to substantiate; we have next to no 'evidence'. The reader will have to decide whether to take our word for it.

The Outcome: Respecting the Process

We (the interdisciplinary project, myself, and Professor Stephen Rowland) would not like to say that we (the programme) formulated 'a science of evidence' – unless one wishes to go for a specific and unorthodox understanding of 'science'. Rather, we all encountered something more fundamental to academic understanding. A key outcome of the interdisciplinary working was not the *solution* of dilemmas but rather this greater degree of *tolerance of lack of understanding* in ongoing discussion. We thought aloud within sets of contestations, and the normal academic process of accumulating knowledge within a recognized framework (or making adjustments to that framework) was inverted: instead of accumulating knowledge, we were accumulating suitably identified areas of ignorance; instead of adjusting a framework in an explicable way, we were deliberately *avoiding* using frameworks that we felt comfortable with.

The obvious – but misleading – comparison that might be made is that of a student learning their discipline (on which we like Polanyi, 1997), but a crucial qualitative difference should be emphasized: it is very different for an 'undisciplined' student to learn than it is for someone *already* expert in a discipline. Indeed, one factor that was thrown up was the question of what is at the heart of academic expertise: is it the accumulation of (disciplinary) knowledge? Or is it the *ability to make sound judgements*? If participants could not participate 'as' academics, then in what sense *were* they participating? This was not a question that could be sidestepped (or definitively answered); it emerged as a pivotal issue that had been fundamental throughout but had gone unrecognized until relatively late.

The chief benefits, if benefits are to be counted, would emerge only when the disciplinarian returned to their 'home' discipline, armed with a more sophisticated mastery of the understandings that they had long had but were previously unrecognized. In a nutshell, what a historian learned through interaction with statisticians, economists, lawyers, etc. was to see the hitherto invisible contours of his (in this case) *own* knowledge. Although this is almost the opposite to the expectations of disciplinary and *multi*disciplinary programmes, it was what united the participants of the Evidence programme.

Epilogue: Thoughts on 'Running' an Interdisciplinary Programme

Perhaps the most obvious recommendation is to remember there is no 'natural' way of running a large cross-disciplinary programme; its organization must be tailored to its purpose. Participants will probably expect things to proceed as they do 'at home' *without realizing it*. Thus, a group that had formed around a common, specific and 'real-life' issue must obviously tend more towards a multidisciplinary approach (but they ignore the interdisciplinary aspects at their peril). On the other hand, a group charged with a more abstract theme, such as 'Is there a science of evidence?', where parameters must be identified *within* the group rather than being provided (usually by the funding bodies), will of necessity find itself in a more 'interdisciplinary' mode of working.

Thus, a qualitative approach to assessing interdisciplinary work should be taken; quantitative assessments will make sense only if apparently *disciplinary* publications 'back home' are also counted as outcomes. And this 'ignorance-oriented' interdisciplinary work affects both academic understanding and teaching; active participants improved at explaining specialist ideas to non-specialist audiences and made new connections within their own disciplinary thinking. As such, 'guidance and suggestion' rather than 'authoritative leadership' of the Evidence programme proved to be a shrewd approach; had there been more aggressive pursuit of 'an integrated science of evidence', the programme would have had to marginalize and virtually silence a number of its disciplines to forge a consensus – and this 'integration' would have been a fantasy. Instead, a rich spread of expertise was kept on board for the lifetime of the programme.

Case-Study References

Klein, J. T. (1990). *Interdisciplinarity: History, Theory, and Practice.* Detroit: Wayne State University Press.

Klein, J. T. (1996). *Crossing Boundaries: Knowledge, Disciplinarities, and Interdisciplinarities.* Charlottesville: University Press of Virginia.

Klein, J. T. (2005). *Humanities, Culture, and Interdisciplinarity: The Changing American Academy.* Albany: State University of New York Press.

Klein, J. T., Grossenbacher-Mansuy, W., Häberli, R., Bill, A., Scholz, R. W. & Welti, M. (eds) (2001). *Transdisciplinarity: Joint Problem Solving among Science, Technology, and Society: An Effective Way for Managing Complexity.* Basel: Birkhäuser.

Polanyi, M. (1997). *Personal Knowledge: Towards a Post-critical Philosophy.* London: Routledge.

Rowland, S. (2006). *The Enquiring University: Compliance and Contestation in Higher Education.* Maidenhead, UK: Open University Press. Online, available at: www.evidencescience.org (accessed 21 December 2008).

Case Study

The Designs for Life Project

PAUL LIAM HARRISON AND MHAIRI TOWLER
University of Dundee

Context

The Designs for Life project was conceived with the intention of providing a framework for a series of collaborations that would explore the process of visualization of laboratory data relating to aspects of cell and gene research: '[O]riginality consists of the achievement of new combinations, and not of the creation of something out of nothing' (Clemence & Doody, [1950] 1966; quoted by Andersen, 1991).

Evolving Social Vehicles

As with most things, the idea for this project did not arise independently. It evolved through many years of meeting with people and chatting – chatting about art with scientists and about science with artists, and about a whole mixture of other things with interesting people, from a whole range of backgrounds and disciplines, with a whole range of different skills and knowledge. It was precisely this activity that was the catalyst for what became this project. The curiosity that initiated this activity, however, is based in the arts practice of one of us (the artist – Paul Harrison) – a practice that had become increasingly collaborative in nature through two parallel threads. First, Paul's practice as a printmaker meant that his work was often workshop based and often involved working directly with other artists and designers, a social activity in itself, towards the 'editioning' of printed art works such as folios and artists' books. And second, it was the result of an intense 'layperson's' interest in the undertaking of the Human Genome Project in the 1990s, and in particular the notion that this was to be developed as a 'map'. This intrigue, driven by the imagined map, mechanics, potential and implications of the project, led Paul directly to the 'Bio-Laboratory'. A chance meeting in 1996 then led him to the Human Genetics Unit in Edinburgh, where he began working closely with a group of scientists. This work developed and culminated in an exhibition titled 'Genome'.

'By creating we think, by living we learn' (Patrick Geddes)

In following years this work seemed to grow organically, with interest from various parts of the world, perhaps benefiting from a growing public interest in this area of research and the potential of funding available to support the emerging genre of 'Sci-Art'. Paul therefore found himself invited to work with an array of interesting laboratory and social scientists engaged in research in this area, including projects with Cold Spring Harbor Laboratory, New York; the Centre for Social and Economic Aspects of Genomics, University of Cardiff; and the Human Genome Organisation. These working partnerships invariably involved Paul visiting and working in the laboratory, or at least within the working space of the partner collaborator. Often it would take the course of discussion, and develop further by Paul taking away material to work on in the studio or workshop – a model that seems to have become established in this form of practice. It seemed, however, that if new work was to be made in a truly collaborative sense, then the work should be made 'together', as the most interesting discussion and decisions were likely to take place at this stage, through the process of making. This became the premise for the Designs for Life project.

'Muscle and movement'

As the University of Dundee is particularly strong in the faculties of Art & Design and Life Sciences, and coincidentally the print publishing facility at the Visual Research Centre, we seemed primed for successful collaboration. In addition, Paul had already done some work with individuals at the laboratory, and the interest and constituent parts of a potential project seemed to be in place. An initial presentation confirmed this beyond expectation. Twelve scientists were recruited and the first collaboration initiated.

Initial ideas for the first collaboration were discussed informally between us. These discussions were based on samples of data or material collected from the lab that were brought to the print studio. A theme began to emerge during the course of these first few meetings, and evolved as the project progressed. Data used as a starting point were images taken of muscle cells stained with fluorescent markers and visualized using a high-magnification microscope. Higher-resolution images of muscle tissue were also produced using an electron microscope. Additionally, photographic films of 'Western blots' were used in the collaboration. A Western blot is a technique used routinely in laboratories to analyse proteins. Mhairi also took photographs of various pieces of equipment in the laboratory, such as the $-80°C$ freezer, where samples are stored, along with the incubator used for growing cells. A sketchbook was developed, cataloguing this material, and the theme of 'muscle and movement' began to develop. Mhairi then spent approximately eight days in total (two days a week over the course of a month) in the artists' studio, taking part in the development of ideas for each screen print, such as the composition, followed by participation in the actual print-making process, including decisions about paint colour, for example.

Reflection was an important part of the process, and sometimes it was more beneficial to stop proceedings on one print and work on another before going back to the initial print.

New Directions for the Collaboration

Through this collaboration an opportunity to work with primary school children arose. This was a very rewarding experience and was coordinated, in a further form of collaboration, with the Dundee City Council Creative Learning Team. This part of the project involved three afternoon trips to the school. During the first visit we gave a synopsis of our roles as scientist and artist at the university and a description of what the collaboration was about. Mhairi then showed the children how to use a microscope and let them have a look down it, after which they made drawings of what they had seen. They were also given words such as 'create', 'imagine', 'discover', 'inspire', 'analyse', 'investigate', and were asked to decide whether those words were applicable to either a scientist or an artist.

To begin with they were very clear about which word matched with which discipline, but through their own reasoning recognized that some words could be applicable to either a scientist or an artist. The children then worked on these ideas using various media, including dance, over the following weeks. The second visit allowed us to see the outcomes of this work. Finally it was decided that there would be enough scope to carry out an Easter holiday project for the children based on the ideas of the collaboration, involving dance and art work. A short film was made of this, and on the third visit we viewed the film with the children and discussed with them how they had found the project, to which one little boy answered, 'It is the best thing ever!' Other comments from the teachers were equally encouraging: 'Made children confident in own ability'; 'Children were able to work in pairs, groups and learned to work cooperatively'; 'Gave children an insight into how scientists, artists, dancers work'; 'It was interesting to observe children working with other professionals'.

The dancer who worked with the children over the lifetime of the project then went on to be commissioned to choreograph a piece of her own dance work in response to the collaboration. This was scheduled to be performed at the same time as the exhibition of screen prints opened. The final gesture in the 'editioning' of the print series was to sign and number the editions in accordance with fine print protocol. In keeping with the social aspect of the collaboration this was enjoyed with a glass of wine.

Thoughts on the Collaboration

Proof of the principle of collaborative working across boundaries is highlighted in this case not only by the successful completion of a set of screen prints, but also by the numerous additional projects that have developed as a result, exemplified by the primary school project described above. For Mhairi, 'Discovering how someone else can interpret scientific imagery was an eye-opening experience . . . and made me realize how closed one can become when only looking at an image from a scientific point of view.' The Designs for Life exhibition offered a chance to reflect on this idea, as all the prints from different scientific areas were shown: 'Although I am a scientist I could look at images from unfamiliar fields of research with a fresh perspective.' For Paul:

> The most important element of this and any collaborative initiative is that it is enjoyable. Each participant should have some fun and take away with them something new. In my view, collaboration allows participants not only to learn from the interests and experience of others, but to share their own enthusiasm for something and find a new place in which to be creative.

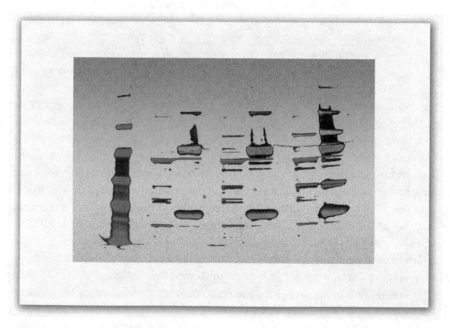

Figure 5.1 *Lighthouse*, a collaborative work by Mhairi Towler and Paul Liam Harrison. Acrylic screenprint in BFK Rives paper (110 × 75 cm), produced in an edition of six at the Visual Research Centre, 2007, as part of the Designs for Life project.

Summary

For a collaboration to be successful, both parties must be committed, and be open-minded when entering the collaborative process as to what the outcomes might be. Collaborators must be willing to take on board each other's ideas and suggestions. They need to meet regularly to throw ideas around and keep in touch via email. It can be easy to lose momentum if your places of work are geographically far apart; face-to-face dialogue is definitely key to keeping a collaboration moving forward.

Acknowledgements

The participating primary school, P5 & P6 pupils and teachers.
Dundee City Council Creative Learning Team.
University of Dundee Wellcome Trust.
www.designsforlifeproject.co.uk (accessed 21 December 2008).

Case-Study References

Andersen, E. S. (1991) *Schumpeter's Vienna and the Schools of Thought.* Aalborg, Denmark: Institute for Production, Aalborg University. Online, available at: www.business.aau.dk/evolution/esapapers/esa90-93/WP70.pdf.
Clement, R. V. and Doody, F. S. (1966) *The Schumpeterian System.* New York: Augustus M. Kelley. (Reprint of the 1950 edn. Cambridge, MA: Addison Wesley.)

Case Study
Working Collaboratively across New Zealand Universities

ALISON HOLMES
University of Canterbury

NEIL HAIGH
Auckland University of Technology

KOGI NAIDOO
University of Adelaide

Context

This project is a collaboration across the universities of New Zealand to explore the impact of the work of academic developers on the outcomes for first-year university students. The project has been set up to try to establish, through systematic data collection and analysis, whether the work of academic developers with faculty has any impact on aspects of the learning of students in large first-year classes. Each participating university is effectively carrying out a self-contained project with its staff and students. It is anticipated that each university will run two or three iterations in either semester- or year-long courses of their designated intervention, which will focus on one or more aspects of the learning and teaching. An agreed standard set of data is then collected from each participating university on each iteration, and these data, when aggregated, form the basis for the systematic evaluation of impact. While we all have retention, successful completion and overall performance data in common, some of the data necessarily vary across the universities because of the differing focus of the interventions. In January 2006 this project won a NZ$400,000 three-year Teaching and Learning Research Initiative grant. The project is hosted and managed by a lead institution. The project manager reports on a quarterly basis to the funding body on behalf of the team, providing cumulative data and individual reports from each collaborating member.

How Was the Collaboration Established and How Is It Sustained?

The timely combination of two key factors brought this project into existence. First, a previous Ministry of Education-funded project (Prebble *et al.*, 2005) identified that there were very few systematic studies of the impact of the work of the academic development community on student learning, thus identifying a large gap in the research. Second, the Academic Staff Development Units in New Zealand, an informal, loose alliance (collaboration, one might say, or, using Hogue's (1993) matrix of relationships, a 'network'), meet annually, and have done so for some years. At these professional development meetings good practice is shared, strategies exchanged and peer support provided. Regularly there are expressions about actively working together during the year, but so far nothing had happened. In November 2004 these intentions were reiterated, with the impetus coming from the members of the Prebble project and other members of the academic staff development network, and a research focus was identified. When the call for funding was published, one member of the project team contacted academic development colleagues at all New Zealand universities to invite them to participate in the development of a joint proposal. The inclusion of a representative from each university at the early stages of the conceptualizing of the project resulted in a strong sense of ownership in the collaboration, as reflected in Mattessich *et al.*'s (2001) definition of collaboration: 'a mutually beneficial and well-defined relationship entered into by two or more organizations to achieve common goals'. In this instance it was clear to all that the case for the proposed research would be strengthened if individual case studies were undertaken at each university. This would also be a way of acknowledging and investigating numerous 'context-related' factors that are likely to influence the academic developer–teacher–student relationship. These factors and their significance would become apparent when we aggregated the data from the individual case studies. We recognized that we could not achieve the project goals individually; we needed to collaborate.

As is typical of many collaborative projects, the efforts required to keep the consortium members engaged and informed are significant. Even where the members all know each other, a consortium cannot maintain its momentum without a guiding hand. The evidence from consortium activity in the Fund for Development of Teaching and Learning projects identified a list of at least five factors that help a collaboration to succeed. These are:

- regular communication;
- shared understanding and values around the project;
- ability to derive benefit from the consortium;
- institutional commitment;
- an effective project manager.

This collaboration was developed by people who all knew each other in a professional capacity at the outset. They also had some insight into the differing institutional environments within which the case studies would occur. The project manager was passionate about the project and had a very strong vision about how to ensure its completion and success. The two-stage proposal development contributed effectively to the emergent, shared understanding of the intentions and potential outcomes of the project. Shared values are harder to develop and articulate, but as the project progressed they manifested themselves in the work ethic, the willingness of participants to contribute, and the understanding that the individual projects have different rhythms, as do the lives of participants. Recognition of the last of these reinforced the need for flexibility as long as it did not compromise purposes, momentum and prescribed timelines. Institutional commitment came from the fact that the directors of all the Academic Development Units were involved from the beginning, either actively or as facilitators of the process. This ensured that each local team had the resources and support necessary to ensure success, although where the director has changed, the local projects seem to be less secure. The endeavours will be sustained beyond the project if the project provides clear evidence that academic development work with faculty leads to improved outcomes for students; then each individual academic development unit can use this information to back up the promotion and implementation of their regular work.

As the project was set up and the logistics planned, decisions were taken that have contributed to the smooth running of the project. These included budget allocation; each consortium member got NZ$15,000 for their participation, to support the individual project. The project manager retained responsibility for communal expenses, in particular for travel for members to central meetings and conference presentations where the team and project is represented. This removes the inequities of project teams located at a distance. Biannual project meetings are hosted by members of the consortium, one of which is linked to the annual meeting of academic staff development units, which also rotates among the institutions, so everyone gets to travel, to host meetings, meet the larger team and showcase the host's project.

One aspect of the collaboration that helps retain its vibrancy, a sign of true and honest collaboration, is the feeling of safety experienced within the team. Team members are able to discuss challenges they are facing and get support. For example, one institution decided to withdraw from the project after about a year, owing to unsustainable demands on the individual academic developer. While the formality of withdrawal and return of funding was managed by the respective research offices, informally the individual academic developer retains a connection with the project. The team decided to reserve the returned funding for a special use later in the project. At a recent meeting it was decided to schedule two additional team meetings to share experiences and strategically analyse data to contribute to the final research report.

Another issue that the team faces is the need to maintain the authenticity of the academic development, and teaching and learning, alongside our wish to obtain relevant and adequate data for our project. This situation has arisen where the teacher partners wish to change their intervention, often for good reason, but the academic developers are then faced with the dilemma of trying to encourage continuation of the intervention or, alternatively, doing what they feel is professionally correct: that is, supporting the desirability of teachers in their context of doing things they want to do. We are wearing practitioner as well as researcher hats, and this introduces some tensions. These are ongoing issues that are regularly aired during meetings as we strive to reach and maintain a common stance.

In reflecting on each project, there are challenges for each team – some of which threaten the success of the overarching project more than others. For example, the apparent unwillingness of one teacher participant to share the work of the project with anyone else in his department does not challenge the overarching project but it does make the sharing of good or effective practice a more significant task for the home team. Conversely, the desire of the teacher participants not to carry out further iterations of the intervention, but rather to do something substantially different, is really good for the teacher participants in improving their practices, but not ideal for the overarching project. Such situations, however, have also prompted us to revisit our original assumptions and concepts and to allow for emergent research questions and changes or shifts in the interventions. For example, we are now exploring the ripple effect that can be engendered from work that an academic developer may undertake with one colleague. At the outset of the project this was not explicitly identified as one of the phenomena that we would focus on. Such shifts are always founded on team-wide discussion so that we remain in synch.

Situations arising in individual universities vary and cause varying amounts of difficulties for the academic developers. Irrespective of the nature of the challenges, these issues can be aired and debated and guidance sought, not just from the project manager but from other team members as well as at the biannual meetings. This level of discussion helps to create and refine shared understandings and values while allowing the academic developers to raise issues that they cannot necessarily discuss in their home institution or with their teacher participants. Understandably, there are agreed-upon protocols concerning discussion of such matters so that privacy and confidentiality are maintained, and in accord with the ethics requirements and conduct of the project. These discussions give the individual academic developers the confidence and strength to go back to address the concerns they face as they run their individual projects. In that way the data keep coming from the collaborating parties so that the overarching project is not at risk. Perhaps the level of benefit gained from the project by individual academic developers is a function of their engagement with the overarching project and their individual project experience.

Barometer of Success

A barometer regarding the level and success of the collaboration is evident in the project management: the receipt of documentation on time and in the required format from each team so that the milestone-reporting requirements of the funding body are appropriately met. The project is kept on track by the project manager and some members of the consortium who contribute more to the joint effort than others. The joint collaborative effort is what keeps the endeavour progressing forward at the overarching project level. While the project manager has a pivotal role, some members of the team have assigned responsibility to provide coordination for an aspect of the project, for example, the dissemination of project outcomes. This not only helps ensure that the project manager does not carry undue burdens, but also acknowledges the expertise and interest of individual members. So, forms of involvement vary, while retaining an overall parity of status. The creation of a consortium presentation at a conference was also a very good example of how the strength of the collaboration is reaffirmed, when participants from each project got together to present their own findings in the context of the overall project findings.

Another key characteristic of this collaboration is that many of the members of the group meet each other in other contexts and groupings. These interactions occur in, for example, another project that successfully developed a bid for a national centre for tertiary teaching excellence; external moderation for postgraduate certificates; other government-funded projects; joint planning and delivery of an accredited course for tertiary teachers; and the committee for the regional branch of a professional organization (the Higher Education Research and Development Society of Australasia). These contexts are varied and range from professional committee-type engagements to real research projects, through to articulating our views and beliefs about academic development and its practice. These more frequent engagements with each other mean that professional perspectives and views are explored and developed and then either are more consistent within this collaboration, or the people know where the areas of tension are likely to arise and will be prepared to accommodate them. Awareness of the realities of different institutional contexts also assists. The values of academic development and developers are surfaced, triangulated within different contexts and brought to the collaboration in a refined form. In addition, the individual personal connections are deepened, and this brings strength to the consortium, which has been identified in the literature on group work as significant. Collaborators in this project find time for these other collaborations and connections, as this project is only a small part of any individual workload.

A final characteristic of our collaboration, and one that has contributed to its development and success, is the duration – an extended period of working together towards a common goal. Despite the fact that all the original participants were known to each other at the outset, the level of trust, understanding and empathy has increased substantially over time. This has been helped, no doubt, by the nature of the meetings we have had. The project manager observed at the fourth consortium meeting a turning point in the way the team interacted. By then the work was well under way and there were the beginnings of real evidence of the impact of our project. Resourcing is also a function of duration. The three-year commitment has allowed more permanent arrangements to be put in place, in particular in the lead institution. As we have observed to one another, it has also strengthened our concurrent membership of a community of practice.

Learning Points

The first learning point from this large three-year collaboration, which has yet to finish, is that there has to be a visionary, persistent and inclusive project manager who can use powers of persuasion and influence to ensure that the project achieves its targets and the participants remain positively engaged. The second is that a project of longer duration gives time for a collaboration to develop and strengthen, and thereby ensure the joint desire for success of the project. This links to the third aspect of learning, which is the benefits of the collaboration that accrue outside of the intended outcomes of the project. These include creating an environment in which other projects and research collaborations can be designed and developed, and the deepening of personal friendships. The desire for success for our collaboration was helped by the fact that even if each individual project were successful in its home location, without the success of the overarching project the impact would be minimal for each university. Some difficulties that have arisen when staff associated with the project have changed have highlighted the need to anticipate the possibility of such changes and to plan for and effectively implement transition arrangements. Those arrangements include a very comprehensive briefing for new members of the team on all aspects of the project. Nothing should be taken for granted. A final learning point is that the collaboration has to be flexible, both in itself and through its funders, to enable the project to deviate from its original plan when unexpected problems or issues arise.

Conclusion

New Zealand is fortunate in having a small number of universities and a compact academic development community, so a nationwide project is feasible. But since many teaching development units are relatively small, the academic developers sometimes need to seek support from outside their home unit, and this project has created a very fertile environment for that collaboration and consultation to take place.

Our key point is that the benefits of a collaboration must outweigh the costs. In this collaboration the costs include ensuring that all the data are supplied by all the participants; ensuring that the travelling and meeting times are productive; ensuring that appropriate ethics clearances were obtained to allow the collaboration to generate data and evidence that as individuals we would be unable to do, except over a significant period of time; the tensions arising between academic developers and teachers in the choice of interventions; and factors external to the project. The benefits, beyond those set out originally in the documentation, include the unexpected outcomes: links for individual project participants to other activities within their institutions, the pleasures of success, and the evidence that our work can be seen to make a difference to students.

Case-Study References

Hogue, J. (1993). Community based collaboration: community wellness multiplied. Online, available at: http://crs.uvm.edu/nnco/collab/wellness.html (accessed 11 February 2009).

Mattessich, P. W., Murray-Close, M. & Monsey, B. R. (2001). *Collaboration: What Makes It Work*, 2nd edn. St Paul, MN: Amherst H. Wilder Foundation.

Prebble, T., Hargraves, H., Leach, L., Naidoo, K., Suddaby, G. & Zepke, N. (2005). *Impact of Student Support Services and Academic Development Programmes on Student Outcomes in Undergraduate Tertiary Study: A Synthesis of the Research.* Report to the New Zealand Ministry of Education. Massey University College of Education. Online, available at: www.education counts.govt.nz/publications/tertiary_education/5519.

6
Proximity and Virtuality in Collaborative Research

In what ways does physical space affect collaboration? Working in a common location offers significant advantages in facilitating emergent working. The issue in part relates to frequency of encounter; and thus collaborations among colleagues who already meet each other regularly can helpfully support a range of exchanges between those involved.

This is not to say, however, that working in close physical proximity with colleagues means that you are always on the same wavelength when it comes to orientations towards collaboration. Gordon Roberts discovered this when he suddenly found himself involved in a funding bid without being asked:

> 'We've put a bid in to do some work for the government, evaluating urban policy. It looked a bit one-sided; so I put your name down, so that it had more weight on this side and it wasn't just me.' So I said, 'Oh, right, OK.'

And although Roberts and his colleague did in fact work together very successfully at the bid stage, he felt frustrated by the 'hierarchy [that] was always there' in their professional relationship, and even by the time Roberts was in a very senior position himself there was still an imbalance in the 'partnership':

> There came a point when he wanted me to take over our research unit. But by that point I was pro-vice-chancellor, and there was no way I was going to do that. I just thought that if he'd wanted me to take over, he should have involved me a lot more, and earlier. Even recently now that he's retired, he's still been trying to get me involved in a bid again. He still wanted to have my name somewhere on a bid.

The Search for Thick Networks

In some situations, however, perhaps because of the focus of the proposed project or the disciplinary context, the immediate pool of colleagues in one's field or potential partners cannot be found on the doorstep, and we need to look further afield in order to facilitate the 'thick networks' identified by Philip Morrison in our second study here. Morrison has identified three major factors that fuel contemporary collaborations: complementarity, creativity and collegiality. He goes on to discuss the challenges of accommodating and working with these drivers in a small country where collegiality depends on being able to communicate with compatible individuals, often specialists in a field, who may not actually exist – 'one of the reasons why staff across New Zealand universities rarely collaborate with each other'.

International research collaborations are on the increase, as is demonstrated by the 50 per cent expansion in joint working with overseas partners experienced by UK university researchers over a ten-year period (UK Higher Education International Unit and Universities UK, 2008). So, this search for more distant partners is clearly proving fruitful. However, that need becomes even more pressing, and something of a necessity rather than a choice, if you live in a relatively small country in terms of academic population, as is demonstrated in our example here from New Zealand.

Virtuality in Collaborative Working

But if international travel is out of the question owing to constraints of time or funding, what alternatives are possible? And in what ways are these issues magnified for individuals who are working in collaboration but have only limited or perhaps no real opportunities to meet physically, or for whom their practice and accompanying opportunities to foster and develop professional dialogues are necessarily focused on the online environment?

The ability to generate and maintain the social relationships, to build the trust and develop the shared values and aims that we have begun to see as central to effective collaborative working, can be frustrated rather than supported in the online environment. Social networking sites, web conferencing and shared e-libraries all contribute to the possibilities; but while these technological tools support *practice*, there is still scope for greater development in relation to developing the *social* side of collaborative working. How can the social vehicle be supported within a virtual environment? Archer (1995: 1) is instructive here:

> Social reality is unlike any other because of its human constitution. Society [has] . . . three unique characteristics. Firstly, that it is inseparable from its human components because the very existence of society depends in some way upon our activities. Secondly, that society is characteristically transformable; it has no immutable form or even preferred state. It is like nothing but itself, and what precisely it is like at any time depends upon human doings and their consequences. Thirdly, however, neither are we immutable as social agents, for what we are and what we do as social beings are also affected by the society in which we live and by our very efforts to transform it.

Essentially, then, there is no real barrier to a virtual reality, a society that is created online, sharing and utilizing the concept of the social as an effective mobilizer of practice. More than this, virtual environments can afford significant opportunities for development of innovative collaborative practice, beyond those available through face-to-face interaction. It may be that virtuality stimulates innovation as much as supporting it. A good example of this kind of innovative collaborative practice is demonstrated by the Stanford Humanities Lab (SHL), 'a loosely structured self-supporting research collaboratory [serving] . . . as a platform for transdisciplinary/post-disciplinary study dedicated to exploring innovative scenarios for the future of knowledge production and reproduction in the arts and humanities', as we saw earlier in Chapter 3. Part of the SHL agenda is an approach based on 'mixed reality' that aims to blend the 'real' and the virtual.

On Towards Mixed Reality

In our third case study Alastair Wilson discusses how the Applied Educational Research Scheme (AERS) project in Scotland engaged in this kind of 'mixed reality' approach, as researchers initially used the virtual research environment (VRE) largely for administrative purposes, yet over time the VRE came to be seen as much more than simply an administrative tool, and became a vehicle in which colleagues could 'engage and generate new forms of knowledge . . . and new opportunities for collaborative analysis, particularly crucial to distributed research teams'.

And on yet Further Towards Hybrid Mixed Realities

There is evidently scope for further experimentation as to how the pattern of our communication with each other might support collaborative working. If frequency of both informal and formal contact is an important feature of the emergent forms of collaborative working that are central to higher education, then scope is certainly present to design social software and working environments that facilitate and encourage such contact.

But these case study chapters are designed in part also to allow us to extend our understandings of collaboration, focusing on interplay between the different aspects of our model for collaborative working or raising points of tension. What then of hybrid software, software that is neither merely social software nor primarily ordered towards completing a specific task? And what also of ways to combine such hybrid software with working together in a common location?

Such advances are needed if technology is to serve the cohesiveness of a group, or to make virtual communication more pervasive within the academy.

References

Archer, M. (1995). *Realist Social Theory*. Cambridge: Cambridge University Press.
UK Higher Education International Unit and Universities UK (2008). *International Research Collaboration: Opportunities for the UK Higher Education Sector*. London: UK Higher Education International Unit.

Case Study

Turner and Roberts, or was it Roberts and Turner?

GORDON ROBERTS *(a pseudonym)*
The Russell Group in the United Kingdom

Turner and Roberts – that was the order of names on the front page, the last page to be written. I just gasped. I didn't say anything, which I probably should have done, but I just gasped; and thought, 'Well, I know you've eventually done a lot of the writing, but I've done most of the research.'

Early Days

We'd been working together for a major local authority, looking at new-build housing and seeing what was actually happening: who was moving into what, and where the housing was going up. We would go out at weekends to look at areas within the conurbation or to select areas in which to interview. We worked away on this for a while, but then Margaret Thatcher [the then UK prime minister] killed the council. As soon as Turner knew they would disappear, he lost interest in the research, even though I thought we still had an audience. We did continue with the research, but it came to the point where I was doing all the work. I thought this was a bit much, and so eventually I held back on my own contribution. I found it all very difficult, but then I also felt very junior in those days. After all, if things had worked out differently he might well previously have been my PhD supervisor. And then years later we found ourselves together again here, when he was the professor and I was a lecturer. And then it all ended with his name first on the final report.

Together Again

So I was certainly surprised when somewhat later I came back from a sabbatical, and he said to me, 'We've put a bid in to do some work for the government, evaluating urban policy. It looked a bit one-sided; so I put your name down, so that it had more weight on this side and it wasn't just me.' So I said, 'Oh, right, OK.'

As chance would have it, we were called in to work up a full proposal. We had three months to propose how to evaluate urban policy across the board. Basically, the message was that if the Treasury didn't think it could be evaluated, then they wouldn't give us any money. So I was desperate to find ways in which we could evaluate it. I came up with a wheeze, I guess, a model that would be helpful in analysing the government policy; and we did get the funding. Only eighteen months rather than the two years we had wanted, but it was still a big project. We had one research assistant, whereas the main guy there had two other co-workers. Then we had Turner, myself and three research assistants here. So, it was a big team.

We had planned to do the detailed work in two specific regions first. I think this was mainly my idea, as we could then have fed the regional information into the national picture. But Turner, and maybe the Department of the Environment, which funded the project, wanted us to look nationally first. Perhaps he and the lead person were more interested in the national scene. But the only data we would get nationally were gross data. One could imagine that there were plenty of tensions. So perhaps it wasn't too surprising that the model didn't work out particularly well. We didn't have the time to use it, because it had been intended for use on the last bit of the work. But in any case I was up at 3 a.m. writing this stuff, and I guess one of the tensions was that I always thought Turner was reflecting deadlines from the government when there was in fact no deadline. I was killing myself staying up and writing stuff, or getting up early and writing stuff.

But there were certainly plenty of compensations. You learned things about the government that were amusing. On one occasion I thought we should look at where the money was going, although Turner wasn't so convinced. But when our first report came through, the reaction of the bow-tie-wearing committee chair was, 'Oh, this is fantastic. I had no idea where this money was going!' 'Very interesting. You mean taking the fifty-seven places that we tried to concentrate on, there are other places getting more money?' And all we could say in return was, 'Yes, in the top thirteen there are at least five that are not part of this fifty-seven.'

It also seemed at times that we were working against the government. There was one big steering committee meeting where, because this was urban policy, we had virtually every department of the government involved. The Treasury was there; and there was an older Treasury guy and a young buck. Part-way through, this guy said, 'We'd like your data.' I'm thinking, 'I'm not giving you our data'; because if we gave them our data they would analyse them and we would have nothing to say. And our steering committee chair said, 'Well, why would you want the data?' And the Treasury guy said, 'Well, we have other data from your department as well.' The chair responded, 'Did you know they had our housing data?' There was sheer fright at the power of the Treasury. This gave us something to laugh about, and defend.

The final report from this project didn't come out for a long time, but Turner mentioned some of our results in a public talk. The government got very upset because he'd effectively leaked stuff, even though the report should have been published a lot earlier. There is a sort of bonding effect when people are against you. One of the steering group meetings immediately after this so-called leak involved a new member from the Department of the Environment. She went through point after point of our report, finding even word-processing faults. Turner was getting redder and redder. But at one point she suggested we should be doing something quite different, and I said, 'I know you weren't on the steering committee, but we never set out to do that.' That's one of the problems with a steering committee: if you have the same steering committee all through, that's fine, but if people keep changing, those at the end don't know what you set out to do. Fortunately, the original chair was still there, and he said we'd never set out to do that, so it would be inappropriate. That deflated this person a bit, and we were much happier after that. So there were ways in which we worked that were complementary and quite helpful.

So, we found ourselves as a duo working together on plenty of occasions, either getting a bid or defending what we were doing. We did in fact bid together quite well, because you'd go down for an interview and they'd ask you questions. Turner would normally lead off, and then I'd come in; or sometimes it was the other way around. While the first person was answering more superficially, the second person was desperately trying to think of the real answer. When we put in a written bid we'd always save something for the interview. So, we'd start talking, and say, 'You can use this kind of transformation', and you could see that you'd caught their interest.

End of the Road

But the hierarchy was always there. I got fed up after a point, because the government would send invitations to bid only to Turner. I seemed just to be a helping hand. Sometimes he'd suggest a bid, and I'd say, 'It's not that good.' But we'd throw it in because we needed the money to keep the research assistants, and those are the ones that you don't want. Every year we'd be asked for a research plan, and every year I'd write one. And then every year I'd write at the end of the year: well, this came up from the government, or this came up from the Greater London Council, or whatever. So in a way I found that the bids deflected me somewhat from my own plans. I thoroughly enjoyed the urban policy project, except for the pressure of trying to do that at the same time as doing lots of other things, but not so many of the others.

At the same time, though, he was very supportive. On one occasion when we were driving up to Sheffield together, he said, 'Sussex have been looking for recommendations – would you be interested in moving there as a chair?' I almost fell out of the car, because he'd never seemed to be interested. He'd never taken on a mentoring-type role until that point. But he said, 'You've been having views.' Then there was a time when the faculty were having problems getting the next senior tutor. He came to my office one day and said, 'Did you see that notice about the senior tutorship?' I said, 'Yeah, I binned it.' He said, 'I'm in charge of getting someone to do that. I thought you would be the ideal person.' He couldn't get anyone else, classic Turner. I said, 'Well, yes. I'll consider it.' And that started me off in academic administration, which got me into other things. He also very much supported my application for an internal chair. I think he lined up the external, someone who owed him a favour. I wouldn't be surprised.

There came a point when he wanted me to take over our research unit. But by that point I was pro-vice-chancellor, and there was no way I was going to do that. I just thought that if he'd wanted me to take over, he should have involved me a lot more, and earlier. Even recently now that he's retired, he's still been trying to get me involved in a bid again. He still wanted to have my name somewhere on a bid.

Case Study

Networks Down Under

Research Collaboration in the Antipodes

PHILIP S. MORRISON
Victoria University of Wellington, New Zealand

Context

The physical isolation of New Zealand from the denser academic markets overseas calls for a variety of strategies to ensure currency and awareness of what is happening in the metropolitan regions of the Northern Hemisphere. The thick networks that many academics take for granted are simply not available in a country of only 4.28 million in the South Pacific over 2,000 kilometres from Australia and almost twenty-four hours by 747 from London.

This case study explores the mix of collaborations across a fairly typical spectrum of geographical research as exhibited by contemporary staff in Wellington, New Zealand, teaching on the Geography programme at the university. It follows on from earlier research into collaboration within the whole of the university's Science Faculty, which covered international work up to 2002 (Morrison *et al.*, 2003). Increasingly, the academy is turning to the views of the scientists themselves (Hara *et al.*, 2003) as opposed to the heavy reliance on bibliometric analysis which has dominated the collaborative literature to date. In addition to looking at who collaborates with each other, as based on an analysis of over 500 items of research published between 2000 and 2008, we thus also explore the key themes to emerge from interviews with contemporary colleagues.

Who Collaborates?

Our university's Research Master Register records publications covering the six-year period of the country's first research assessment exercise from 2000 to 2006 as well as most of the first two years' entries for the second assessment period, 2006 to 2012. There are several advantages in using such a data set, including the wide coverage it offers of research outputs beyond journals and books covering conference presentations and poster sessions; reports to external bodies, including government; and oral presentations – each of which must be made available for verification should an audit be carried out. Even acknowledging the under-reporting in more recent years (our updating issue), the sheer volume of output is impressive, amounting to over 500 separate outputs over the almost nine-year period for Geography alone.

It is common practice to define collaboration on the basis of two or more authors (e.g. Babchuk *et al.*, 1999). By this definition almost two-thirds of the outputs were the result of collaborations, so that only 3.6 out of every 10 were sole-authored outputs. This is consistent with contemporary figures such as those observed in Canada for social sciences (ibid.). Almost two-thirds of the joint publications by staff in geography were the result of a collaboration of two people, with only 10 per cent of the joint publications involving four or more authors. The instance of collaboration and number of collaborators per publication varied by staff member, ranging from 4.4 to 1.2. For research articles in journals the average was 2.23 authors. The single most frequently authored output is the journal article, over one-third, followed by the full abstract in published conference proceedings (see Table 6.1).

While we are not able to report the full details of an extensive modelling exercise here, it was clear from the modelling that full professors engage in collaboration across the entire range of academics and that collaboration is not necessarily associated with the peer-reviewed outlets that yield the highest return on investment. It was also clear that the subdisciplinary distinction is important in geography, where both physical and social phenomena and the interaction

Table 6.1 The distribution of published research outputs, 2000 to September 2008, over publication outlets

Publication type	Frequency	Percentage
Peer-reviewed		
Authored book or monograph	5	0.98
Edited book	9	1.77
Chapter in book	21	4.13
Journal contribution – research article	174	34.25
Journal contribution research	43	8.46
Edited journal	10	1.97
Often not peer-reviewed		
Edited conference proceedings	3	0.59
Conference paper in published proceedings	47	9.25
Full abstract in published conference proceedings	94	18.5
Conference Poster Presentation	13	2.56
Report for external body	66	12.99
Articles in edited volumes of papers	2	0.39
Oral presentations	21	4.13
Total	508	100.00

Source: VUW Research Master, September 2008.

between them are studied. The technical requirements of physical geography on the other hand did have a measurable effect, with their outputs being over twice as likely to be co-authored. The argument for greater collaboration among physical geographers reflects their greater reliance on particular specialisms. Also, physical geographers are more likely to apply a quantitative methodology, and the evidence suggests that quantitative research is more likely to be performed in collaboration (Moody, 2004).

Motives for Collaboration

One can, though, ask whether there are other possible motivations for collaboration if it is not necessarily associated with peer-reviewed publications. The interviews suggested that three major factors drive contemporary collaborations, which I condense here as the three Cs: complementarity, creativity and collegiality. Together they explain a great deal about the way that collaborations work in New Zealand, but they also take a particular twist because of our physical isolation.

Complementarity

As Adam Smith observed, the division of labour is a function of the size of the market. In a country whose population hardly exceeds that of a second-tier metropolitan centre in the Northern Hemisphere, the local market is small, and maintaining a narrow specialization is very difficult. Academics in New Zealand spend most of their lives fighting local pressures to broaden and move into adjacent unpopulated fields. Those unable to resist this temptation, with its accompaniment of immediate local gratification, often pay the price in terms of international recognition.

Maintaining the narrow specialization so necessary to compete on a world market requires the harnessing of complementary skills: the theoretical and/or modelling expertise to drive the interpretation of local data, for example – data that may be unique internationally, or simply different enough to be attractive to academics from the European Union or the United States seeking exotic case studies (*touché*). Complementing personal skills, which may be straightforward in very large metropolitan universities in Europe or the United States, in the tiny New Zealand case requires international collaboration.

Creativity

Creativity is the generation of new ideas and, in academia at least, productivity is the division of creativity by a unit of time (published output per annum). It is difficult to separate any discussion of productivity from research assessment rounds, which are now applied in New Zealand as they are in Australia and elsewhere. Performance in research in New Zealand is based not on depart-mental performance but on individual performance (from which assessments to higher reporting units are aggregated). This places additional pressure on research planning and strategy, and hence on collaboration. Collaboration was widely agreed by colleagues to enhance creativity. Although the international biometric work shows variation in the strength of the evidence on the rela-tionships between collaboration and creativity, as do the results of our own (Table 6.1), the sheer growth of collaboration in the social and physical sciences itself constitutes a strong case for pay-offs.

Collegiality

Colleagues further suggested that they collaborated to secure sympathetic critics – colleagues (in the widest sense) who are prepared to read and comment constructively on a draft. The opportunity cost of this form of collegiality has risen as the research assessment exercises have taken hold, to the point where collaboration and hence joint authorship is exacted as the price. But collegiality is also driven by the need to have someone with similar expertise and interest to whom one can talk. In a small country like New Zealand such people may simply not exist. And the more specialized you become, the greater your dependence upon higher-order centres and the greater your need for international travel. This is one of the reasons why staff across New Zealand universities rarely collaborate with each other – a feature that, we noted in our earlier work, was exacerbated in the early 2000s when *competition*, not collaboration, among universities was thought to be the route to higher productivity. Staff within departments do collaborate in publication but to a much lower degree than propinquity would suggest. From a strategic point of view the pay-offs from international collaboration are believed to be relatively much higher.

Revisiting the Research Register

In the light of the strong personal cases for collaboration, it is worth revisiting our Research Register data again in this case to see whether collaboration (which, as we have seen, is heavily weighted to overseas) is associated with publication in overseas journals, which are typically those more highly regarded in performance evaluations. While, again, we do not report the full modelling here, it was clear within the class of peer-reviewed outlets that collaboration (whether within or outside New Zealand) is positively associated with overseas publication. Collaborative research in peer-reviewed outlets is 1.7 times more likely to end up being published outside New Zealand, and full professors are 4.4 times more likely to publish overseas, as are physical geographers. Over this time period at least, female staff exhibit no discernible difference from their male colleagues. And despite a slight growth in collaboration overall, there is little evidence of a greater tendency over the period to publish overseas. We can, though, say in summary that academic survival in New Zealand does still depend upon collaboration, as the quantitative evidence and the qualitative stories do match up.

Conclusions

We have explored the nature of contemporary research collaboration in a small to medium-sized academic department in the Antipodes, showing how the physical isolation of the New Zealand academic calls for a variety of strategies to ensure currency and awareness of what is happening in the much denser knowledge-intensive metropolitan regions of the Northern Hemisphere. Indeed, we picked out three main drivers of collaboration: complementarity, creativity and collegiality. There is a prevailing belief that when applied to an Antipodean setting they generate research strategies that favour international collaboration, enhancing the global at the possible expense of the local. The result of centring collaborations offshore and the constant quest to render the local relevant to a much larger international agenda may, it is argued, serve to downgrade attention to the local and domestic issues in favour of internationally favoured frontiers.

I would like to end with a short anecdote from the economist Tim Hazeldine in his book *Taking New Zealand Seriously: The Economics of Decency*, because it illustrates the way many collaborations down under just 'happen':

> Four years ago at a conference in Sydney, I ran into a professor from Nashville, Tennessee, by the name of John J. Siegfried. 'So you're a Kiwi,' he said. 'Do you guys have a Rich List in New Zealand?'
>
> 'Of course we do,' I replied huffily. 'We are a modern developed economy, you know.'
>
> 'That's just fine,' said Siegfried soothingly. 'So let's you and I write a paper about it.'
>
> (Hazeldine, 1998: 127)

Acknowledgements

I wish to thank those of my colleagues who gave up their time to be interviewed for this project. I also wish to thank graduate student Eunica Aure for her work in searching the post-2000 literature and in preparing the data for the modelling that the case study reports. I especially wish to thank Sara Kindon, Ralph Chapman, Mike Crozier and Nick Preston for their insightful reflections on their own experience within the academy.

Case-Study References

Babchuk, N., Keith, B. & Peters, G. (1999). Collaboration in sociology and other scientific disciplines: A comparative trend analysis of scholarship in the social, physical and mathematical sciences. *The American Sociologist, 30,* 5–21.

Hara, N., Solomon, P., Kim, S.-L. & Sonnenwald, D. (2003). An emerging view of scientific collaboration: Scientists' perspectives on collaboration and factors that impact collaboration. *Journal of the American Society for Information Science and Technology, 54,* 952–965.

Hazeldine, T. (1998). *Taking New Zealand Seriously: The Economics of Decency.* Auckland: HarperCollins.

Moody, J. (2004). The structure of a social science collaboration network: Disciplinary cohesion from 1963 to 1999. *American Sociological Review, 69,* 213–239.

Morrison, P. S., McDonald, F. & Dobbie, G. (2003). Research collaboration among university scientists. *Higher Education Research and Development, 22,* 275–296.

Case Study

Using a Virtual Research Environment to Support New Models of Collaborative Research in Scottish Education

ALASTAIR WILSON
University of Strathclyde, Scotland

Context

In common with other areas of social research, the past few years have seen a rapid rise in educational research teams using a virtual research environment (VRE) to facilitate their collaborative research activities (Wilson *et al.*, 2007). The need for more effective collaboration has been highlighted in recent years in many quarters (Smedley, 2001; Baron, 2004–2005; McLaughlin & Black-Hawkins, 2004; Furlong & Oancea, 2005) and is based on views about the continuing gaps between policy, practice and research and the difficulties of effective cumulation of research findings. In Scotland the Applied Educational Research Scheme (AERS)[1] has been funded to help build educational research capacity and, crucially, to develop more effective collaboration among researchers, policymakers and practitioners. The AERS structure involved three substantive research networks based in three universities, supported by a capacity-building network and a small management and administrative team. Initially it was envisaged that this structure would be supported by the use of a static website. However, the potential of virtual environments was soon recognized as a possible means of both supporting the research infrastructure and, possibly, engaging more effectively with the policy and practice communities. Working in collaboration with the Centre for Applied Research in Educational Technologies at the University of Cambridge, AERS began to develop a VRE in late 2004 as a platform for a diverse range of research activity.

In the early developmental stages of AERS the VRE was envisaged as supporting individual research teams and providing a platform for these teams to communicate with each other and contribute to their broader network and AERS communities. The VRE supported both individual research teams and networks, including a capacity-building network. The most effective use of the

VRE was made by small, often dispersed higher education research teams, usually of fewer than ten colleagues, working collaboratively on funded research projects. These teams initially used the VRE as a means to collate, store and share data, communicate and manage research administration more effectively. Other groups made use of the environment as a purely administrative tool. For example, one editorial group employed the environment as a means of reducing the frequency of meetings in order to reduce their carbon footprint. As use of the VRE by research teams developed, it proved a very effective research tool, facilitating the sharing of data and collaborative working, but also, in allowing other participants access to the research environment, permitting new forms of participation in the research process. This provided researchers with new forms of data and challenges to analysis. The VRE also offered a potential means of engaging policymakers, practitioners, pupils and higher education staff in different forms of collaborative work in education.

The AERS Virtual Environment

Figure 6.1 is an example of a virtual worksite designed to engage pupils working towards their Higher exams. 'Worksite' is the key unit within the Sakai virtual environment and it comprises a distinct virtual space, accessible by username and password and equipped with a set of tools selected to support the activities of collaborative groups. As is illustrated in Figure 6.1, the tools are presented on the left-hand side tool panel and include various synchronous and asynchronous communication tools (e.g. Discussion forum, Chat Room, Announcements, Email Archive, Mail Tool, or a Blog). In addition, the worksite can offer tools geared to support collaborative working, including a Resources area for sharing and storing digital files (texts, audio, video, etc.) and a Wiki tool for collaborative writing. There is also an integral Schedule for organizing dates and deadlines. A web content tool enables the collation of relevant

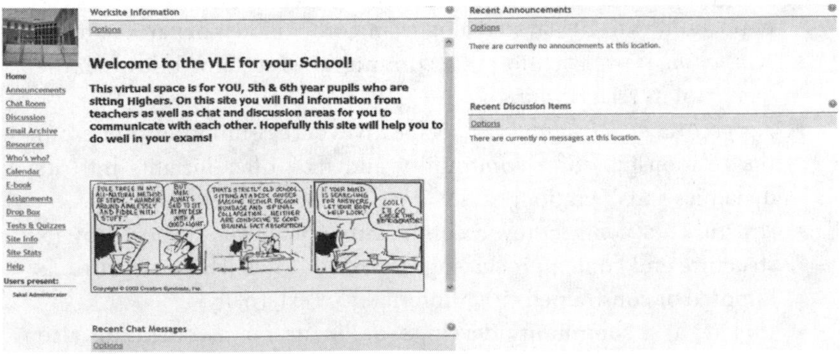

Figure 6.1 Example of a virtual worksite from the AERS project.

external websites, which can be accessed without users having to leave the Sakai environment.

Access to the environment is password controlled, which makes it a secure collaboration space. The worksites can be either private, available only to those registered on the site, or publicly joinable by anyone registered in the environment. There are two main types of users within the environment, maintainers or accessors, whose permissions can vary from being equal to being highly differentiated, depending, again, on the purpose of the worksite and nature of the participating group. For example, in school-based worksites teachers can moderate the use and availability of resources for their pupils (Rimpiläinen & Carmichael, 2006).

Understanding and Realizing Collaborative Working

Within AERS, one of the substantive networks, the Learners, Learning and Teaching Network, had a particular focus on developing communities of inquiry involving researchers and other stakeholders. The network developed a dual purpose in terms of providing collaborative groups with virtual spaces, nurturing and, also, researching their ongoing development. To inform this process the network undertook a review of the concept of 'community of inquiry' and of a wide range of related literature (see Cassidy *et al.*, 2008). The review demonstrated the existence of a diverse and rapidly growing multi-disciplinary literature on the subject and suggested the value of adopting an eclectic approach to research on communities of inquiry, including electronic communities and those making use of virtual environments alongside other forms of communication. From a process of progressive filtering and interpretation of the literature, seven factors were identified by the research team (ibid.) as important considerations for anyone seeking to establish a collaborative community of enquiry in the context of educational research:

- *dialogue and participation*: a community depends on its members' opportunities to engage in dialogue and other modes of participation;
- *relationships*: participation in a community is sustained through the quality of its relationships;
- *perspectives and assumptions*: perspectives and assumptions underpin the relationships of a community and may offer insights into its dynamics and operation;
- *structure and context*: how a community operates is governed by its structure and context, including the extent to which its structure is imposed or constrained either internally or externally;
- *climate*: as a community develops, a climate for its operation also emerges, involving aspects such as tone, environment and potential conflict;

- *purpose*: the purpose of an inquiry will influence this climate, and there may be a need to accommodate or harmonize a multiplicity of purposes arising from the complex interrelationships, perspectives and assumptions involved;
- *control*: a key issue for all communities, in relation to who has access to the community, to resources, constraints and power within it.

The network research team used these factors as a framework for initial analysis of emerging communities of inquiry. The findings of this analysis indicated the need for developing communities to have genuine 'relevance of the purpose of the enquiry to the interests of participants and mutual potential benefit in terms of the outcomes of the shared activity'. In addition, the research indicated the demands of such collaborative working in terms of time and resources and the need, where possible, to build on existing collaborative working (Christie *et al.*, 2007). These factors and questions remained in the background of investigations of the operation of collaborative groups that made use of the AERS virtual research environment.

A Vignette from the Network

The following vignette is drawn from one of the research teams using the AERS VRE as a platform both for collaborative research and for engaging with the wider policy and practice communities.

An action research project was funded for two years to develop and explore the potential for enhancing literacies learning for adults with learning difficulties by engaging with their systems of care and/or support. A key feature of this project was the way in which its development evolved into an action research project. The researcher played a key role not only in contacting and recruiting participants, both tutors and learners, but also, crucially, in shaping their understanding and participation in the project. The researcher acted as a catalyst in terms of encouraging and facilitating tutors' effective contact with participants and their carers or support workers. Throughout the course of the project the researcher provided ongoing feedback to tutors, and facilitated meetings between support workers, tutors and a range of other relevant people necessary to progress the aims of the project.

In the early stages of the project a virtual research environment was constructed to facilitate the work of the project. This VRE was accessible via the web to the research team, a representative of the funding body and all tutors participating in the project. It contained a variety of tools such as chat or discussion areas, a file store, an announcement function and a group email address. Tutors were encouraged to use the VRE as a means of contacting and discussing ideas with the research team. In addition, it provided a means for tutors to record their experiences and share them with each other.

As an administrative tool the VRE proved invaluable to the research team. The group email address allowed all researchers and other project participants to keep up to date with communications, which could be sent to all or selected members of the VRE. Emails were also collated in the VRE for reference, allowing participants to keep up to date with communications. Different forms of data generated by the project (interview recordings, film, research notes) were immediately stored in the VRE, giving the research team immediate access. Transcripts were later collated in the VRE file store, meaning that all data generated by the project were collated and easily accessible via the web. In addition, the location of the VRE within the wider AERS virtual environment, protected by login and password procedures, ensured that the data were secure. Such access to emerging data, both in the form of dialogue on the site and stored in various formats in the file store, enabled distributed members of the research team to engage in ongoing analysis. This greatly facilitated the work of the project as an action research project. The following extract from a tutor's diary illustrates the way in which the VRE collated information that was essential to the project's development:

> I [tutor] had a brief meeting with [the carer] afterwards and went through what each of the learners was working on. She said that she had met one of his [the learner's] support workers and asked her if she could start getting him to calculate his own money. She emphasized that he still may need support even if he tried. She also said that when [the learner] goes to the gym she tells him (and the other clients) to get their money ready to pay. [The learner] normally waits with his wallet expecting her to sort it out for him but she's been telling him to try himself. So far she has found that he can work it out on his own but just expects other people to do it for him.
>
> I've said I am going to try and call [the learner's] mum and see if we can get her to encourage him as well so that he is getting reinforcement everywhere.
>
> [The carer] also asked if there was anything extra they could do with [another learner] but I've said for the moment he's doing enough in the group and at home. I've said I'll speak to him and [the carer] is going to as well in case there is anything extra he wants to do.
>
> I've arranged to have a meeting on Monday to go over the VRE.

There was variation in tutors' interest and available time to make use of the VRE, and some corresponded with the researchers using phone calls and email. Where the VRE was used, tutors felt it helpful both in enabling communication with the researchers and as a means of learning about other tutors' practice. For example, several tutors kept online diaries of their experiences of the project, with daily and weekly accounts of project progress and developments. This greatly facilitated the action research dimension to the project as it enabled researchers to clarify issues and respond to emerging difficulties.

As these forms of communication and dialogue increased, the VRE became a vital hub for the research activities. Access to emerging findings in terms of tutor experience of the project allowed an iterative process of inquiry and clarification to develop between researchers and tutors. Likewise, a key part of the collaborative dimension of the project was to assist tutors in working with parents or carers and care providers to support opportunities for literacy development in people's everyday lives. Tutors made use of the VRE to identify opportunities for this to occur, and some of the carers involved in the project used the VRE to correspond and clarify with tutors, an essential activity for the project. Equally, all members of the research team had immediate access to data and were able to observe the project developing. In particular, those leading the research were in constant touch with its development, rather than, as in other projects not supported by a VRE, having to rely on researchers gathering data and reporting at specific project meetings.

In summary, the VRE soon became crucial to the development of the project by continually generating data that all members of the research team could analyse, reflect on and use to shape future steps in the project development.

The collation of tutor material and experience on the VRE was of interest to the funders of the research, who wanted to explore the producing of training materials from the data to help other tutors develop their practice. Use of the VRE enabled the funders to see the project develop, to collaborate with the research team and to address emerging difficulties.

As the amount and nature of the data generated by the project increased and changed, ethical issues had to be addressed in terms of the degree of access that participants had to different forms of data. While all participants were aware of and understood the ways in which data would be stored, used and made visible on the VRE, the research team was not comfortable storing all of the data where they were accessible to all participants. The site was subsequently differentiated into those having research team access rights and others having more restricted access to data. Furthermore, the research team sought to engage participants with learning difficulties, and this raised a number of problems in terms of making the site sufficiently accessible, as well as ensuring that participants understood and were comfortable with procedures. The use of the VRE by this project was not unproblematic and was facilitated by intensive researcher support. However, it provided an innovative and extremely valuable platform for collaborative working.

Implications for Future Development

The developing work of the network has been ambitious in terms of striving to realize new forms of collaborative working, of communities of inquiry, while simultaneously providing and supporting different groups and communities in the use of VREs. Initially this work conceptualized VREs as tools supporting higher-education-based research teams as communities of inquiry. The seven key considerations for communities of inquiry listed on pp. 146–147 were employed both as considerations to be shared with developing communities of inquiry and later as an initial framework for analysis. However, as is illustrated in the vignette above, it is clear that VREs, when used in the context of communities of inquiry, are not simply tools to support group communication and inquiry. They are new environments in which participants engage and generate new forms of knowledge. For researchers, VREs initially offer secure, practical spaces for the organization and administration of research. However, experience within AERS indicates that as their use develops, researchers have realized their potential as environments providing alternative ways of conducting research and of engaging with participants and practitioners. Such activity has, then, generated new forms of data and new opportunities for collaborative analysis – particularly crucial to dispersed research teams.

Practitioner use of VREs has been less straightforward, with barriers, such as demands on practitioner time and access to adequate IT support, affecting their engagement. The experience within the network is that practitioner use of VREs needs recognition as a legitimate, alternative and effective way of collaborative working. While engagement with policymaking communities is developing more slowly, early analysis indicates the ways in which VREs can offer channels for communication and dialogue that provide a new and immediate interface between policymakers and practitioners. Research within the network indicates the use of VREs as potentially transformative to the processes of collaborative inquiry and research in education.

Case-Study Note

1.   The Applied Educational Research Scheme (AERS) is a five-year programme of research funded by the Scottish Executive Education Department and the Scottish Funding Council. The AERS aims to build educational research capacity in Scotland and to harness that capacity to carry out high-quality research relevant to the Scottish National Priorities in Education.

Case-Study References

Baron, S. (2004–2005). The Applied Educational Research Scheme: A real opportunity for Scottish educational research. *Education in the North, 12,* 41–44.

Cassidy, C., Christie, D., Coutts, N., Dunn, J., Sinclair, C., Skinner, D. & Wilson, A. (2008). Building communities of educational enquiry. *Oxford Review of Education, 34* (2), 217–235.

Christie, D., Cassidy, C., Skinner, D., Coutts, N., Sinclair, C., Rimpiläinen, S. & Wilson, A. (2007). Building collaborative communities of enquiry in educational research. *Educational Research and Evaluation, 13* (3), 263–278.

Furlong, J. & Oancea, A. (2005). Assessing quality in applied and practice-based educational research: A framework for discussion. University of Oxford. Online, available at: www.aare.edu.au/05papc/fu05018y.pdf.

McLaughlin, C. & Black-Hawkins, K. (2004). A schools–university research partnership: Understandings, models and complexities. *Journal of In-Service Education, 30* (2), 265–284.

Rimpiläinen, S. & Carmichael, P. (2006) 'Sakai: An environment for virtual research', Ennen ja Nyt 2006. Online, available at: www.ennenjanyt.net/2006_2/rimpilainen.pdf.

Smedley, L. (2001). Impediments to partnership: A literature review of school–university links. *Teacher and Teaching: Theory and Practice, 7* (2), 189–209.

Wilson, A., Rimpiläinen, S., Skinner, D., Cassidy, C., Christie, D., Coutts, N. & Sinclair, C. (2007). Using a virtual research environment to support new models of collaborative and participative research in Scottish education. *Technology, Pedagogy and Education, 16* (3), 289–304.

7

Challenging Patterns of Practice through Collaborative Working

Collaborative working provides an important stimulus for the development of new forms of practice, indeed for innovation. Indeed, the relationship between innovation and collaboration is clearly a synergistic one, and we explore in the round-table discussion how the need for innovation also acts as a driver for collaboration. But in this chapter we consider first of all the way in which a collaboration may lead to changes in practices. We thus look to explore ways in which forms of working that favour emergence actually result in innovations, filling out this aspect of our model for collaborative working in higher education.

All three case studies presented here illustrate elements of challenge to established practice and ways of working. Some of these challenges are rooted in disciplinary identities, some within approaches to teaching and learning, and others reside within the collaborations themselves. All three demonstrate ways in which the inherent adaptability and innovative approach within collaborative working can address a range of challenges within and across the academy.

Disciplinary Knowledge-Making

The first of these case studies, by Jan Parker, provides an illustration of this based on a programme of writing in the disciplines. Initially highly successful, the original programme closed when the forms of *practice* developed were felt to be threatening to the established order on a number of levels, as a result of dis*engagement* from the management structures in the idea and concept of the programme, and when the disciplinary community became less receptive to the developing *professional dialogues*. But we can also see that the maintenance of the *social vehicles*, the networks of committed colleagues in both the United States and the United Kingdom, has allowed the idea of the programme to continue.

The Parker example raises questions for the academy with regard to accommodation of difference and accepted routes to the creation and inclusion of new knowledge within the disciplines. As we discussed in Chapter 1, collaborations can have a focus on the product or the process, or perhaps both to a greater or lesser degree. In this case the process of developing the collaborations between faculty and students was approved of by management and disciplinary communities, initially; but the product of the joint working was not, as in Parker's reflections it was deemed to be threatening on a number of levels.

Some successful collaborative ventures change over time from what may have been a fixed-life, fixed-purpose entity to a different kind of joint working, with potentially much greater longevity and influence. Certain kinds of successful collaborative activity become threatening to others, as some individuals or groups become excluded from the process. Is there a tipping point (Gladwell, 2002) in collaborative activity – where initial short-lived collaborations and associated innovations are tolerated but more long-lived ventures that begin to threaten or challenge the established order are reacted against by those who are not part of the collaborative activity? Are collaborations themselves also affected in this way?

'Are we living what we talk about?'

Our second case study in this chapter also reflects the idea of a tipping point in collaborative activity. The Professional and Organizational Development (POD) Network in Higher Education is identified by Lee and Ouellett as the 'largest professional organization in North America that fosters human development in higher education'. Already posing a challenge to established practice over its thirty-year-plus history 'by providing a non-dominant perspective in counterpoint to traditional academic values', the POD collaboration itself was threatened by increasing membership far removed in time from the ideas and ideals of the original founders. Lee and Ouellett explore in their case study the ways in which collaborative difference can be addressed in order to support inclusion, especially where a group is able to maintain an egalitarian edge whereby newcomers are allowed to contribute new ideas yet respect the attitudes of others already involved.

'Regularity without rules'

Peter Goodhew's case study from the world of engineering demonstrates how engagement on a mass scale – thirty universities on five continents – has allowed a common approach to supporting the teaching of engineering to be implemented across the globe. As Goodhew notes, commitment to 'all or most of the implications of the .. standards', plus the support of the respective heads of department or school, was 'crucial both to the success of local Conceive, Design, Implement and Operate (CDIO) implementation and to the value to be gained from collaboration within the CDIO network'. There is thus a significant challenge evident here to notions of competition between institutions, with the future of the engineering profession as a whole, and alongside the interests of students, playing an important role in this. Clearly, one of the strengths of higher education is that our infrastructure for collaboration, including that of disciplines and professions, provides genuine motives for academics from different institutions to work together.

Room has still been left, though, for individual ownership within the collaboration – 'A number of methodologies of collaboration have developed and it is perhaps the existence of this range of approaches which has ensured success' – although Goodhew also points out, in his discussion of the relationship between the regional and international groups, the potential tensions involved in going too far down this road.

As well as providing challenges to practice, we can see that each of these case studies tackles head-on established notions of collaboration. We can thus see ways in which collaborative working may take one beyond an exclusive focus on the interests of institutions or enable one to confront the values and practices of otherwise dominant academic hierarchies. Even if much of what we do currently within collaborative practice is recognizable as such, and broadly supported and

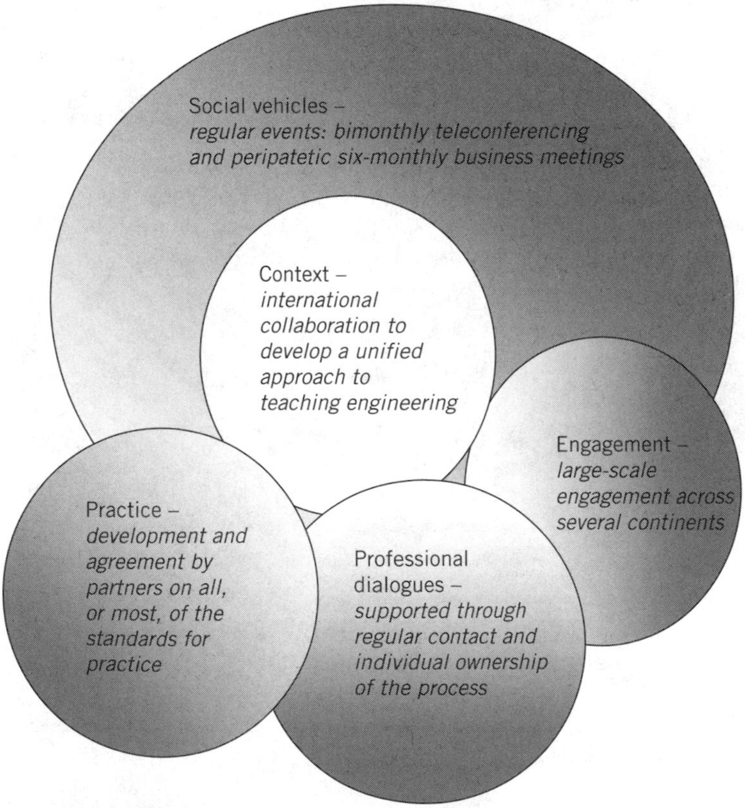

Figure 7.1 Model for collaborative working in higher education applied to the Goodhew case study.

encouraged by management, there is still plenty of scope for collaborative work to address entrenched interests and power relations, even if the outcomes that emerge from such critique are harder to predict.

Reference

Gladwell, M. (2002). *The Tipping Point*. New York: Back Bay Books.

Case Study

Collaborative Academic Work

Writing in the Disciplines

JAN PARKER
Open University, United Kingdom

Context

Research assessment and accountability exercises in the United Kingdom, but also in Australia and South Africa, and increasingly in other European countries, have tended to militate *against* collaborative working. Single-author publication is prized, despite an honoured tradition in the sciences that all those who did the work should present and publish the results. Academics', no less than students', identity rests on individual achievements built into a personal profile.

Knowledge-Making in the Disciplines

The issue is far more than one of an exercise in accountability – for the collaboration that is in question is one of disciplinary knowledge-making. The lone scholar model in the humanities and the magisterial and authoritative journal article both posit knowledge as finally created by a sole voice. Others may have contributed to the project, to the 'work', but the knowledge is created and disseminated in authoritative, sole-author writing. That is what 'monograph' of course means: not 'single worked' but 'single written'.

It was in reaction to this perception that Cornell University's Knight Institute for Writing in the Disciplines was set up. It started with the Nobel Prize-winning chemist who suddenly realized he did not 'do' chemistry and then 'write it up', as his discipline usually formulated it; he 'wrote chemistry'. But that also meant that knowledge was being created in all disciplinary writing, not only that of the professor or principal investigator charged with and credited for 'writing it up'.

The 'Writing in the Disciplines' Programme

The result was a radical experiment in collaborative disciplinary knowledge-making, the Knight Institute for Writing in the Disciplines, which won for

Cornell University the *New York Times* 'Best College' award for two years running. It is usual for US college students to have 'Comp Rhet' classes in their first year; organized by the Composition and Rhetoric staff of, usually, an English department, they are basic writing courses run by non-tenured writing instructors. Assignments can be creative, reflective or in academic writing genres such as book reports; they can aim to develop students' writerly voice, but the focus is on development and the correction of basic skills of grammar, punctuation and argument. The underlying model is the same as that developed in Europe as 'English for Academic Purposes': that writing is an applied and essentially context-free skill whose appropriate deployment can be taught.

Writing in the Disciplines, rather, built a community of practice as well as of discourse on a radically different concept: that first-year students as well as senior professors make meaning in their writing. Rather than the professor making knowledge and the student absorbing it, all can be brought into a common, discipline-renewing activity. To turn this vision – of academic collaboration across all levels of faculty (including research students, who were brought into the institute as Endowed Junior Fellows) and all four years of student cohorts – into reality required collaboration of a different kind. It required endorsement of the vision by senior administration – the president and university committee chairs – and by a benefactor. In fact, it seems that they were easily convinced, and the John S. Knight Institute was founded. It attracted extremely prestigious senior academics (the book *Writing and Revising the Disciplines*, edited by the director of the institute, makes fascinating reading about how and why they became involved), and the competition from research students to be accepted onto the summer 'training' school was fierce.

The problems came in the ongoing implementation of the programme. These problems were due to external factors but also, perhaps, arose as the collaboration became so established and well regarded that it became threatening to those not already involved. But before returning to the history of the institutional collaboration that was necessary to keep the project – and any project? – alive, I want to turn back to the multilevel academic collaboration I saw working.

As befitted the overarching belief – that disciplinary knowledge is a collaborative meaning-making exercise – the 'writing in each discipline' involved disciplinary writers at all levels. 'Writing-intensive' courses – disciplinary courses focused on the students as practitioners of the discipline and focused around topics developing and questioning the knowledge-making (rather than -acquiring) in the discipline – ran for all four years of the undergraduate course. Unusually, these courses departed from the almost universal 'Harvard System' whereby the senior academic lectures to large cohorts, and the 'teaching' – the small-group work, the grading of assignments – is left to graduate student 'teaching assistants' with no role in planning the course. The Writing in the Disciplines courses, rather, were quintessentially the idea of the teacher, who designed the course, set the reading and assignments, and marked both formative papers (response papers, reflective logs, venturesome disciplinary writing of all sorts) and a summative term paper. Although without the underpinning theoretical consideration of the 'aligned curriculum', the teacher was also encouraged to design an integrated course where weekly writing assignments were capped or patched into something greater. But, much more radically, each entered the programme to think through again the relationship of writing in their discipline. This involved proposing and teaching often quite innovative courses. But, more, it involved them in a larger movement to develop writing in their discipline.

An essential element in the Knight Institute's programme was the development of Institute Special Fellows. Any research student can submit a proposal for a 'writing in her/his discipline' course and can over two weeks in summer work with senior faculty and institute staff to refine and develop the submission. At stake are named, endowed research student fellowships, and the acceptance into the programme of the course that the research students have worked so hard to develop. The involvement of discipline 'stars' in the development of both their own and research students' courses is, as far as I know, a unique academic collaboration in developing not just innovative courses but also innovative explorations of disciplinary knowledge-building.

One physicist decided to start with what it was to popularize physics, be it Great Physicists' 'autobiographies or Feynman's or Hawking's 'popular' accounts. After critical and reflective writing on such topics, the students were asked to 'write up' a set of data for *Nature*. In 500 words. Then in 250 words. What it is to communicate physics, and what physics is communicated, was the rationale for the course. An anthropologist teaching a course entitled 'Constructing Gender' built that into one about representations: the students' own and their reaction to and modulation of texts by feminists and queer theorists when asked to give their own 'take' on their reading. Constructing Gender, that is to say, became the medium as well as the matter of the course: how gender is constructed in texts and what then happens in the 'gendered' reader.

'Troublesome Knowledge' in the Disciplines

Such courses were evaluated and their outcomes researched; they were very highly rated by students and enjoyed by staff and students alike. But the importance of the collaboration across academic levels is an epistemological as well as a pedagogical one. Senior professors and research students writing their doctorates (which have to be a significant contribution to disciplinary knowledge) alike report that designing such courses forces them into asking the most central questions about their discipline's meaning- and knowledge-making processes. Students spend the semester asking and answering such questions, and some of their answers can change, perhaps profoundly, their professors' understanding of the discipline that they may have fronted for a decade.

A different model of what might be happening is Carl Perkins' model of 'troublesome knowledge'. He posited that students, especially in subjects such as physics, may come up against a 'threshold concept' that they need to learn in order to make disciplinary sense of the data they are wrestling with. Of course the teacher, seeing this, appends the relevant formula or concept and puts a red line through their writing. But what interests Carl Perkins is what sense and meaning the student makes in the absence of the disciplinary concept he or she lacks. This 'troublesome knowledge' is potentially troublesome to the discipline because it makes an alternative meaning that the student's more 'disciplined' teachers would not be able to generate for themselves. The next great paradigm shift, said physicist Perkins, may come from some such alternative meaning-making.

The Writing in the Disciplines programme, rather, involves senior professors, doctoral teachers and students in making 'collaborative troublesome knowledge'. The writing is shared with the group, the questions put back to the discipline constantly present; many senior faculty reported that their ideas had been in some ways turned upside down by their involvement in the programme.

For writing in the discipline to contribute to the knowledge-making of the discipline, it has to reach and affect all levels of the discipline community. A not very creditable, though traditional, route is for the professor to publish the results of a collaboration with junior faculty as his or her own, with their names lined or relegated to footnote acknowledgement. The multilevel collaborations in Writing in the Disciplines are published under the students' name in a special Cornell journal and often in disciplinary journals.

The key to the successful integration of all levels of students and academics in the programme came from skilful mediation and facilitation by the 'writing development' staff at the institute, who were in fact operating also as academic developers. The institute provided coordinators who were expert both in writing and in disciplinary understanding. The coordinators mediated between institute and disciplinary staff, co-designed and taught joint courses, and ran doctoral students' training courses. Equally important was the directorship of the institute – a recognized academic, he could constantly reinforce the message that these courses were not some low-level, add-on 'skills' courses but, rather, centrally concerned with disciplinary process. As well as publishing and publicizing the involvement of senior academics, he ran an annual international five-day consortium where the 'Cornell Method' was critiqued, investigated and frankly evangelized to institutions in North America and Europe. Importantly, he set up research and evaluation projects that were properly reported to the academic community of writing researchers and educationalists. Several doctoral students completed theses on aspects of the project: it looked like and was a major research project.

'Space for a backlash'

The importance of disciplinary validation and of a skilful and high-profile director became clear when both were removed. Circumstances and policies changed, central university support became less univocal and opposition started to grow. In a development that can be recognized in several cases in the United States and one high-profile one in the United Kingdom, the withdrawal of central committee backing made space for a backlash. In the United Kingdom the relevant academic development/disciplinary research centre staff were moved off academic contracts, emphasizing that even the Professor of Higher Education Studies should see himself as a servant of the disciplinary academics, not a peer. The parallel US cases – of a free-standing academic unit being cut back to a service function – may equally be the result of a concatenation of circumstances, personal and political. But in any case it brings to the fore a prejudice *against* the collaborative meaning-making described in this case study, of which all of us who so clearly see the benefits must be aware.

Prejudices are rarely overtly expressed, but some of the factors in trying to limit such collaborations seem to include:

- A sense of threat, personal and institutional. Such initiatives are outside the experience of many academics, who will usually have been stars in a conventional system. Alternative research, teaching and writing projects demand flexibility of approach to one's academic practices and in turn energy and openness to the new. In pressurized times, that can be a lot to ask.
- A sense of threat to academic standards. The conventional model of knowledge acquisition and accretion is a top-down, 'another brick in the wall' one: the professor or principal investigator lays out the problem to be solved and is responsible to the funding authorities that it is solved. Collaborative working involves a certain laying down of authority; collaborative knowledge-making much more so.
- A sense of threat to disciplinary standards. While disciplinary knowledge is seen as owned by senior academics and validated by publication in peer-assessed journals, knowledge production and transmission is 'safe'. It is acquired by undergraduates, engaged with by Master's students and added to by trainee academics – that is, doctoral students. The expression of such knowledge is also canonical and bounded – the undergraduate essay, the Master's dissertation, the PhD thesis. All are single-voiced documents submitted for assessment to and by the 'masters' of the discipline (the craftmaster–apprentice model). Collaborative working of any sort threatens such a system; collaborative meaning-making between master and apprentice even more so! It can seem peripheral; if it is adopted by the discipline, then it is even more to be feared as taking the discipline into other directions.

Conclusion

Many of those who were part of the programme or the annual consortium still keep in touch. Several of the doctoral Endowed Fellows are now, as tenured disciplinary faculty in other institutions, trying to implement a version of the programme in their new institutions. Participants in the consortia have set up programmes of the own – Johns Hopkins and Dartmouth in the United States and Queen Mary College London, notably (www.thinkingwriting.qmul.ac.uk). Reunions are marked by nostalgia but also the recognition that something remarkable happened. Once one has been part of such a collaboration – one that brought together writing developers and disciplinary staff, that encouraged cross-fertilization between student and professor, that gave structured support but essential autonomy to doctoral students, that involved all kinds of support staff, disciplinary academics and international partners in a common vision – it is hard to go back to being a lone scholar, gate-keeping journal editor and module deliverer. Radical collaborative academic work, with a shared vision and common purpose, is difficult to set up and even more difficult to forget.

Case-Study References and Further Information

Monroe, J. (2001). *Writing and Revising the Disciplines.* Ithaca, NY: Cornell University Press.

Perkins, D. (2006). Constructivism and troublesome knowledge. In J. H. F. Meyer & R. Land (eds) *Overcoming Barriers to Student Understanding: Threshold Concepts and Troublesome Knowledge.* Abingdon, UK: Routledge.

Thinking Writing: A guide to writing-intensive teaching and learning. Online, available at: www.thinkingwriting.qmul.ac.uk (accessed 22 December 2008).

Case Study

Collaborative Workings within Communities

The POD Network in Higher Education

VIRGINIA S. LEE
Higher Education Consultant

MATHEW L. OUELLETT
University of Massachusetts Amherst

Context

The Professional and Organizational Development (POD) Network in Higher Education is the largest professional organization in North America that fosters human development in higher education through faculty, instructional and organizational development. Central to POD's philosophy is belief in the value of people as individuals and members of groups, and a commitment to lifelong, holistic, personal and professional learning, growth and change for the higher education community. Further, POD believes that the development of students is a fundamental purpose of higher education and requires an orchestrated response on the part of colleges and universities. To support a faculty prepared to respond effectively to rapidly changing student needs, faculty and educational development opportunities in key areas, including teaching and learning, advising, leadership and management, are essential.

The POD Network provides support and services for its members through publications, conferences, consulting and networking; offers services and resources to others interested in faculty development; and fulfils an advocacy role, both nationally and internationally, seeking to inform and persuade educational leaders of the value of faculty, instructional and organizational development in institutions of higher education.

How the Collaboration was Established and Sustained

POD began more than three decades ago when Bill Bergquist (Council for the Advancement of Small Colleges) and Bert Biles (Center for Faculty Evaluation and Development, Kansas State University) organized a T-group at a workshop on faculty development at the College of Mount Saint Joseph (Cincinnati, Ohio) in 1976. At this same conference, Jack Lindquist held a plenary calling for the creation of a formal organization dedicated to professional and organizational development in higher education. Interest in the organization was sufficiently high that about twenty people at that meeting contributed dues for it immediately.

POD was formally created two months later in March 1976 at the annual meeting of the American Association of Higher Education. At this same meeting, Joan North was appointed as POD's first coordinator (now president), the Core Committee (i.e. POD's board) was created, and members agreed to sponsor an annual workshop or conference.

Key Characteristics of the Collaboration

According to Bergquist (1992), the emergence of a developmental perspective in the culture of the academy (of which faculty development is a conspicuous exemplar) arose out of the ferment of the 1960s human potential movement as a direct answer to the perceived inadequacies of the dominant culture of most research universities and liberal arts colleges. In other words, our work as faculty developers is inherently and historically countercultural. The emphasis we place on human growth and development contrasts sharply with the legacy of the German research university: the objective, analytic and experimental ways of knowing (cf. Parker Palmer), supported by the research agenda of the academic disciplines. In this emergent developmental culture, for example, collegiality trumps autonomy; autonomy is a core value from the Oxford and Cambridge University models of education from which our liberal arts colleges derive (Lee, 2008).

By the nature of their roles, early POD members often worked on their campuses as sorts of 'one-person bands'. When members came together at annual conferences, there was therefore a real desire for community. At POD conferences, members found colleagues who understood the challenges of working as an insider or outsider on one's campus and the challenges of swimming against a current that privileged research over teaching. POD was both a disciplinary home for early faculty developers (providing support, sharing resources, finding innovative ideas, and offering social support and affiliation) and the incubator for the development of the field writ large.

POD members have long prized organizational norms that emphasize innovation in teaching and learning, self-growth, collegiality and mutual helpfulness. As well as participating in the development of the core models of practice and the literature of faculty development, over the years members created organizational traditions addressing members' social and relational priorities such as having fun together (Saturday night dances at the annual conference), respectful and inclusive decision-making (the POD 'nod'), and a high-spirited celebration of innovation and creativity (the Innovation Award, an unfortunate-looking lamp passed along annually to the next winner).

Related to POD's commitment to pedagogical innovation and honouring diverse learning styles is a strong belief in the importance of honouring social and cultural diversity within the organization. Many early POD members brought to the organization strong social activist roots and commitments to organizational change and development in higher education. These commitments have evolved with the times. As a result, POD has played a critical role in teaching and learning in higher education over the decades by providing a non-dominant perspective in counterpoint to traditional academic values (i.e. individualism, specialization and personal autonomy).

Working Practices Involved in the Collaboration

Today, POD has grown to an organization of about 1,800 practitioners of faculty and educational development professionals in colleges and universities. Members continue to be drawn predominantly from the United States, with the number of members from other countries increasing slowly. POD continues to operate on a volunteer system that includes fifteen active committees; a nineteen-person Core Committee that meets twice annually; an executive committee comprising President, President Elect, Past President, Executive Director and Chair; a Finance & Audit Committee that acts on behalf of the Core between meetings; and, most recently, a central office run by a paid Executive Director. The work of POD is sustained through an annual conference, a highly active listserv, an energetic volunteer committee structure, publications, and much informal interaction and collaboration between members.

Learning Points

Since our origins, teaching and learning have moved more centrally into the higher education agenda, and the field of educational development has become far more complex. Sub-fields such as the scholarship of teaching and learning and assessment and accountability have sprung up and quickly become more sophisticated. High-end technologies have opened up an array of platforms for learning, and issues such as globalization and the growing diversity of college students are changing the very nature of higher education (Lee, 2008). Consequently, faculty development centres today respond to an increasingly complex set of campus-wide challenges and constituencies.

With growth in membership and the scope of faculty and educational development, critical tensions have developed within POD's collaborations in three key areas: consensus and leadership; becoming a more multicultural POD; and the need to expand organizational capacity to support POD's values, vision, mission and goals.

Consensus and Leadership

Recently the convergence of several factors has challenged POD's historical commitment to consensual decision-making and a collaborative leadership model with a one-year rotating presidency and a volunteer Core Committee and committee structure. As POD membership has grown, more and more people are coming into the organization unfamiliar with its history and culture, and the spirit of the founding members. They come from increasingly complex institutional environments with mounting pressures on centres to provide more programmes and services on their own campuses, often with fewer resources. At the same time, with the increasing sophistication and complexity of the field of faculty and educational development there are an increasing number of interesting opportunities, both nationally and internationally, to contribute to the field in important ways and achieve recognition. Consequently, as POD confronts a more complex environment with more opportunities to which it could respond, its volunteer leaders, increasingly pressed for time, represent an ever-widening range of values, motivations for participation, expectations, and preferences in communication and leadership style. Under these conditions, conflict is a certainty.

More recently, POD has struggled with individuals assuming leadership roles who hold a more individualistic and entrepreneurial perspective and more traditional views of advocacy and persuasion (as opposed to building constituencies and consensus). As a result, open conflicts between a range of co-leaders, Core members and individual members have pockmarked recent work of the Core. In addition, some members have different aspirations for the mission of POD, such as desires to see the organization take on an increasing advocacy role nationally and internationally. POD has also seen the emergence of a greater presence of independent education consultants clearly committed to developing entrepreneurial opportunities, both domestically and around the world, and to using POD as a platform to accomplish this.

Finally, communication between face-to-face meetings, so central to cohesion in the past and necessary in order to get things done, has presented difficulties with the growth of the organization. While email and other modes of electronic communication such as online conferencing software have enabled meaningful interchange between face-to-face meetings, virtual communication poses challenges when it becomes the primary mode of communication among people who do not know one another very well. In addition, members have varying levels of commitment to the online process and tolerance for extended email exchanges around complex issues that require well-considered decisions. There are also varying perceptions of what levels of etiquette and collegiality may be appropriate in different online contexts and relationships. Specifically, unanticipated degrees of incivility have dogged isolated, but central, interchanges between Core members, executive committee members and online participants, skewing organizational dynamics and causing disequilibrium and ill-feeling. Governed by past practices and a still-vigorous commitment to collaboration, POD has responded to such flaming with informal mentoring and, more recently, direct feedback, as well as a larger call to POD members to consider values embedded in our communication style preferences (Ouellett, 2008).

Multicultural Organizational Change and Development

Related to the tension in values detailed in the previous section are efforts to create a more multiculturally inclusive POD. One example of this tension emerged at a national conference in the late 1990s. In the midst of a move to reinvigorate POD's commitment to research efforts, the annual conference organizers invited a plenary speaker much admired for his research acumen. In the course of his presentation, this speaker made remarks that members of the audience viewed as clearly racist. When questioned by participants about his comments, he became defensive and eventually left the conference early. To hear a senior white academic make such comments from the podium (whether intentional or unconscious) seemed to exemplify a collision between our long-standing commitments to social justice and diversity and tradition-bound higher education practices and values. The moment became an important milestone in POD's pathway to becoming a multicultural organization as conference organizers and Core worked to find appropriate responses in the context of the conference.

Budget allocations for travel grants have became another site for conflict. POD initially funded the programme to support the participation of under-represented groups in educational institutions within the United States (historically black colleges and universities, Hispanic-serving institutions and Native-serving colleges). More recently, some members have advocated that we allocate similar organizational resources to encourage the internationalization of POD by supporting travel grants for participants from overseas countries. At the root of these discussions are differences in values and priorities, both personally and for POD's future direction. The question 'are we living what we talk about?' becomes unavoidable.

Our commitment to collaboration demands that we create the time to support a sustained dialogue about what we are doing and to bring as many perspectives as possible into the dialogue. The central challenge playing out in these conflicts is how we might effectively adapt our traditions (or create new traditions) to sustain the organizational qualities that have made POD such a unique and powerful experience for members (e.g. commitment to collaboration, inclusion, generosity and mutual respect) while expanding and diversifying our membership and continuing to develop the organizational infrastructures required of a much larger, more complex membership and mission.

Examples of Collaborative Strategies in Action

POD values collaborative strategies because we have seen them in action and can attest to their efficacy. For example, POD's Diversity Committee has provided members with opportunities for self-reflection and growth rather than becoming enmeshed in the politics of a cause or advancing a particular cause within the organization or nationally. While this is accomplished in a number of ways, two examples illustrate our commitment to self-growth and capacity-building especially well. The first is our long-standing history of sponsoring experiential pre-conference workshops and concurrent sessions designed to encourage participants to explore affective domains of teaching inclusively (i.e. values, beliefs, residual feelings based on prior experiences) to better understand the preconceptions of and patterned responses to others we bring to the teaching environment and to the instructional development consultation process. Through these efforts we regularly mentor each other's capacities and skills. The second example is our ongoing adherence to models of multicultural organization development within POD and the Diversity Committee as a model for building centres for teaching and for other initiatives to build institutional capacity for diversity. Similarly, POD as an organization has avoided advocating a particular teaching method in favour of best practices supported by research and a catholic, or inclusive, method in both practical and research-based strategies.

Our succession of leadership (i.e. the one-year rotating presidency with the President Elect, President and Past President serving concurrently and a staggered three-year term for Core members) and the success of the organization under it also testify to the effectiveness of collaborative strategies. Developing strategies include carving out more time for leadership development; sharing common readings consistent with POD values (e.g. Diana Chapman Walsh's *Trustworthy Leadership*); and having a member of the Executive Committee call new Core members, bring to the surface their concerns about Core membership and find out their interests in serving the organization. We are also investigating ways of clarifying our values as an organization, linking these more explicitly to our mission, creating a more extended narrative around both our mission and our values, and finding ways to share the narrative and make it more visible to the wider membership (e.g. the website, a newsletter, conferences).

At the same time, as a volunteer organization with increased scope and scale we need to build organizational capacity in any number of ways. These ways include creating clearer lines of reporting, greater accountability, and organizational efficiencies that respect the burgeoning responsibilities of our volunteer leadership. With growth in membership over the past several years, we now have a larger budget, more complex finances, and financial assets that we need to manage for the benefit of the organization. Among other things, we need to develop ways to identify programmatic priorities and align them with our budget. In this context, the organization's strategic plan and widespread investment in the plan have become even more important as we try to ensure organizational integrity both in the present and as the organization moves forward with a one-year term, rotating volunteer presidency. Doing all of this while still preserving the core values that are central to POD's organizational identity is very challenging.

Our developing plan to build organizational capacity comprises both structural and financial components. Structural components include contracting with a paid Executive Director five years ago to manage POD's central office and support the volunteer Core Committee; re-examining the roles of the members of the Executive Committee, particularly the President Elect and Past President, and the relationship between the Executive and Core Committees; strengthening POD's committee structure; and creating additional strategies for rewarding and recognizing the considerable efforts of our volunteer membership and extraordinary service to both POD and the field of faculty and educational development. Financial components include establishing an ongoing relationship with an accountant and providing additional financial training to the Executive Director; conducting monthly online finance meetings with the Executive Director, President, and Chair of the Finance and Audit Committee; segregating funds earmarked for specific purposes and establishing clear guidelines for the management of each fund; and investigating ways of diversifying POD's revenue stream, including the establishment of a gifting programme and an endowment.

A very recent effort to strengthen POD's strategic planning process is a good illustration of how we are trying to orchestrate clarification of values and organizational priorities with appropriate structural and financial supports. While POD has had a five-year strategic plan for many years, we have never really linked it to a detailed long-range plan and corresponding five-year budget until now. In late spring 2008 we formed a Long-Range Planning Committee to oversee this effort. This committee has assigned responsibility for various aspects of the strategic plan to appropriate committees and issued them a charge in early summer to develop a plan with researched cost estimates of proposed projects in the five-year period. To coordinate the efforts of committees with overlapping responsibilities for a given objective and/or strategy of the plan, we have strengthened the role of members of the Executive Committee as liaisons to the various committees; the liaisons will try to resolve any confusion arising from overlapping responsibility at the Executive Committee level. Once committees have submitted their plans, the Long-Range Planning Committee will consolidate the plans; establish priorities for proposed projects; develop additional revenue streams, if necessary; and prepare a detailed plan and projected budget for submission to the Core Committee at its fall meeting. Because planning in this way is a new venture for us, we anticipate unforeseen snags and difficulties, which we hope to greet with openness, tolerance and patience. In the end, we feel a process like this that balances our traditional commitment to collaboration with enhanced accountability is necessary in order for POD to respond with hospitality to the possibilities of the teaching and learning agenda in higher education today.

Case-Study References

Bergquist, W. (1992). *The Four Cultures of the Academy: Insights and Strategies for Improving Leadership in Collegiate Organizations.* San Francisco: Jossey-Bass.

Lee, V. (spring/summer 2008). President's Message. *POD Network News.* Nederlands, CO: POD Network in Higher Education.

Ouellett, M. (winter 2008). President's Message. *POD Network News.* Nederlands, CO: POD Network in Higher Education.

Case Study
CDIO

A Case Study in International Collaboration

PETER GOODHEW
University of Liverpool

Context

At the turn of the century it became clear in a number of countries that engineering education had become dominated by the teaching of engineering science, and threatened to marginalize engineering practice. In particular, many educators were concerned that graduates in engineering had not been exposed to the full life cycle of the products they were hoping to spend their professional lives developing, producing or improving. The CDIO initiative was created to emphasize the full range of the engineering process – the acronym stands for Conceive, Design, Implement and Operate. A decade later we might have chosen to add two further stages – Decommission and Recycle – but the CDIO label has now become established.

In 2000 the Wallenberg Trust funded a consortium of four universities in the United States and Sweden to develop the framework for a new engineering curriculum which, while retaining the academic and technical rigor of each engineering discipline, reinstated some of the central attributes of the professional engineer. A systems approach to engineering was advocated, and this was intended to apply equally to the process of engineering education. To support these objectives, twelve 'standards' were developed (see the appendix). At the time of writing (April 2008), engineering departments or schools in thirty universities on five continents have formally agreed to use the CDIO standards as the context for their undergraduate engineering programmes. These collaborators form a network of between 100 and 200 committed engineering academics working in a wide range of education systems across the world. In this short case study we report on the nature and impact of this collaboration.

The key characteristics of the individual collaborators are:

- an interest in implementing change in engineering education;
- active engagement in teaching at undergraduate and (in many cases) postgraduate levels;

- commitment to all or most of the implications of the CDIO standards;
- the support of their head of department or school.

The last of these is crucial both to the success of local CDIO implementation and to the value to be gained from collaboration within the CDIO network. There is, evidently, a very clear focus for collaboration, although individual topics for detailed discussion can be quite varied (e.g. assessment techniques, design of laboratories and workspaces for team work, enhancement of faculty skills).

Methodologies of Collaboration

A number of methodologies of collaboration have developed and it is perhaps the existence of this range of approaches that has ensured success – at least by the simplest short-term criterion available to the group: others regularly apply to join, and no school or department has left the initiative. The collaboration is underpinned by two important sets of regular events, which are never postponed or cancelled. There is a bimonthly teleconference among a (quite large) group of 'leaders' – essentially just one or two people from each collaborating institution. Not every collaborator can join every teleconference, but it always takes place and always seems to last about an hour. In the teleconference, agreement is sought (and reached) on such issues as the admission of new members, progress in planning CDIO conferences and meetings, and updates on regional activities. A dozen or so 'core' members almost always participate, but they are defined not by their formal roles but by their willingness to take part. Perhaps surprisingly, although the teleconference has a designated chair, the discussion does not require robust supervision and can be quite free-ranging without disintegrating into chaos. As with many examples of collaboration, it helps greatly that the vast majority of participants actually like each other as individuals.

The second regular series of events is a six-monthly business meeting of collaborators. This is held in different countries, hosted by a different CDIO institution each time. Although this is relatively expensive (in dollars and carbon), its benefits are huge: collaborators meet face to face; they see each other's facilities and workspaces; and they have to report on their progress on agreed tasks only a few months after their last meeting! At these meetings major decisions are taken, nominally by the 'leaders' but in practice by whoever shows an interest in attending the business meetings. Such decisions would include the locations for the next business meetings and the annual conference and (were it to arise) changes to the CDIO standards.

A third series of meetings occur at the annual CDIO conferences, scheduled to coincide with the first business meeting each year. This is a conventional academic conference at which we aspire to be a little more 'active' than is often the case. Presentations, workshops, round-table discussions and posters feature, as at many conferences, but CDIO members try to practise what they preach, in the context of CDIO Standard 8 'Active Learning'. Participants come both from the CDIO community and from other departments and schools interested in the latest developments in engineering education. This provides a very healthy discussion and collaboration base, particularly during the round-table discussions, at which new ideas often emerge.

Three other types of activity have helped to cement many of the collaborators together. In the early days of the collaboration a number of thematic groups were established, with specific defined tasks and a duty to report on progress to every six-monthly business meeting. This worked well while there were only a handful of participating departments and it was simple to define just a handful of themes (assessment, workspaces, curriculum development, etc.). However, because of the vast geographical scope of the CDIO movement it was decided after about five years to establish regional groupings – principally to reduce the cost of face-to-face discussions. There are now half a dozen regional groups (North America; the United Kingdom and Ireland; Continental Europe; Scandinavia; etc.), which are encouraged to have their own meetings and activities. These two approaches do to some extent conflict: it is difficult to manage overlaps between the topics addressed by regional groups while at the same time it is hard for participants (even the most enthusiastic) to sustain active commitment to the international group and to a regional group in parallel. This tension has not been satisfactorily resolved to date.

Collaborative Output

A final powerful example of collaboration was the production of a multi-authored book on CDIO. This project offered a number of key positive points: the collaborators had to set down carefully and precisely the principles, practices and benefits of the CDIO context. This served to clarify ideas while at the same time providing a handbook of guidance for new CDIO adopters and a textbook for our introductory course/workshop. It was also an opportunity to involve, via case studies, some of the more recent members of the collaboration to supplement the core material provided by the original team. Progress and content issues were regularly discussed at the teleconferences, thus informing the whole collaboration of progress.

The benefits of the type of collaboration described here are manifold. Those that I have found to be most useful are as follows:

- It is a powerful driver for the global reform of engineering education.
- It enables learning from the experience of others (e.g. examples of design–build–test exercises, design of laboratories, use of students as developers of learning materials and as guardians of safe practice).
- It provides a worldwide sounding board for our own ideas before we commit to trying them on students (e.g. virtual projects in a project management module, clearing the conventional timetable in order to

run full-time design–build activities, use of simulations prior to laboratory classes).

- It represents a repository of evidence for the success of approaches we propose to adopt (principally in order to persuade sceptical colleagues that we are neither alone nor crazy).
- It provides access to a range of students in a variety of countries.
- It links a network of institutions that would in principle be willing to engage in exchange of students and/or staff.
- It provides an understanding of curricula and systems elsewhere.
- It is a network for my colleagues to plug into for support, career development and reassurance.
- It enables participants to make new friends.

Conclusion

Why does this collaboration work well? I believe that its most important characteristics are as follows:

- It represents a common cause, passionately espoused and to some extent revolutionary – in other words, we join together to fight a common enemy. In most cases the common enemy is the dominant research culture in universities, which leads to the undervaluation and sidelining of teaching – although, of course, many of the participants (including this one) have strong research career paths in parallel.
- It offers a clear agenda for change; the CDIO standards were developed at an early stage and provide clarity in what the collaborators are trying to achieve (although there is no prescription of the method-ologies they might choose to use, or of the technical content of their programmes).
- It has a regular pattern of events (teleconferences, meetings, etc.), so that there is never a period of much more than a month before the next active involvement.
- It has no formal rules.

In a single phrase: regularity without rules.

This particular example of collaborative working has been successful by any number of metrics. The number of participants has grown continuously, and continues to grow. It has survived the transition from a small number of people who knew each other well to an international group in which many participants have never seen some of the others. The group has produced tangible outputs: a book; course materials for an introductory workshop; a website; a repository of useful published materials and evidence; and changes in education policy (e.g. in Sweden) and the beginnings of global reform. Most important of all, it has produced documented improvements in the engineering education experiences of thousands of students. Both I and my institution have gained tremendously from participating, and I believe at least a hundred colleagues around the world would say the same.

Appendix: The CDIO Standards

The twelve CDIO Standards address programme philosophy (Standard 1), curriculum development (Standards 2, 3 and 4), design–build experiences and workspaces (Standards 5 and 6), new methods of teaching and learning (Standards 7 and 8), faculty development (Standards 9 and 10) and assessment and evaluation (Standards 11 and 12). Of these twelve standards, seven are considered *essential* because they distinguish CDIO programmes from other educational reform initiatives. (An asterisk [*] indicates these essential standards.) The five *supplementary* standards significantly enrich a CDIO programme and reflect best practice in engineering education.

A brief outline of each standard follows.

Standard 1 – CDIO as Context*
Adoption of the principle that product and system life-cycle development and deployment – Conceiving, Designing, Implementing and Operating – are the context for engineering education

Standard 2 – CDIO Syllabus Outcomes*
Specific, detailed learning outcomes for personal, interpersonal and product- and system-building skills, consistent with programme goals and validated by programme stakeholders

Standard 3 – Integrated Curriculum*
A curriculum designed with mutually supporting disciplinary subjects, with an explicit plan to integrate personal, interpersonal and product- and system-building skills

Standard 4 – Introduction to Engineering
An introductory course that provides the framework for engineering practice in product and system building, and introduces essential personal and inter-personal skills

Standard 5 – Design–Build Experiences*
A curriculum that includes two or more design–build experiences, including one at a basic level and one at an advanced level

Standard 6 – CDIO Workspaces
Workspaces and laboratories that support and encourage hands-on learning of product- and system-building, disciplinary knowledge and social learning

Standard 7 – Integrated Learning Experiences*
Integrated learning experiences that lead to the acquisition of disciplinary knowledge, as well as personal, interpersonal and product- and system-building skills

Standard 8 – Active Learning
Teaching and learning based on active experiential learning methods

Standard 9 – Enhancement of Faculty CDIO Skills*
Actions that enhance faculty competence in personal, interpersonal and product- and system-building skills

Standard 10 – Enhancement of Faculty Teaching Skills
Actions that enhance faculty competence in providing integrated learning experiences, in using active experiential learning methods and in assessing student learning

Standard 11 – CDIO Skills Assessment*
Assessment of student learning in personal, interpersonal and product- and system-building skills, as well as in disciplinary knowledge

Standard 12 – CDIO Program Evaluation
A system that evaluates programmes against these twelve standards and provides feedback to students, faculty and other stakeholders for the purposes of continuous improvement

Source: www.cdio.org/tools/cdio_standards.html (accessed 2 February 2009).

Part III

Developing the Social Academy

8

Squaring the Circle

Round-Table Discussion on Collaborative Working

We have chosen in this book to explore collaboration in a number of ways through our model for collaborative working in higher education, outlining potential indicators for collaboration and situating our discussion within a framework of illustrative case studies from across the globe. This chapter offers another distinctive approach by engaging two leading figures in the fields of contemporary thought and higher education, Matthew Taylor and Ron Barnett, in a round-table discussion on collaborative working.

We met for the round-table discussion at RSA House in London in September 2008. The discussion ranged over issues such as the context for collaboration, the engagement of individuals, thinking beyond higher education, external partnerships, opportunities and challenges, and criticality in collaboration. This chapter provides the transcript from the discussion, highlighting a depth and breadth of thinking around collaboration as it impacts on twenty-first-century working and practice in higher education.

The Context for Collaboration

Lorraine Walsh: We wanted to start by thinking about the complexity of twenty-first-century working, and to ask you both, perhaps Matthew first and then Ron, to think about this complexity in the way that we work in a globalized world where technology features very large, virtuality, in terms of our working practice. Whether you think this kind of environment lends itself to a more collaborative rather than an individualistic approach to working.

Matthew Taylor: I think there are aspects of current time which don't favour collaboration. On the one hand, there is more explicit competition between higher education institutions, and you could argue that, inasmuch as the opposite of collaboration is competition, there are forces driving competition. Certainly, for example, universities themselves, our sense is that in recent years they've been much more willing to be aggressive in the way in which they recruit star academics as part of global expansion strategies.

So I think there's a kind of set of forces there. I think you could also argue that whilst higher education is being encouraged everywhere in the world to collaborate more closely with industry, in some senses that collaboration with industry makes collaboration between higher education institutions more difficult. Because if, as it were, part of what you're trying to do is to generate value, then again that pushes you towards a slightly more competitive framework.

On the other hand I think there are other forces which drive towards collaboration; the complexity of research drives towards that. And I think the scope offered by the internet in particular, to reduce the frictional costs of collaboration, is an enormous force here. But possibly what that aids is informal collaboration, collaboration of people, emailing each other, visiting each other's websites, rather than the slightly more formal collaboration that one is used to. I have a model, an updated kind of notion of higher education and collaboration being about professors going to conferences in various parts of the world, producing learned papers. And that was a method of collaboration, but now it's something much more informal and ad hoc. There are all sorts of ways of people working together which don't involve them having to engage in these kinds of set pieces.

And then I think the other – and it's interesting in that it certainly seems to be the case in the States and certain areas – is the emergence of new disciplines which span old demarcations and which by their very nature are quite collaborative. But that's kind of written between institutions or between subjects. So you see, for example, in America the emergence, particularly around neuroscience, of a whole set of new disciplines which span social science and science, social neuroscience, neuroeconomics. Now if – and I suspect it will be – the brain becomes an incredibly prominent part of the research agendas, then the fact that this is the kind of area which requires one to span scientific and social scientific insights will be a spur to collaboration. And I don't know whether there are other examples of this in other parts of higher education in the world, but certainly that's an area that I took a lot of interest in and it is fascinating to see the emergence of these new disciplines.

Peter Kahn: Is that more true in the sciences, in social sciences, than it is in the arts? Because the arts draw on more of a tradition of the lone researcher at work in their archive or office.

Taylor: Yes, I think there's certainly less sense that there's a change, and I'm not sure there's anything fundamentally changing the nature of studying literature or studying history, or whatever it might be. What has happened at the boundaries of brain science has been a collaboration which is based upon an intellectual process, which is understanding behaviour and then looking for the explanations of behaviour in the brain, understanding the brain, and then looking for behavioural expressions of the understandings of the brain. So there is a symbiotic relationship between the study of behaviour through behavioural economics, social psychology, the study of the brain through neuroscience, but also part of that conversation is evolutionary psychology, bringing different scientific disciplines to linguistics, anthropology. So I think there's a lot of dynamism in the study of human behaviour and that is bringing people together across boundaries. I don't think there's any kind of similar drive for collaboration taking place in the kind of arts emerging.

Walsh: Ron, what are your thoughts on this? You've written a lot about supercomplexity in higher education. Do you think collaborative working can be seen as a response to that supercomplexity, or do you think perhaps it is as a result of it?

Ron Barnett: A good question. I think I'd just like to start in a more mundane way really, if I might. I want to start by addressing the context. I think there are wider global and universal features of the context here which weigh towards collaboration. Some of the problems facing us on this planet are so mega that they're only going to be addressed collaboratively, both across disciplines and across agencies. So that's the first thing that I think is beginning to be understood.

Secondly, we live in a networked world, increasingly networked. There's an increasing literature on the idea of networking, and, as you probably know, Manuel Castells has developed a name for himself around this whole idea of the 'network society'. We live in a networked globe really, and the way in which academics talk to each other is just one feature of that. You've only got to look at what's happening in the world financial systems and so forth.

Figure 8.1
Professor Ron Barnett,
Institute of Education, London.

We are literally living in a tiny little village – and I constantly feel that, I actually feel it kind of emotionally – it's a tiny, tiny little village, where we're all interconnected. So I think those forces for networking, for interconnecting us, are going to be bringing people together, almost against their will.

And that, too, is driving towards a sense where, as I say, issues are themselves interdisciplinary in character, and it's very interesting what Matthew was saying about the spawning of new disciplines, new fields, which are sort of transdisciplinary in a way. There's again a vocabulary regrowing around disciplinarity, interdisciplinarity, multidisciplinarity and transdisciplinarity. And we've hardly got a vocabulary to describe this messy knowledge world that we're in.

Another feature is one that's been well commented on in the last ten to fifteen years, and that's the growth of what one might call 'knowledge modes'. In other words, our sense as to what counts as knowledge itself is becoming more complex. Michael Gibbons and his associates have developed a thesis about Mode 2 knowledge, which is a much more hands-on, in-the-field kind of knowledge, knowledge that grows out of wrestling with practical problems. It's not a knowledge applied *to* a field, it's knowledge that's actually *in* a field. And that's an intriguing thesis, but it seems to me it's just totally inadequate, it just doesn't go anywhere near far enough.

For example, we have seen the emergence of the virtual world, and the creation of virtual life. Further, people have sort of virtual personas – a sense that professional life itself embodies practical knowledge that is plural in nature; we're worrying about what it is to be a doctor or a surgeon these days. And we're understanding it isn't just a matter of technique. So, picking up on what Matthew was saying, we're seeing the spawning of a new interdisciplinary field around medicine and the humanities, for example. So all this is to say that knowledge itself, the very category of knowledge, is problematic now, and that, I think, is increasingly so. All of these, I think – social, medical, technological and professional developments – are going to make for more collaboration.

And on top of that you have the repositioning of higher education. Higher education now is much more a service for society, and we're trying to work out what that means. And universities are increasingly collaborating with industry, commerce and business in all sorts of ways, and that's giving rise to some very interesting issues about the nature of that contract, that collaboration and what its goals are – what its values are, indeed.

So this interconnecting, this is happening in a practical way as well, but it's giving rise to very nice issues. For example, if you're trying to develop a curriculum with professional or commercial interests, what is that relationship to be? Who is going to define the field and the questions, the mode of the curriculum? So I think there are forces for collaboration, certainly. But I think they're giving rise to some very interesting issues which we're coming to recognize.

Models of Collaboration

Kahn: Part of the context in higher education is that you're working at the boundaries of knowledge, and we see that in the comments here about reshaping what knowledge is. And that demands something of the individual as well: they have to generally give something to make that happen, it doesn't just arise from the coming together, someone has to actually be creative or inventive. And the same thing is true when working with students in the educational side. In order to help someone learn, there has to be engagement from the tutor, the lecturer, that draws the students with them; you can't just manage that learning. So those are two particular features that demand the individual to still be invested in a constant collaboration. So I want you to think about what is it that engages someone's energy and investment, their agency, in making the whole thing work, rather than people free-riding or just following the jet stream or just complying with something? So where does that personal engagement come from?

Taylor: I always find it helpful in exploring dimensional change and people's attitude to change to draw on Mary Douglas's framework, understanding social relations within a prism of four frames: hierarchical, individualistic, egalitarian and fatalistic. I always find that an interesting starting point, and I think that, without wanting to be too schematic, you can apply that to collaboration interestingly. So your reasons for collaboration could be hierarchical, and CERN is an example of that. That is to say, a group of greater people get together and say there's going to be a huge project, and it's a kind of a planned system and if you want to be part of that project you have to be part of the collaboration. So it's very much a kind of top-down model based upon the kind of model of leadership.

And an individualistic model of collaboration is one in which my interests are served by working with others and therefore there's a clearer sense of my career development; the achievement of the particular directives I've got will be fostered by collaboration. And then an egalitarian perspective is one which says that there is a shared sense of purpose of solidarity which drives that collaboration.

Kahn: That tends towards the emphasis, I suppose, we're heading towards in the book.

Taylor: Yes, and so I think that in the engineering case study, you give an example that looks like there's a group of people around the world who share the solidaristic sense of wanting to improve their subject, coming together to do that. But I think you can also see fatalistic collaboration, which in a sense is people collaborating because they've always collaborated and they'll just carry on collaborating, and they've always had their annual conference and they go to the annual conference and nobody ever asks whether there's any particular point to it; you just kind of do it. But one shouldn't. I mean, I think we can talk breathlessly about the new and amazing world, but there's a lot of academics going to a lot of conferences where if you asked a really tough question about the purpose of this, you'd probably find, 'Well that's what you do, we've always done that. We have our journal and we meet together.'

So I would be, I think, sceptical of any model of collaboration which sought to privilege one of those impulses above the others, because I think it would reflect more the idealism and enormity of dispensation with the kind of writers than it would the reality. And I don't think there's any reason to believe that kind of egalitarian collaboration should be privileged above individualistic collaboration or hierarchical collaboration. And individualistic collaboration might have a contradiction in terms, but of course it isn't, you can pursue collaboration if you're entirely self-interested. And that may be, in some ways, the most robust form of collaboration because in those contexts there will be complete clarity about the purpose of the collaboration, for example.

Kahn: But even in a hierarchical collaboration you still want the individuals involved to be investing themselves in what's going on.

Taylor: Yes, they may be – but what I'm saying is that the investment, the sort of quantum of investment, may be the same in each of these different contexts. Maybe my commitment to CERN, because I know, because I've been kind of told to do it, may be no less than my commitment to this engineering collaboration because I love engineering and want to save my solution, may be no less than my commitment to collaboration because actually I think by working with you I can get a bloody good research grant, and so I don't really like you but I'm going to work with you. And I don't think these things should be, as it were, privileged, one against the other. I think they should be analysed coolly, and then you can see what are the drivers of those different systems of collaboration. And I think possibly argue that the most robust forms of collaboration have all those elements in them.

Barnett: I really like that, if I can say so, but of course it then prompts one to wonder if there are other forms of collaboration, and recent bank mergers come to mind; how do we explain that? We might call that a kind of disruptive collaboration; in other words, it happened as a result of major disruption.

Taylor: Defensive collaboration.

Barnett: Defensive is perhaps a better term. Collaboration comes about very often, not only out of a position of strength but as a position of weakness; you suddenly realize how vulnerable you are and you look around for a fellow traveller with whom you can collaborate and shore things up a bit. So I think that is a feature of increasingly turbulent times and you see that in the academic world where universities start to feel the pinch a bit, they look around for a possible amalgamation, and that can spill over into more external forms of collaboration, arguably.

Another word I've jotted down here I've simply called opportunistic. In a market-led environment, universities are having to sing for their supper and generate income, and all that kind of thing. And this may encourage more universities to get into cahoots with people very much on an opportunistic basis: who comes along, who do they think they can do business with at this moment? And those might be quite short-term or quite ephemeral kinds of collaborations, where some of the others, I think, that we are talking about may be more durable.

Taylor: Is there a contrast here between what I'm describing as forms of collaboration and you're describing as moments of collaboration? So I think in a sense if you were to direct those into a theoretical framework, you might say these are the kinds of drivers of collaboration which are universal. And Douglas and colleagues have argued that those kinds of frameworks for social relations are ubiquitous, and can be found in families and organizations and nations. But that, what Ron's pointing at, is that there are kind of moments. So a form of collaboration will, in some ways, reflect the moment of that form, but is it a defensive moment? Is it a moment of opportunism? Is it a highly structured moment? Is it a kind of an ephemeral one? So the moment of the gestation, the moment of the emergence of the collaboration – the point I'd make, I think, is the value of the Douglas framework if you take a recent bank merger. Now it's unclear as we speak whether that's a hierarchical collaboration because the UK prime minister told them to do it. Or an individualistic collaboration in the sense that one bank might think they're going to get a good deal and the other bank has got no choice. But the point would be, if it is individualistic and hierarchical, it lacks an egalitarian basis in the sense that it lacks a kind of sense of common purpose, and it will be vulnerable, therefore. Because if it is merely opportunistic or hierarchical, if the hierarchical leadership goes, or the self-interested argument disappears, then the collaboration will be weak because there will be nothing to sustain it.

And similarly, however, a collaboration based upon a kind of mere egalitarianism will be vulnerable because it will lack the kind of glue of individualistic ambition and therefore it can become quite kind of soggy. And indeed when Mary Douglas applied this framework to higher education, I think she contrasted the London School of Economics and University College London (UCL), and she said unless these are all about egalitarian collaboration, and therefore it's soggy, kind of not thought through, and actually it's not really very real. Whereas at UCL it's a hierarchical, individualistic frame, very, very driven, people are absolutely clear what they want, very strong leadership. And therefore, actually, much more kind of functional. And she was kind of raving against the attempt to assert a hierarchy of frames for social relations and saying actually these are ubiquitous.

Walsh: What we have found in terms of our work so far is that the social vehicle for collaboration and personal investment in something does appear to be absolutely critical. In terms of sustaining the collaboration, in terms of driving it forward.

Taylor: I'm not going to argue against that, but what is the nature of that personal investment? It could be a personal investment for career development, or simply personal . . .

Barnett: I think the category of the personal is perhaps problematic and needs to be broadened out a bit, because once you start thinking in terms of disciplines and fields and institutions, more collective needs and possibilities come into view. So again this example of this bank collaboration, you can see it's in the interests of those institutions almost irrespective of the people involved. So I think when we talk about commitment, I think we want to open up space for broader categories of commitment. I think you can talk about organizational or institutional commitment.

Kahn: So that we have different forms of engagement at different levels, whether for groups or individuals.

Barnett: But going back to the general issue that Matthew was raising, there are issues about the values underpinning collaboration. And I think if you could chart differences and values, that could be helpful. But as I say, there are very interesting issues about how you bring differences and values into a positive juxtaposition. And I'll give you an example of a student paper I'm just reading, and the student actually has an example of collaboration in developing an MBA curriculum between the university and local regional businesses. And that does raise very nice value issues about what a curriculum is for. And that's where much of the challenge of modern life comes in, the extent to which, and ways in which, different value positions can be brought together in some kind of positive relationship.

Tensions in Collaborative Working

Taylor: I think one of the things that's interesting to explore here is the kind of view you take on the purposes that a collaboration serves. The question then is, well what would lead to the suboptimal type of collaboration? And the tendency is to focus primarily, and probably rightly, on the barriers to collaboration. One can argue that collaboration is suboptimal because institutional barriers, frictional costs or whatever stop collaboration from developing. And I think that's true.

However, I also think that you should explore the possibility of suboptimal collaboration coming about as a consequence of a kind of a fashion for collaboration, in the sense that one has to collaborate – which may sometimes have dysfunctional outcomes. I mean, it's a different issue because we're not talking about collaboration, but it has been now well attested that there is no demonstrable benefit at all from acquisitions and mergers in the market. Why do acquisitions and mergers in the market take place? Well, they take place because people who organize acquisitions and mergers make money from acquisitions and mergers.

Now similarly, one needs to look in collaborations as to whether there are brokers – collaboration brokers – who gain from promoting collaborations, regardless of the substantive content of those collaborations. And I don't know enough about it, but I can't help feeling that when there's a kind of epidemic, or there's a huge fashion, you do get dysfunctional collaborations. Every university being required to have links with industry – I wonder how many of those links are kind of daft, to be honest, but they're just kind of led, driven by the fashion. Or the other side of this is the danger that the drive towards collaboration in the field of study means that those who are not part of the collaborative consensus are excluded, to the danger of the development of knowledge.

So it's an argument I understand, either in terms of its content or indeed understand enough about the case on either side. But certainly there were a couple of books last year about particle physics which argued that the kind of hegemonic position of string theory in physics was problematic in the sense that everyone was working in this area, everyone was working on new defined theory, and there wasn't really a space for anybody outside that consensus to get funding, or to be listened to. And the argument there was that in science there have always been two ways of advances taking place. One

Figure 8.2 Matthew Taylor, CEO of the RSA.
Courtesy of David Devins.

is people all coming together, working at a problem and coming up with a solution. And the other has always been mavericks, simply outside the consensus, viewing things from completely different perspectives.

So I think another thing I would kind of urge you to do when you look at collaboration, because the danger is it just sounds like a lovely word, doesn't it? You know, who would not want to do it? But there's a possibility of a suboptimal situation, not just being suboptimal in terms of barriers to collaboration, but collaboration which is not driven by a clear sense of purpose and may, indeed, have a dysfunctional outcome.

Walsh: I wonder if we're using 'collaboration' in too broad a sense. We've talked a lot about – and it's very current in the news just now – about bank mergers. Is that not more, perhaps, a cooperation rather than a collaboration that's arisen out of a real need to react to a situation? Do you see a distinction between cooperating and collaborating, which a lot of authors have drawn?

Taylor: Well, I certainly think you need to be clear about the kind of typology here. Where do cooperation and collaboration ultimately kind of merge? There's a point at which collaboration ceases to be collaboration and actually a new entity is created.

My view is that collaboration implies an ongoing relationship between different entities or different individuals, which is goal oriented. The notion of collaboration suggests to me goal orientation, and it suggests organizations which otherwise are separate, which are coming together, but are not in the kind of process of merging; it is a goal-orientated cooperation. But I'm sure there are lots of typologies or lots of definitions which you'd use, that's something we'd need to know.

Kahn: For us the joint nature of the process is quite important, and this involves avoiding situations where one person simply imposes their view on others. We're not talking about management of higher education; we're talking about a more collaborative process that has a more egalitarian edge to it rather than a fully imposed edge. And that does have certain demands on what's involved. There is an exchange of ideas that maintains that direct process, rather than one person taking direction and the other person or other institution saying, 'No, thank you.' So there's a challenging process to maintain.

Barnett: If universities are being encouraged and required to collaborate with external bodies, those external bodies have huge amounts of leverage. And one is thinking of examples of industries which manipulate academic research to serve their own ends. There are real issues about where the weight of the power relationship lies. We need to be aware of that, otherwise we can talk about values for as long as we like, but in the real world money talks.

Kahn: Our notion of collaboration implies that the parties involved all have some influence on proceedings. Otherwise the process stops being a collaboration and becomes something else.

Taylor: Yes, I would be looking for a further term, I suppose; it depends on where we're putting the boundaries. But collaboration is often used in a wider sense as well, so it's being careful about exactly what we mean, it's quite an important part.

Barnett: There are more scientists outside of the universities than there are in universities. Which again comes back to the position of why collaboration? It's just in the interests of the universities in that sense of if they want seriously to be in certain fields then they collaborate with certain parts of industry. And there are some people who have developed really quite fancy typologies of knowledge production in industry, with this set of relationships having gone through different stages.

There are opportunities to do new things, to be literally at the cutting edge of things, because it's just not happening anywhere else. But at the same time it may bring some difficulties with it. It may, as I say, be seen as skewing the character of academic research. If, for example, there are restrictions on the extent to which the research can be made public, and that sort of thing, then one's into difficulty, we're into issues about value systems here.

Catalysing Collaborative Initiatives

Walsh: Bringing two of these areas together and thinking about external partnerships and the role of older-established bodies in collaborative work, I wonder, Matthew, what role you see, as Chief Executive of the RSA [the Royal Society for the Encouragement of Arts, Manufactures and Commerce], for the RSA to take a leading role, to be the initiator of collaborative ventures across the sectors? Do you see that as being key to what you do, or something that just comes along and is useful?

Taylor: I don't think it's something that we set out to do; I think sometimes the role that we can play is kind of like someone who stumbles into a party of people who are having a huge argument or falling out, or in camps, and doesn't understand any of this and simply says, 'Let's walk in and do something together.' And therefore, almost by shaming people, by the kind of context they create, [they] overcome these things. So if we're doing a piece of work, we will blunder into organizing an event where we will have philosophers and neuroscientists and economists and social psychologists, and kind of say, 'Well, look, you all seem to be interested in this issue from different angles.' And they may become quite horrified because they don't normally spend time with these other people, let alone talking about their work in front of the other people.

We did a dinner a few months ago where we had Steven Pinker here and we had philosophers of the mind in the same room as neuroscientists, and you really kind of felt outside it. I kind of naively assumed these people would

Figure 8.3
RSA House, London.
Courtesy of the RSA.

always be talking to each other because they seemed to have so much interest. Because a neuroscientist had just written a book which raised philosophical questions, and his starting point was particular neurological pathologies and understanding those physiologically, but then he moved on to some quite philosophical musing at the end of it. And of course the philosophers of the mind should, if they've got any kind of pride in their work, should understand sufficiently the kind of physical basis and neurological processes. But yes, these people are in a room together, you really felt that this was two completely different cultures.

So I don't think organizations like us set out to make collaboration happen, but in a sense we are a client. And so therefore I think that's actually what it's akin to. It's akin to the process in which the client says, 'I want this package of services', and the people who want to sell the service realize that they have no choice but to work together because that's what the client's demanding. And so that's the main thing that goes on here, that we kind of foster collaboration simply because we blunder into it, and we're not interested in discipline, we have different objectives in which we're seeking to produce useful work which will change the world.

I think the other aspect of this is that organizations, like think tanks, span academia, policymaking and practitioners, so part of the boundaries which we help to overcome from time to time are disciplinary boundaries, and part of the boundaries are part of the chain which goes from the grand theory through to grubby practical action. A big part of what we did really was getting the academics to come and talk about their work in front of policymakers and get the academics to reflect on the practical implications and try and get the policymakers to think about some rigour in their work. So I don't think it's because we have a mission here, I think it is the nature of us as clients for what's being produced in the kind of knowledge industry, as it were.

Innovation, Specialization and Timeframes in Collaborative Working

Kahn: We've raised a number of opportunities and challenges as we've gone through, but innovation is one thing that sometimes drives collaboration. Is that the need for innovation and to come up with something new rather than something you can produce on your own, or might not quite meet what we need? So that demand, that drive for innovation, is that one of the things that, in higher education particularly, serves to force us to come together?

Barnett: I'd put it slightly differently, moving on from what we've already been saying, that innovation is going on anyway in a complex and virtual world. Everybody's innovating, in a sense, all the time! And so if one is serious about doing serious work, then one will want to collaborate, perhaps because there are other people – and Matthew's given us a nice example – doing work, cognate work, in other fields.

Taylor: You've got two drivers in opposite directions, it seems to me. There is a drive to innovation, absolutely, and I do think that fear and innovation suggests that bringing people together with different perspectives is concretely implicated in successful innovation. And on the other hand, the process of specialization continues and it hasn't stopped. It is still the case that there is a kind of natural process whereby academic disciplines become more and more specialized, that the division of labour within them becomes a bit . . that where one starts with kind of quite simple distinctions, one ends up with the distinction within disciplines which is highly obscure.

So these impulses are kind of driving in opposite directions and I don't know whether . . . but I would imagine, as it were . . . managers, planners and overseers of kind of the academic enterprise have to work with these two impulses which are driving in opposite directions. And I don't think one's going to try and further the other.

Now I think there are some interesting examples of these kinds of innovative processes. Malcolm Gladwell wrote a piece in *The New Yorker* about very interesting methodology developed in the States in which they get together scientists and designers and programmers, and they look at a particular problem all day, in order to, as it were, see whether some intuitive leap can take place.

An example that Gladwell gave was a discussion about cancer, in which a non-scientist in the conversation discovered something that non-scientists had never discovered before, which is that secondary cancers are not caused by . . that if you have cancer, millions of cancerous blood cells rushing round your body, but through a kind of quantum process some of those blood cells will then attach themselves to other parts of your body and develop secondaries. So if you could simply reduce dramatically the proportion of cells, you could reduce the possibilities of secondaries. He had previously had a notion of cancer that a small number of cells, bad cells, immediately latched on.

From this idea developed the notion that if cancer cells are going round your bloodstream, and the blood is circulating incredibly quickly, could you provide, could there be some kind of system blocking those cells, which then led to the development of the technology which is now being tested by two companies. Which is to do with whether or not you can kind of create a filter within an artery, so that as the blood rushes past you can effectively catch the cancerous cells, which are differently shaped and therefore won't go anywhere.

Now there's something very interesting in that process, which is people who are designers are computer programmers when they understand the medical problem, because they push away at it until they understand it in their terms, being able to innovate. But I think the only question is one answer; I think you could argue that the technology of innovation is developing and that therefore what we may start to see is an evidence base for the value of interdisciplinary collaboration, which in the past, as it were, we've done out of a kind of sense of intuitive sense of hope or interest. But it could be that people start to say there is actually strong evidence that putting people together from different perspectives, to work at a problem and a particular process, does actually produce better results. I don't know; we'll see about that.

Barnett: Innovation, that too is a problematic notion, isn't it, when talking about innovation and product innovation and process? Innovation in an organization – one can start to understand that. And increasingly, of course, we're developing tools and techniques and theories, perspectives, in under-standing innovation itself. And those understandings in innovation are increasingly multidisciplinary, so there's that, trying to unpack innovation.

But just picking up on what Matthew has been saying, simply to press the point, that innovation sometimes comes about when you have a clash or collision of different frames of understanding. So the advantage of space that the RSA offers is it opens up the possibility of new frames coming together and colliding. And that's what we're desperately short of, it seems to me, in society: spaces for allowing different perspectives – call them ideologies, call it what you will – to be forced to give an account of themselves to others, to let the light of others in.

Taylor: And of course that begs the question, which I have no idea of the answer to, which is, is the kind of incentive system within academia aligned in the right place to encourage that kind of innovation and collaboration? It's a long time since I was an academic, and I was a failed academic, but it seemed to me that the rewards were all towards ever-greater specialization, more and more abstruse kind of theorizing! And that kind of innovative work we're talking about is not the kind of work which produces academic papers; it produces intuitive leaps. But who gets some research assessment exercise points for intuitive leaps?

Walsh: In your role as a senior manager at the Institute of Education, Ron, can you see – I'm sure you can see – but to what extent are you finding there's a difficulty, the competitive aspect of universities having to carve out a niche in society, but wanting to generate that collaborative and innovative approach to working?

Barnett: Well, there are challenges, which we touched on earlier, about the academic mindset. A research-intensive university is fortunate because it often has people knocking at the door wanting to collaborate, and the question is to what extent can we encourage academics to open themselves up and take more practical perspectives? There are also issues of timeframe, often more practical missions and projects. You come out of a meeting with the clients and you have to start writing the draft report almost on day one! And that kind of approach doesn't sit well with some academics, for understandable reasons.

I think the question of time, time horizons, is another very interesting issue here; how do they play out? And having an increasingly professional life is no barrier to having to operate amid competing in different timeframes, time horizons. That's a very interesting feature and it might be something that the RSA might want to pick up on: how do we organizationally and personally handle and live in different timeframes all at once?

Taylor: I can give you an interesting example of that, Ron. I have seen, when I worked at the Institute for Public Policy Research, the policy think tank, and one was acutely aware of the fact that academic timeframes were not really suitable for policymakers. Academics would want, quite reasonably, would want years to evaluate a policy, and the policymakers are demanding instant feedback on the operation. And I've since seen that think tanks themselves now suffer from the same process, which is that to get a think tank project off the ground you've got to get funding, you've got to employ a researcher. Meanwhile, the UK prime minister can commission a strategy unit to do a piece of work now and have it in two weeks' time.

So think tanks are now caught in the same dilemma that they used to catch academics in, which is that they are too slow off the ground and the policymakers aren't very interested in research institute projects. I partly got out of that business because what was the point? When I was in government I wasn't very interested in think tanks because they were too clunky and too slow to give me what I wanted. I had very clever people who were willing to work very long hours to give me what I wanted immediately.

That is to say that it is simply not realistic from a policymaker's perspective to say, 'Well, let's set up a common intellectual collaboration and come back to me in two years.' So it's absolutely right that different timeframes will foster different forms of collaboration. So yes, absolutely, this kind of clash of time, and I certainly think that in a world of – and I know it's a cliché, but I think it's genuinely a world of accelerating change and complexity, what one needs is processes and intellectual engagement which are real-time.

Walsh and Kahn: Matthew, Ron – thank you very much.

9

A Collaborative Future for the Academy

> And we've hardly got a vocabulary to describe this messy
> knowledge world that we're in.
>
> **Ron Barnett**

Speculating on the future can be viewed as something of a fool's game. And it is therefore not something in which we plan to indulge. However, there is merit in considering emerging drivers of collaborative working, directions of travel and potential areas for development based on our consideration and exploration of current practice. In this concluding chapter we discuss several features of the sectoral landscape that are increasingly affecting our patterns of collaborative working: globalization, inclusivity, emerging technologies, and new and developing disciplines.

As Ron Barnett comments in Chapter 8, 'We are literally living in a tiny little village . . . it's a tiny, tiny little village, where we're all interconnected.' The influence of *globalization* will doubtless continue to be felt, although its impact on practice has the potential to create 'defensive collaborations' (identified by Matthew Taylor in the round-table discussion) as much as those that are more supportive and innovative in their approach. Allied to this is the idea of inclusivity. *Inclusivity* within collaborative working should involve the articulation of professional values and the development of ethical approaches to practice. As part of any collaboration, this should translate into open and honest communication, transparency around processes and genuinely joint working towards agreement on aims, actions and outcomes. The third feature of the sectoral landscape under discussion here is *emerging technologies*, which have much to offer collaborative partnerships, and will continue to have implications for practice in higher education. Beyond improved opportunities for communication with distant colleagues and the provision of a platform to facilitate joint working practices, technology is already offering us new virtual spaces for developing practice, the potential for a redefinition of collaborative working through alternative virtual communities and the opportunity to embrace multiple identities online. *New and developing disciplines* also have a role to play in our discussion, providing further spaces for re-creation of knowledge and academic practice, and the realization of new forms of collaborative relationships. We reflect on the impact of these and related features by considering them through the lens of our model for collaborative working.

Perspectives on Practice

In the round-table discussion in Chapter 8 we posed the question: does the complexity of twenty-first-century practice lend itself to a style of working that is more collaborative than individualistic? And leading on from this: is it likely that collaborative activity will increase or decrease; to what extent will the idea of collaboration be reconceptualized by future colleagues; and what purposes will it be deemed to serve?

Our model (Figure 9.1) demonstrates a number of issues affecting the practice element of collaborative working. One trend at least is towards international collaboration, a move that is driven more than from geographical considerations alone, as we saw earlier in Chapter 6 regarding collaborative working in New Zealand. As we noted earlier, one recent study in the United Kingdom has found that over the past ten years the number of collaborations involving researchers from UK universities has increased by 50 per cent (UK Higher Education International Unit and Universities UK, 2008). Alongside this, employers may play increased roles in curriculum development, and international institutions may be drawn more fully into pan-global approaches to research, teaching and development, with students taking a more active role

Practice

- A focus on global problems

- Exclusion of others through inclusion

- Working across disciplines

- New conceptions of collaborative practice through technology

Figure 9.1 Model for collaborative working in higher education focused on practice.

in university management systems. Joint working between teachers and learners is already becoming a feature of the academy, in a more collaborative rather than hierarchical approach. Examples of initiatives developed within these working approaches include joint conferences between staff and students in order to address key issues, for example, the 2008 Enhancing Student Success Conference held by Newcastle University, Australia; and learning agreements developed to clarify expectations on both sides of the learning and teaching divide, written in collaboration with students and staff, for example, the Learning and Teaching Partnership Agreement from the University of Leeds, England.

But in a climate of globalization, which is becoming increasingly more about 'glocalization' (global perspective, local focus), and its concomitant concerns with regard to finite resources, is collaboration more about risk-taking or consolidating positions? In Chapter 2 we raised the concept of 'competitive collaboration', an example of which can be seen in the Northern Consortium of Universities in the United Kingdom, where higher education institutions, which are all in the market to recruit increasing numbers of overseas students, pool their resources at the information-gathering stage about a new international market but with the clear understanding that they all remain in competition for the potential students. 'Competition' and 'collaboration' are more commonly viewed as being at odds with one other. In Chapter 8, Taylor suggests that collaboration is at the opposite end of the spectrum to competition. Yet it could also be argued that collaboration is the epitome of competition, as it leads to the exclusion of individuals or institutions from the inner circle of collaborative practice, and, often, from associated funding. This may be a changing situation, based on the perceptions and realities of both collaborative and competitive practice, as competition may be giving way, in the face of escalating costs, the need to embed sustainability within practice or the need to develop a solution to a global challenge, to a viewpoint that embraces collaboration as a first, or perhaps only, choice.

Addressing Global Challenges: Researching Wheat Trust

One source of future trends in collaborative working in higher education comes from the academic goals that we look to meet. In this, globalization is indeed likely to play an important role, as problems are increasingly seen to affect the entire world. Not only is globalization resulting in an increase in the range of organizations, foundations or companies willing to address issues of worldwide concern, but coordinated action across the globe is also becoming a realistic possibility, as we see in the following illustration.

World wheat supplies are currently threatened by rust diseases, a problem that is especially acute in parts of Africa and Asia. Indeed, over 80 per cent of the world's wheat supplies are potentially vulnerable to new types of stem rust disease emerging out of East Africa. A problem on this scale can hardly be solved by a single country working on its own, but rather requires coordinated global action. This is where the Durable Rust Resistance in Wheat project comes in, managed by Cornell University and funded by the Bill & Melinda Gates Foundation, with the close involvement of the Borlaug Global Rust Initiative.

The immediate academic challenge that the project faces is to develop new varieties of wheat that are resistant to the emerging virulent strains of disease. This requires close coordination of a variety of research goals, including tracking of pathogens, effective screening facilities, and identification of new sources of disease resistance, for example, from wild wheat plants. Monitoring the spread and evolution of the rust fungus requires different types of expertise, whether monitoring disease incidence through visual observation, collecting samples and recording the location using GPS units, or through straightforward visual observations. And then for stem rust disease, after a disease sample has been collected from an infected wheat plant in a field, it must be carefully analysed, with follow-on infection assays in glasshouses to determine what type of rust fungus is present, and this may be supplemented by DNA marker analysis. Mistakes are easily made at several steps, such as in mixing up wheat varieties, and so it is important to build in quality control and confirmatory analysis to ensure that data publicized are of a high standard. And if this research project is actually to affect the livelihoods and practices of farmers in the developing world, then advocacy, effective seed policies and close involvement with farmers on the ground are all required as well, so that farmers obtain access to new, protected varieties of wheat. Collaboration with a range of partners is thus inevitable in all of this work, with the project involving teams in Kenya, Ethiopia, Mexico, Syria, Canada, China, Australia, South Africa, and elsewhere in the United States.

Clearly, a project of this nature involves far more than allocating the work across these many partners. Consistent and considered ways need to be found to open up communication across divides between elite researchers and small farmers, and between staff in developing countries and the global research partners involved. How does one ensure that a scientist in Canada or Australia is fully aware of the challenges of working with a GPS unit in Kenya? There is a need for all those involved to appreciate the specialist contributions that other team members can make. Brokers are clearly essential in this, but so also are the understanding and trust that can only come from working together in a genuinely joint process or from exchanging views on what matters. Emergent working will be important too, with space and occasions for partners to come to understand each other and develop connections. The Food and Agriculture Organization of the United Nations already has a role in this project, but looking more widely we can also see a role for further social vehicles to help bridge these divides between the local and the global, or the academic and the farmer, in a stable fashion. If we are to develop capacity for addressing global problems, then the social structures that underpin collaborative working also need to reflect this.

For further details on the Durable Rust Resistance in Wheat project, see www.wheatrust.cornell.edu.

The changing academic territory also needs to be taken into account in any consideration of future drivers, where the decline of some discipline areas and the increase in others, owing to the proclivities of research funders, the rise of interdisciplinary working and the unsustainability of single-discipline areas in any one institution, will impact. The effects of the last of these can already be seen where resource-intensive disciplines, such as chemistry and physics, are witnessing the decline of institutional departments and the rise of national collaborative centres of excellence. The ultimate driver here of course is not the decline of the discipline but the pressures of supporting individual units where costs are high but corresponding resource is relatively low. Some discipline areas may, however, be in decline and others on the rise. We saw in Chapter 1 how new academic disciplines are being forged through collaborative working. Allied to this is the professionalization of new categories of staff working in academic environments in areas such as learning technology, academic skills and information literacies, which also open new avenues for collaborative working. In such an environment there may be a move towards collaboration as a first-choice approach to practice, rather than one option among many. The corresponding impact may be significant in disciplines where the personal monograph, and the emphasis on individual interpretation as the acknowledged scholarly medium, continues to persist.

Emerging technologies are already supporting collaborative developmental spaces, for example, through web conferencing and wikis. More complex and sophisticated approaches include virtual reality environments, such as Second Life, where multiple permutations for partnership working exist – between colleagues working face to face or at a distance from one another, collaborating with individuals or groups within the virtual environment, or perhaps conducting their joint working entirely as a virtual collaboration. The possibilities appear endless, but what is the direction of travel? Will virtual reality become commonplace within everyday life? And if so, will it involve a translation or integration of our face-to-face models of social reality to the virtual reality? What new conceptions of professional practice might emerge; whether in face-to-face or virtual spaces for practice? And to what extent might taking on a virtual identity support individuals in undertaking specific roles within a collaboration or, alternatively, create a collaborative dissonance? Collaboration may come to form a bridge between the real and the virtual, and current and future practice, within the academy.

Exploring Engagement

We have seen that engagement on a number of levels is key to effective working in collaborative activity. Without it the practices are hollow and on shaky ground, while with it such collaborations can go from strength to strength. Figure 9.2 highlights a number of future directions and drivers in relation to engagement within the collaborative process.

As we have discussed, a collaboration may come together, but that in itself is not sufficient to stimulate effective joint working; the personal element provides the spark of ingenuity or creativity, and intellectual curiosity the catalyst. What effect, however, does engagement in a collaboration have on the participants, whether individuals or institutional groups, and perhaps, in the future, nations? And what might that look like for future partnership working if collaborative working practices are to become the norm or the practice of choice for most academic endeavours? What role will more personal patterns of collaboration play in this, where it is personal engagement that takes centre stage, rather than a social vehicle or the work in common driving this (or at least the work in common is shaped through the nature of the personal collaboration). Matthew Taylor, commenting in the round-table discussion on the potential of the internet in supporting collaboration, notes that 'possibly what [the internet] aids is informal collaboration, collaboration of people, emailing each other, visiting each other's websites, rather than [any] more formal collaboration'. The emphasis here is on the personal, on the engagement of individuals with one another.

Yet collaboration may become a metaphor for action in a global village of increasing partnership working where the emphasis is less on the individual and more on the group as the locus of activity. This in itself may carry potential

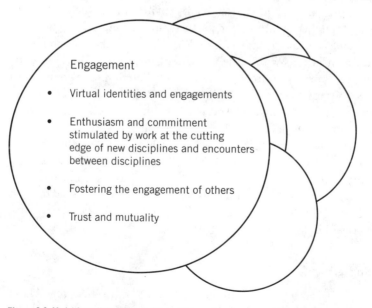

Engagement

- Virtual identities and engagements

- Enthusiasm and commitment stimulated by work at the cutting edge of new disciplines and encounters between disciplines

- Fostering the engagement of others

- Trust and mutuality

Figure 9.2 Model for collaborative working in higher education focused on engagement.

challenges, or perhaps even dangers, in relation to the inclusion of diverse groups and with regard to where responsibility lies. Who is responsible for work or actions carried out by multi-member, international collaborations? Who decides which individuals or which groups are 'allowed' to take part in collaborative activities and which are not? And, ultimately, who benefits? Collaborations can be empowering; but for whom? At the expense of whom? And perhaps most importantly, with respect to the academy, against whom? As Matthew Taylor notes in Chapter 8,

> the other side of this .. is ... the danger that the drive towards collaboration in the field of study means that those who are not part of the collaborative consensus are excluded, to the danger of the development of knowledge.

The 'we' within a collaboration can provide something to hide behind, or to react against, as much as something to take forward. Although pan-global collaborations aspire to address and, one hopes, to resolve global problems and challenges, as noted earlier in the wheat rust illustration, ultimately knowledge is power: the ethics of collaboration is a field worthy of future study.

Future forms of engagement may come through the medium of technology. Social software is already providing us with increasingly rich forms of engagement and patterns of adding value to work – and also the potential to develop multiple identities and to redefine ourselves within a virtual medium. We already have many 'identities' in our day-to-day life and work, whether as parent and child, teacher and researcher, learner and creator of knowledge, which creates a matrix of complexity and sometimes opposition, but all these identities are ultimately visible and identifiable in some tangible manner by both ourselves and others. The possibilities afforded by multiple identities within a virtual world add a new dimension to the concept of engagement, as identified by Barnett in Chapter 8:

> For example, we have seen the emergence of the virtual world, and the creation of virtual life. Further, people have sort of virtual personas – a sense that professional life itself embodies practical knowledge that is plural in nature; we're worrying about what it is to be a doctor or a surgeon these days. And we're understanding it isn't just a matter of technique.

In what ways can we develop trust and a sense of mutuality either in a virtual environment or with virtual colleagues? How can we gauge levels of engagement within a virtual environment? Challenges akin to these are already posed by teacher–learner interaction in virtual learning environments as part of learning and teaching approaches, where moving the students to a position of readiness and commitment to group work with their peers needs significant initial investment in socialization of individuals within the online environment through introductions, sharing of personal information and collaborative activities. Ultimately, however, one is aware that a real person lies behind the postings. Moving into a collaboration within an environment where the 'individuals' with whom one collaborates are represented by avatars complicates the element of reality. Again, ultimately, a real individual is behind the online representation, but the potential for multiple virtual identities within virtual environments, each potentially represented by a different avatar with different 'personalities' and perhaps changing physical appearance, places new stresses on the elements of trust and mutuality that are key to the successful underpinning of collaborative working – as we know it currently.

Beyond the virtual, we need also to consider innovations within and across disciplinary areas and the ways in which this might bring renewed enthusiasm and engagement to the academy. Cutting-edge work is already going on in new interprofessional areas such as interactive media design, forensic art and specialized law programmes. Specialization is therefore increasing in some fields, as identified by Matthew Taylor in Chapter 8:

> You've got two drivers in opposite directions, it seems to me. There is a drive to innovation, absolutely, and I do think that fear and innovation suggests that bringing people together with different perspectives is concretely implicated in successful innovation. And on the other hand, the process of specialization continues and it hasn't stopped. It is still the case that there is a kind of natural process whereby academic disciplines become more and more specialized . . . that where one starts with kind of quite simple distinctions, one ends up with the distinction within disciplines which is highly obscure.

Increased specialization brings its own challenges for collaborative working. Might we all become so specialized within our fields that we will not be able to 'communicate' with anyone outside that sphere of interest? Or will it in fact promote cross-disciplinary working as we seek partners who can take a fresh look at our practice and bring new ideas and insight? As Taylor goes on to say, the direction of travel may all depend on the institutional drivers:

> And of course that begs the question, which I have no idea of the answer to, which is, is the kind of incentive system within academia aligned in the right place to encourage that kind of innovation and collaboration? It's a long time since I was an academic, and I was a failed academic, but it seemed to me that the rewards were all towards ever-greater specialization, more and more abstruse kinds of theorizing! And that kind of innovative work we're talking about is not the kind of work which produces academic papers; it produces intuitive leaps. But who gets some research assessment exercise points for intuitive leaps?

Dialogue, Inclusion, Criticality and Culture

Professional dialogues are the lifeblood of academic communities. Without critical dialogue a contextualized understanding of new research and new knowledge cannot be achieved.

As we can see from Figure 9.3, professional dialogues may be stimulated in a variety of ways, but central to them all is criticality. Criticality is rooted in a dialogue around ideas and knowledge generation that leads to enhanced or to new (whether in form or content) professional learning. Collaborative working is particularly supportive of the development of professional dialogues, as Sachs (2000: 84) describes:

> These new kinds of affiliation and collaboration move all parties beyond traditional technical notions of professional development and create spaces for new kinds of conversations to emerge. They provide opportunities for all groups to be engaged in public critical dialogues and debates about the nature of practice, how it can be communicated with others and how it can be continually improved. All parties move from peripheral involvements in the individual and collective projects to full participation. Dialogue is initiated about education in all of its contexts and dimensions, and about how people can learn from the experiences and collective wisdom of each other.

Professional dialogues

- Discussion across cultures in global working

- Inclusion of varied perspectives

- Virtual dialogues

- Interprofessional dialogues

Figure 9.3 Model for collaborative working in higher education focused on professional dialogues.

Collaborative professional dialogues are beginning to be generated and supported by emerging technologies, using both synchronous and asynchronous approaches, and including blogs, web conferencing and virtual research/ learning environments. The creation of such spaces for critical interprofessional dialogue will in itself create new opportunities for professional learning and the development of meaningful and authentic relationship-building both within, across and outside the collaborations themselves in order to engage with wider communities on local, national and global stages, leading to the development and integration of different conceptual models of collaborative practice. There are also opportunities here for re-creation of personal academic identity *within* the collaboration on an individual level – a developmental space – which can allow for the adoption of the mantle of 'the other': the individual academic and the collaborative persona in action. We need not immerse ourselves in the virtual in order to develop a new identity. Indeed, such re-creation of identity may above all be fostered by the increasing mobility that is a feature of our global world, and as individuals immerse themselves in their new (local) world. And Archer (2007) also points out the consequences of such contextual discontinuity for the way even in which we communicate with others and think about courses of action that involve others.

New Platforms on Which to Collaborate

Academic life stimulates and supports numerous opportunities for social – and, through this, intellectual – engagement ranging from simple day-to-day interactions around teaching and research through to more complex and (semi)formalized communities of practice and disciplinary networks. The resulting social vehicles that underpin these interactions provide a range of platforms and positions from which to engage in collaborative activity. Future conceptions of community, methods of engagement and shifts in practice, as discussed above and reflected in Figure 9.4, may impact on the nature of the role of the social in collaborative working.

As we have seen, moves in this direction are already taking place in the rise of virtual sites for practice, whether the virtual research environments discussed in Wilson's case study in Chapter 6 or the yet to be fully realized opportunities and accompanying challenges for the social and for individual agency presented by virtual realities. Mass collaboration through technological media means that we discuss, share and often develop ideas with electronic messages as opposed to 'real' people. We assume that living, breathing human beings are generating these messages, and we interact with their text on this basis, but we often have no evidence of this and can collaborate with forever unseen, unknown entities who remain closed to us beyond their writing. Yet we still strive to create the social online through the use of humour, sharing photographs, emoticons, etc. in an effort to develop interpersonal bonds that construct the trust and an

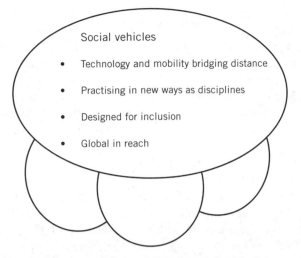

Social vehicles

- Technology and mobility bridging distance
- Practising in new ways as disciplines
- Designed for inclusion
- Global in reach

Figure 9.4 Model for collaborative working in higher education focused on social vehicles.

accompanying sense of connection and responsibility that is vital to effective collaborative working.

Wikipedia and other mass-scale collaborations are focused much more directly around working practice, with technology substituting for the social as the primary vehicle. We have yet to harness such mass-scale collaboration for the purposes of research and teaching anywhere near as directly as we could. Certainly, with scope for larger-scale collaborations among institutions there is perhaps a way to work between the issues of confidentiality that come with genuinely mass-scale movements linked to web 2.0. In twenty, fifty, one hundred years' time, academics may be using very different kinds of technological interfaces, but our reflections in this chapter are less about specific examples of interaction and more about the opportunities raised through use of them and the expectations placed on the ways in which partnerships are facilitated and knowledge created through collaborative engagement.

The Shifting of Disciplines: A Digital Humanities

We can also expect that institutions will project to students more directly the nature of the experience that they are likely to receive if they embark on a given programme of study. On one level this pertains to the marketing and branding of education, and to claims for the distinctiveness of one's educational provision. Technology clearly provides one way to arrive at such a unique position, given the pace of change and the huge range of possible applications of technology to education. Clearly, there are other ways to create a distinctive learning experience, and offering a new subject is a classic example. We will always expect to see the arrival of new disciplines and of novel interactions between existing disciplines. But it is clear also that all of this will demand new ways of working together in the academy. One person can hardly create a distinctive programme on their own, but many have the potential to realize new opportunities, as the following short case study from Umeå University in Sweden demonstrates.

The HUMlab at Umeå University in Sweden provides an example of distinctiveness, technology and the shifting nature of the discipline all in one. The main thrust behind this venture is to bring together the humanities and information communication technology, drawing together domains of practice that are often kept far apart. Information and communication technology (ICT) thus becomes a focus for new developments within the humanities, whether as a medium or object of study or a focal point for people to come together.

We thus see students from Museum Studies working in the lab on a project in Second Life, building structures within this virtual world. There is a streaming of archives, a flow of seminar speakers, regional collaborations around new media, a digital culture technology class and a computer lab fostering links between modern languages, statistics and cultural studies. The lab is looking also to develop an international standard database for environmental archaeology data in collaboration with another part of the university, the Environmental Archaeology Laboratory. The challenge here is to develop a system that will store, extract, analyse and visualize data about past climates and environments – all online. Several postdoctoral researchers are involved, as are a number of digital art fellows. One of these is looking to develop a project related to open-source embroidery.

The notion of open-source embroidery opens for us one window onto what a digital humanities might look like. The first part of this notion stems from open-source software, where a programming code is made freely available so that others can understand it and adapt it for themselves. A piece of embroidery, similarly, can be left in a state that allows others to see the underlying structure of the pattern. Or someone can seal the reverse side of the fabric so that the system employed in the stitching is hidden. The challenge in this project is thus to develop a more social process of embroidery, involving such strategies as workshops and social software.

There is a clear need within all of this for professionals from these various tribes to work together. The intention is indeed to bring people rather than simply ideas together, in that as people meet and work together, we can expect new ways of working to emerge. The lab itself thus constitutes a substantive studio environment that is based at the centre of the university's campus. The building is open 24/365 – all day, every day of the year. And all of this requires extensive funding (from a range of national bodies or foundations) and institutional commitment. Part of what is at stake in the lab as a whole is to draw together a range of different initiatives through a single institutional focus, but in ways that encourage a catalysing of further innovations.

Given all this, it is perhaps no surprise that the HUMlab features strongly in the university's strategy, and also in the image that it wishes to portray of itself to the wider world: as an institution at the cutting edge of interdisciplinary working. The lab also serves as a focus to attract international visitors – to draw others into this novel way of working. Such a prioritization of the lab is clearly important if new development is to be sustained, with a recent doubling of space and such features as the installation of multiple screens, and a dedicated environment for digital and cultural heritage; as well as participatory media and digital art. For further details of HUMlab, see www.humlab.umu.se/about.

Although early twenty-first-century contemporary perspectives on the virtual are largely located in technological constructs, the idea of the virtual goes beyond this, and indeed can be identified in much earlier examples of collaborative working. De Solla Price & Beaver, writing in the 1960s, outlined the idea of the virtual or 'invisible college' as identifiable groups of researchers who spanned college boundaries but who created a nexus of activity around their collaborative practice in a shared space without walls. Many other such 'invisible colleges' exist currently and represent virtual collaborations, for example, virtual graduate schools found at several UK institutions and the SHED (Scottish Higher Education Developers) group, which connects colleagues from across Scotland. Yet although these groups are not fixed in terms of location or habitus, they do utilize social vehicles as a medium for collaboration. Ultimately, however, all modes of engagement that involve discourse – whether face to face, at a distance, virtual or other-worldly – are necessarily forms of social interaction, and thus a place remains for social vehicles as the lubricant for collaborative action.

Conclusion: Realizing the Potential of Collaborative Working

One of our opening questions – and it was a big one – for the round-table discussion was whether increased collaborative working can be seen as a reactive response to dealing with supercomplexity within working practices, or whether it has emerged positively as a result of it. Another way to look at this question is to consider whether we are naturally inclined or conditioned by society to choose collaboration as a positive strategy for life and work. For some colleagues, collaborative working can provide the doorway or portal to new fields of understanding, the unleashing of creative or innovative potential, and to greater achievement and satisfaction in both the practice and personal dimensions. Collaborative activity may even take the form of a 'threshold concept' (see Land *et al.*, 2008) in that it leads 'not only to transfigured thought but to a trans-figuration of identity and adoption of an extended or elaborated discourse'.

For other colleagues, however, collaborative working may continue to present itself as a troublesome activity, not only for individuals who engage as participants in collaborations but also for those who aim to manage and

understandings of collaborative working are required if the academy is to address the challenges that we have explored in this chapter, and across the rest of the book. In this way we hope that the academy itself will become, more truly, a *social* academy.

References

Archer, M. (2007). *Making Our Way through the World: Human Reflexivity and Social Mobility.* Cambridge: Cambridge University Press.

Cooke, R. (2008). *On-line Innovation in Higher Education.* Report to the UK Government Secretary of State for Innovation, Universities and Skills. Online, available at: www.dius.gov.uk/policy/world_leader_e-learning.html (accessed 19 December 2008).

De Solla Price, D. & Beaver, D. (1966). Collaboration in an invisible college. *American Psychological Association, 21,* 1011–1018.

Durable Rust Resistance in Wheat project. Online, available at: www.wheatrust.cornell.edu (accessed 21 December 2008).

Enhancing Student Success Conference, Newcastle University, Australia. Online, available at: www.newcastle.edu.au/news/2008/12/workingcollaborativelytosupportstudentdiversity.html (accessed 19 December 2008).

Gajda, R. (2004). Utilizing collaboration theory to evaluate strategic alliances. *American Journal of Evaluation, 25* (1), 65–77.

HUMlab. Online, available at: www.humlab.umu.se/about (accessed 22 December 2008).

Knowledge Transfer Partnerships programme. Online, available at: www.ktponline.org.uk/academics/default.aspx (accessed 19 December 2008).

Land, R., Meyer, J. H. F. & Smith, J. (eds) (2008). *Threshold Concepts within the Disciplines.* Rotterdam: Sense.

Learning and Teaching Partnership Agreement, University of Leeds, UK. Online, available at: www.leeds.ac.uk/aqst/tsg/1pa.htm (accessed 19 December 2008).

Meads, G. & Ashcroft, J. (2005). *The Case for Interprofessional Collaboration in Health and Social Care.* Oxford: Blackwell.

Presser, S. (1980). Collaboration and the quality of research. *Social Studies of Science, 10* (1), 95–101.

Sachs, J. (2000). The activist professional. *Journal of Educational Change, 1,* 77–95.

UK Higher Education International Unit and Universities UK (2008). *International Research Collaboration: Opportunities for the UK Higher Education Sector.* London: UK Higher Education International Unit.

Universities UK (2008). *Demographic Change and Its Impact on the Higher Education Sector in England.* Report to the UK Government Secretary of State for Innovation, Universities and Skills. Online, available at: www.dius.gov.uk/policy/documents/UUK%20contributions%20to%20the%20HE%20Debate%20-%20demographics.pdf (accessed 19 December 2008).

Index